Law and Ethics
for Today's Journalist

D1519784

Law and Ethics
for Today's Journalist

A Concise Guide

Joe Mathewson

Routledge
Taylor & Francis Group

LONDON AND NEW YORK

First published 2014 by M.E. Sharpe

Published 2015 by Routledge
2 Park Square, Milton Park, Abingdon, Oxon OX14 4RN
711 Third Avenue, New York, NY, 10017, USA

Routledge is an imprint of the Taylor & Francis Group, an informa business

Library of Congress Cataloging-in-Publication Data

Mathewson, Joe, 1933–
  Law and ethics for today's journalist : a concise guide / by Joe Mathewson.
    pages cm
Includes bibliographical references and index.
ISBN 978-0-7656-4075-8 (hardcover : alk. paper)—ISBN 978-0-7656-4076-5 (pbk. : alk. paper)
1. Press law—United States. 2. Journalists—United States—Handbooks, manuals, etc.
I. Title.

KF2750.M37 2013
343.7309′98—dc23   2013009458

ISBN 13: 9780765640758 (hbk)
ISBN 13: 9780765640765 (pbk)

To my students

Contents

Preface

This "user-friendly" text grows out of years of teaching media law and ethics to bright, aspiring journalists. Law and ethics intertwine in journalism; as such, they should be taught and discussed together. Creating quotations, publishing a rape victim's name in derogation of state law, or plagiarizing another's work are ethically dubious if not totally unjustifiable, yet the U.S. Supreme Court has sanctioned these practices as protected by the First Amendment to the U.S. Constitution. So journalists need to know the essentials of both law and ethics to help guide their daily work. This is not to suggest that journalists must become experts, but rather that they need to recognize a legal or ethical dilemma anytime it arises in their work and, if under deadline pressure, must weigh the options and make a decision. Should I photograph the dead body? Should I not mention that I'm a journalist? Why or why not?

In some situations, such as deciding whether to go undercover in an investigation, there may be time to consult editors or even the company lawyer. Any such deliberate deception must be carefully weighed, typically to consider whether the harm of the ethical deviation is likely to be outweighed by the benefit of the resulting story. But when the journalist is in the midst of an urgent, breaking story, with no opportunity to consult others, law and ethics still apply and must be evaluated by the journalist on the scene.

This book is designed to help the working journalist recognize legal and ethical issues, and to provide guidance in making such decisions. It emphasizes the pitfalls of the profession, specifically the legal and ethical limitations within which a conscientious journalist must operate on a daily basis.

This book is not intended to be a comprehensive treatise on all aspects of communications law and its development to its present form. Matters such as obscenity (which has no First Amendment protection) and advertising law, important though they may be to certain professions and to legal scholars, are of no importance to the working journalist, and so are omitted. Other matters that a journalist needs to be aware of but does not need to interpret or apply, such as the Federal Communications Commission (FCC) technical requirements for operating a broadcast station and FCC rules on multiple ownership of television and radio stations, are mentioned but not emphasized.

Accordingly, in both content and style, this book is addressed to the working journalist; it is highly practical. Its end game is the current state of the law and ethical thinking in journalism. This necessarily entails some history and consideration of monumental, decades-old decisions that still apply, such as the Supreme Court's bellwether 1964 libel decision of *New York Times v. Sullivan*. But the working journalist does not need to know every twist and turn of libel law from 1964 to the present day, so the cases presented here are selective rather than comprehensive.

This approach permits the book to be shorter than most textbooks of communications law and ethics, or even just law alone, and makes the often-complex reasoning of judges considerably more accessible. The text may be supplemented, and should be, by reading of at least some of the important court opinions summarized in the book. The selection is left up to the instructor.

Most of the book is organized by the well-recognized areas of the law that are most relevant to working journalists—prior restraint, libel, invasion of privacy, fair trial, journalist's privilege, access to government documents and meetings, and broadcast indecency. These are subjects the journalist must know and sometimes apply quickly.

Then there is one chapter that the journalist won't be expected to apply, but must know in order to understand how broadly the First Amendment, as interpreted by the U.S. Supreme Court, affects vital aspects of our democracy: *Citizens United v. Federal Election Commission*. This, of course, is the Court's 2010 ruling that struck down most limitations on political campaign finance, opening the door to unlimited contributions by corporations, unions, and wealthy individuals. The resulting huge new flow of unregulated contributions, amounting to billions of dollars, was a major, and sometimes irrefutable, factor in the 2012 elections. Journalists must understand this phenomenon, which seems likely to fuel special-interest candidacies for the foreseeable future. It also provides a virtually unlimited opportunity for revelatory journalism.

Although the research, the case selection, and any errors in this text are the author's own, acknowledgment is due to David Abrahamson of Northwestern University's Medill School for his encouragement of this project, and to two other Medill colleagues, Jack Doppelt and Craig LaMay, whose teaching preceded and helped to guide my own.

To the Reader:
An Introduction

> *This above all: to thine own self be true,*
> *And it must follow, as the night the day,*
> *Thou canst not then be false to any man.*
> —Shakespeare, *Hamlet*, Act 1

Journalism is a joy. Where else can you be paid for stimulating daily engagement in the affairs of your neighborhood, your city, your country, even the world? And your work makes a difference, right from the start. You help focus your audience and its leaders on things that matter, things they should know about, maybe even *do* something about. More personally, you'll enjoy enormous gratification from deploying your multiple skills in such a visible, public way.

Especially in the United States, journalism is favored, both by law and by long practice. It is protected by state constitutions and laws and most notably by the First Amendment to the U.S. Constitution (1789), which guarantees a panoply of human rights never before accorded by any government to its people. The First Amendment (1791) states:

> Congress shall make no law respecting an establishment of religion, or prohibiting the free exercise thereof; or abridging the freedom of speech, or of the press; or the right of the people peaceably to assemble, and to petition the Government for a redress of grievances.

This text will show how favorable laws are applied in court cases to buttress the freedom of the press that the founders of the country treasured and adopted as one of its most basic precepts. There are limitations along the way—the laws of defamation, personal privacy, fair trial, uneven testimonial privileges accorded to journalists, access to government documents, copyright and broadcasting—as well as ethical concerns that will challenge your own personal sense of what's fair and what's right. For instance, should you misrepresent yourself to get your story? Should you alter the name of a source to fulfill your promise of confidentiality? The broad landscape of this profession is not primarily restrictive; on the contrary, it is a delicious invitation to the curiosity, the initiative, and the imagination of people who care about the world in which we live.

The norms, the practices, and the history of our society also favor journalism, and especially private journalism. There are no government newspapers, television channels, or "news" services spewing the official line; no government censors, and no media affiliated with political parties with the sole purpose of disseminating their message. From colonial times, journalism has been the heartbeat of America, informing the citizenry of significant public events and public-policy arguments. It is arguable whether this country would even exist without newspapers. In the beginning the enterprising printer/ journalist spread the word about the indignities and discrimination foisted on the colonists by Britain. In Boston an inflammatory newspaper publisher and pamphleteer (and, yes, a brewer) named Samuel Adams sounded the alarm and pointed the way toward rebellion. The gifted Thomas Jefferson of Virginia, eloquent author of the Declaration of Independence (1776) and the third president of the United States (1801–1809), once remarked, "Were it left to me to decide whether we should have a government without newspapers, or newspapers without a government, I should not hesitate a moment to prefer the latter."

Fortunately, the United States has enjoyed both government and newspapers—not always exemplary, far from perfect, but both strong and effective —for over two centuries. Government and the press need each other. Public officials and opinion makers need the news media to communicate with the public. At the same time the media, always looking for a good story, relentlessly monitor the affairs and the quality of American life and especially our governments at all levels—national, state, and local—in an endless effort to expose corruption and to elevate the level of government and business ethics and services. Four decades after it happened, there's still no better example of media impact than the Watergate break-in and subsequent scandal, assiduously investigated and reported by two young journalists, Bob Woodward and Carl Bernstein of the *Washington Post*. President Richard Nixon's inept efforts to cover up the White House role in the tawdry affair eventually induced him to resign, in 1973—the first time a U.S. president voluntarily relinquished the office in midterm. The power of the press!

Of course the media have changed over these two centuries. Newspapers are now supplemented (and sometimes replaced) by broadcasting and the

Internet. But the role of the media in American life remains vibrant, indeed essential. This book will help you position yourself in the exciting profession of journalism. Whether you want to write, produce video, design websites, start your own Internet business, or whatever, you will need to grasp the essence of journalism law and ethics; they always apply. A false defamation or unauthorized copying of someone else's work on the Internet is just as unlawful as in your hometown newspaper, and unprincipled Internet whiners who like to rant anonymously and falsely are finding that their victims are getting support from courts in uncovering their identities. Moreover, if you create your own blog or website inviting comments from your audience, you may be personally liable for defamations or other illegal material posted there by others.

Of course, there are more than just rules to journalism, there is also a very practical consideration here: A journalist needs to act both ethically and within the law, since the *sine qua non* of good journalism is credibility. If a newspaper, TV station, website, or an individual journalist isn't credible, their work is useless. However, credibility isn't easy to come by. Each news organization and journalist must earn credibility with consistently fair and accurate work over a period of time. If you seriously misquote or misrepresent a source, you've probably lost that source. On the other hand, a source who has been treated fairly (and that doesn't necessarily mean favorably) will probably continue to talk to you. A journalist must be trustworthy and must continuously earn that trust.

But back to the predominant and very best side of journalism. In your studies you will enlarge greatly your grasp of the basic skills and techniques of good journalism. If you like to write, you'll hone that predilection by focusing on a specialty or two, like business writing or magazine writing. If your yen is video, you'll both sharpen your pictures and produce a substantial video or two that requires you to gain knowledge by reporting on challenging subject matter. As for the Internet, new sites are being created every day, and although not all are top quality or economically viable, they all require knowledge and skills.

While gaining that knowledge and those skills, take time to think about yourself. *You* are important. Your ambitions and your passions are important. Not just for your future professional life, but right now. The skills you are acquiring are vital to conducting yourself well as a journalist, but so is your own senses of balance, fairness, integrity, and truth. That's what journalism law and ethics are all about. What you learn here will always be with you, growing and ripening as you move along your journalism journey.

Law and Ethics
for Today's Journalist

1

Courts and the Legal System

"Equal justice under law"
—United States Supreme Court façade

The inscription over the entrance to the U.S. Supreme Court's impressive Greek temple in Washington expresses an ideal that everyone can readily embrace. It has three important implications for journalists.

1. American law provides both freedoms and restrictions for journalists, and these are the subject of most of this book.
2. The courts that administer American law are the operative locus of many of the frictions, controversies, and disputes that inevitably arise in a free and complex society. Many of the conflicts that bubble up in the United States give rise to lawsuits, trials, and appeals. The stories of these conflicts and how they're resolved are often the stuff of great journalism, evoking human failings and triumphs as well as the fundamental standards of our democracy. Anyone can sue, and these days it seems that everyone does. Courts are open to journalists. This book will help you to take advantage of that access, and not incidentally, to contribute to equal justice under the law.
3. Covering legal disputes and working responsibly as a general assignment journalist require some basic knowledge of United States law and courts, which is addressed in the following sections.

Sources of American Law

Ours is a common-law system derived from that of England. Common law is judge-made law, differentiated from constitutions and from statutes enacted by a legislature. However, when the United States became an independent nation, much of the English common law that had governed here was expressly adopted, or codified, by the state legislatures and by the United States

Congress. Take, for example, the law of contracts. Contracts are written agreements between two or more parties, such as a retailer's agreement to purchase certain goods from a manufacturer, and they may be enforced in court if necessary.

In a common-law system, legal disputes, called lawsuits, are presented to a trial court, which produces a decision, either by a judge or a jury. That decision may be appealed to an appellate court, which has the power to overrule or modify the ruling of the trial court. Whether the appellate court affirms the ruling of the trial court or rejects it, the decision by the appellate court establishes a "precedent" that is followed by the trial courts of that district in similar future cases. So the law builds on itself over time. This process differs from that of European countries, for instance, most of which have a "civil" law system. In that system, each court decides each case based solely on its interpretation of statutory law, without reference to prior decisions by other trial or appellate courts. In other words, in a civil system there are no binding precedents. Another difference is that common-law judges decide only on the evidence presented to them in court, whereas civil-law judges have investigative powers as well, thus assuming a function of prosecutors in our common-law system.

State and Federal Courts

Within our common-law system there are two court structures, state and federal. They are quite similar. Most of the action is in state courts. They are more numerous, and they handle most of the lawsuits, from personal injuries and traffic violations to murder and high-stakes disagreements between powerful corporations. Federal courts, located in every state, adjudicate cases brought under federal law, meaning primarily the statutes passed by Congress that apply nationwide, such as those governing immigration, labor, and broadcasting. The federal courts also interpret the U.S. Constitution, our basic law from which all federal powers flow, including its guarantees of individual rights and freedoms such as the freedom of speech and the right to a fair trial. (Each state has its own constitution, too, but legal disputes over the meaning of state constitutions are fewer than those involving the federal Constitution.) Each court has a clerk who maintains the court's docket and can answer questions about the court's schedule, procedures, and rules.

The federal trial courts are called U.S. District Courts; each covers a portion of a state, or, in less populated areas of the country, an entire state. The district courts adjudicate disputes arising under federal law; they may also hear cases arising under state law when the parties (the plaintiff and the defendant) are residents of different states. Federal appellate courts are U.S.

Courts in the United States

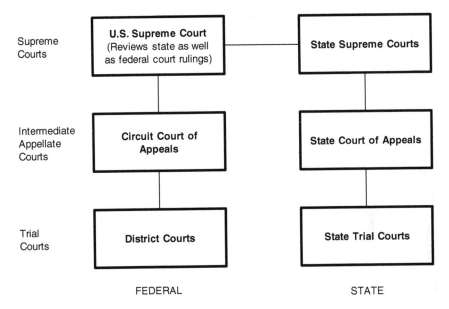

Circuit Courts of Appeals; each covers a multistate area, except the Circuit Court of Appeals for the District of Columbia, which keeps quite busy with appeals from the many cases tried in the U.S. District Court for the District of Columbia, plus appeals from rulings of federal regulatory agencies like the Federal Communications Commission, which go directly to a Circuit Court of Appeals.

The structures of our federal and state court systems are much the same: a trial court hears and decides each case; an intermediate-level appellate court may review the trial court's ruling; and a higher-level appellate court, typically called the supreme court, is the final authority in that jurisdiction, meaning that state or judicial district or, in the case of the United States Supreme Court, the nation as a whole. Some decisions of state supreme courts may be appealed to the U.S. Supreme Court, if there's an interpretation of the U.S. Constitution or other federal law involved. Recent examples of U.S. Supreme Court rulings on state cases are decisions on gun control (applying the Second Amendment to the U.S. Constitution) and student protests (First Amendment). A request that the Supreme Court review a lower court ruling is called a petition for a *writ of certiorari,* a Latin word meaning to inform or to certify. If at least four of the nine justices vote to hear the case, the writ is granted and the case is docketed for review. If the petition gains no more than three votes, the writ is denied, which leaves the judgment of the lower court standing. In common parlance, these actions by the Supreme Court are called *cert denied* and *cert granted*. Note that a denial does not constitute an affirmation of the lower court's ruling, nor is it even a decision or ruling of the Supreme Court. The justices simply decline to consider the case. Of the thousands of petitions for a *writ of certiorari* presented to the Supreme Court every year, it grants only about eighty.

Types of Law

Our law has four sources:

1. Federal and state constitutions
2. Statutes enacted by the U.S. Congress and state legislatures
3. Rules and regulations promulgated by regulatory agencies such as the Federal Communications Commission, the Nuclear Regulatory Commission, the Securities and Exchange Commission, the Federal Trade Commission, the Food and Drug Administration, and the National Labor Relations Board
4. Court rulings, characterized as common law

Let's elaborate a bit on each of these.

Federal and State Constitutions

Each constitution was written and adopted by a constitutional convention representing the citizenry. A constitution has two basic functions: it broadly describes the powers of the government, separating them into legislative, executive, and judicial functions and setting forth the authority and responsibilities of each (the "separation of powers"); and it prescribes limitations to those powers in the form of individual rights and liberties which the government may not violate. Many of the individual-rights guarantees of the constitutions are similar. The federal Constitution and all state constitutions, for instance, proclaim freedom of speech, freedom of the press, and the right to a fair trial. But there are differences, too. Most state constitutions declare a right of personal privacy; the federal Constitution does not.

Statutes

Acting in accordance with the authority granted by the constitution, the legislature enacts statutes, sometimes called acts or simply, laws. They generally require the signature of the president or the governor as well. Some of the grants of constitutional authority are very broad, for instance, the federal Constitution's empowerment of the federal government to regulate interstate and foreign commerce. Congress often invokes interstate commerce as the legal justification for statutes that are only distantly related to it, such as the Civil Rights Act of 1964, and the Supreme Court usually affirms such broad interpretations.

Regulations

Both federal and state laws create regulatory agencies empowered to apply and enforce specific statutes enacted by the legislature. The most important regulatory agencies, those with the broadest scope and the greatest authority, are federal. For instance, the federal Communications Act of 1934 established the broad outlines of federal regulation of broadcasting and created the Federal Communications Commission to carry out that mandate, which encompasses licensing of television and radio stations and then regulating their broadcast content, e.g., with rules to prevent indecency and mandates for children's programming.

Court Rulings

Common law, though the phrase inevitably invokes remembrance of the law that the United States inherited from England, still exists today. It's judge-made law, but now most of those rulings are based on constitutions, statutes, and rules that have been carefully crafted and are usually intended to limit judges' discretion. For instance, most states (but not the federal government) have "shield" laws that exempt a journalist from testifying in legal proceedings under certain circumstances, but in the few states that lack such a statute, the state supreme courts have recognized a common-law testimonial privilege that's the equivalent of a shield law. Federal versions of this journalist's privilege have been fashioned by several U.S. Courts of Appeals in a number of cases, despite an important Supreme Court ruling that the First Amendment does not give rise to a journalist's privilege and therefore journalists summoned by a grand jury must appear and testify about what they know.

Civil Law and Criminal Law

Criminal and civil cases are both under federal and state law. A criminal case, of course, is one in which an individual is charged with violating a specific provision of a statute, such as prohibitions against murder, attempted murder, battery (striking another person), larceny, burglary (stealing from a home, office or other building at night), fraud, narcotics dealing, reckless driving, and so forth. In such cases, the plaintiff (the party initiating the lawsuit), is typically a state or the United States. So, if John Smith is charged with murder in Chicago, the case would be entitled Illinois versus (or simply v.) Smith. Smith is the defendant. A guilty finding must be "beyond a reasonable doubt." Penalties for violating a criminal statute may include a fine or a jail sentence; sentences greater than one year are imposed for major crimes, called felonies, while sentences of less than a year may be ordered for relatively minor infractions, called misdemeanors; public drunkenness, for instance. Maximum fines and jail terms are specified in each criminal statute, and the specific penalties for each conviction are determined by the judge. Criminal defendants usually are entitled to a jury trial; so most cases are tried by a jury, but on occasion may be tried by a judge alone.

Civil cases may be initiated either by a government agency or by a private party, such as a person or a business. They usually involve an alleged violation of a civil statute or a written agreement between the parties, for instance, a breach of contract, or an accusation of libel (defamation) by a person against a newspaper; or an allegation of an injury to a person caused by a defective vehicle, power tool, or other manufactured product (products liability). Civil cases may be tried by a jury or by a judge alone, and a guilty verdict usually requires the defendant to pay money damages to the plaintiff. The damages awarded usually compensate the plaintiff for any out-of-pocket expense or loss, such as wages lost through inability to work (compensatory damages), but may include damages for pain and suffering (from an automobile accident, for instance) and also, in egregious cases, punitive damages explicitly intended to punish outlandish behavior. If the case is brought by a government agency, under federal securities law, for instance, the judge may order a fine and also impose an order forbidding the defendant to engage in such illegal conduct in the future. However, violations of civil law are not punishable by jail sentences.

Anatomy of a Lawsuit

A plaintiff, public or private, initiates a lawsuit by filing a document called a complaint in a court, or more specifically, in the office of the clerk of that court. The complaint names the defendant and sets forth one or more accusations of wrongdoing. If it's a criminal case, the defendant is arrested and arraigned before a magistrate, at which time he pleads guilty, or more likely not guilty, and a trial date is set. If it's a civil case, the defendant has thirty days after receiving the complaint in which to file an answer or reply; often the defendant will simply deny each accusation in the complaint. The defendant may request a jury trial.

In a civil case, the judge then calls the opposing lawyers to a hearing to set deadlines for pretrial proceedings, particularly for what the lawyers call "discovery," a sometimes-lengthy process of gathering evidence to present at trial. That's done in part through depositions (formal questioning under oath, with an opposing lawyer and a court reporter present) of prospective witnesses (including expert witnesses to testify about acceptable professional practices, by a doctor accused of malpractice, for instance) to determine what they know and will say at trial, and through written interrogatories, questions submitted to prospective witnesses to be answered in writing, also under oath. Whatever each side learns in the discovery process is made available to the other party.

In our system, the jury decides the facts of the case—who actually pulled the trigger—and the judge decides questions of law, whether a given statute applies, for instance. Civil disputes are decided by the preponderance of the evidence, a lesser proof than the "beyond a reasonable doubt" requirement of a criminal case. It sometimes happens in a civil case that there's no disagreement about the facts—about what actually took place—so the only question is whether those facts constitute a violation of law. In that instance, the case may be decided by what's called a summary judgment, a determination of guilt or innocence by the trial judge alone. For instance, if a journalist uses a concealed camera to get a story, and those facts are uncontested, the judge may decide without a trial whether that tactic constituted an invasion of someone's personal privacy.

The verdict, or judgment, in any case, civil or criminal, decided by judge or jury, may be reviewed by an appellate court. If the loser in the trial court feels that the verdict was somehow improper or unjustified, he or she may request such a review. The petition for review must state the reasons for seeking review. The reasons may include, for instance, an allegation that the trial judge's rulings on whether to admit or bar certain evidence were incorrect, that her instructions to the jury were unclear or insufficient, or that her interpretation of a statute or regulation was incorrect. But the facts determined by the judge or jury can't be questioned on appeal. If the appellate court, consisting usually of at least three judges, agrees with the appellant (the party seeking review) the court may reverse or set aside the judgment of the trial court, and may order a new trial. However, if the appellate court finds no grounds for upsetting the trial court verdict, it affirms that judgment. The party that loses the appeal may seek review by the supreme court, which has the same options to reject the case, or to affirm or set aside the ruling, possibly including an order to retry the case.

Court Opinions

Appellate courts, and on occasion a trial judge who has tried a case without a jury, announce and explain their judgments in a written opinion. They may summarize their ruling orally from the bench, but the written opinion is the final word on the case in that court. This is what journalists base their stories on, and if the loser requests review by a higher court, that petition will be based on the written opinion, contending that it's somehow mistaken or unjust. (There's no written opinion in a jury trial, so a petition for review, as explained above, will be based on the trial judge's rulings on evidence, instructions to the jury, some other procedural aspect of the trial, or the judge's interpretation of law.)

Next to actually witnessing a trial or an oral argument by lawyers dueling before an appellate court, courts' written opinions provide the best insight about our legal system. Each opinion sets forth the facts of the case, quotes the applicable law, cites prior court decisions (precedents) that are deemed relevant or perhaps determinant, analyzes the application of the law to the facts at hand, and announces the court's findings and judgment. This may be accomplished in a few pages or very many, depending on the simplicity or complexity of the case.

Although this book will cite many more cases than we have time to read, perusing a few opinions will be instructive. Each opinion bears a citation, in this fashion: *New York Times Co. v. Sullivan,* 376 U.S. 24 (1964). This is the Supreme Court's opinion in the great case setting forth new, press-friendly rules for determining libel of a public official. New York Times Co. is the appellant or petitioner (reflecting that it lost in the lower court), Sullivan is the appellee or respondent; 376 is the number of the volume of the official United States Reports in which all Supreme Court opinions are published; U.S. indicates U.S. Supreme Court, 24 is the page number of that volume, and 1964 is the year in which the judgment was rendered. Supreme Court opinions, especially more recent cases, are sometimes cited this way: *Citizens United v. Federal Election Commission,* 130 S.Ct. 876 (2010) (the case allowing unlimited campaign contributions by corporations and unions); it's a different reporting service, but the opinion is the same as in the United States Reports. Most major opinions can be found on free Internet services such as the Legal Information Institute of Cornell Law School, and all opinions are available through subscription services Westlaw and LexisNexis Academic (perhaps accessible through your school library). LexisNexis also references cases with its own citation, such as 2012 LEXIS plus the page number; it may be especially useful in a search for a very recent decision, before it has been printed in the report volumes.

Similarly, opinions of the federal appellate courts, the U.S. Circuit Courts of Appeals, are cited thus: *Masson v. New Yorker Magazine, Inc.,* 501 F.3d 1394 (9th Cir. 1996) (another important libel case), where 501 is the number of the volume of the Federal Reports, third series (or in another, earlier appellate case it might be 2d, second series), page 1394, decided by the Ninth Circuit Court of Appeals (in San Francisco) in 1996.

An opinion citation that includes the abbreviation of a state name is by that state's supreme court, such as 194 Neb. 783. State appellate court citations include the abbreviation App., as in 154 Cal. App. 4th 97. State cases also are commonly cited to a regional reporting service, such as *Gore v. Harris,* 772 So.2d 1243 (Fla. 2000), appearing in volume 772 of the Southern Reporter, second series, page 1243. (This was the Florida prelude to the decisive 2000 presidential election case, *Bush v. Gore,* 531 U.S. 98 (2000), at the U.S. Supreme Court.)

When reading a court opinion, first make sure you have the right one, for some cases pop up multiple times with different citations and dates, either before or after the key decision for which you're looking. Supreme Court opinions and many others include a number of brief "headnotes" at the top, sometimes several pages long, which you may skip; they're references to specific legal issues or questions addressed in the opinion, intended to facilitate research by lawyers, but they're not a part of the actual opinion and have little or no value to journalists. However, read the Summary or Syllabus (also at the top) carefully. As the names suggest, they provide a brief statement of the issues presented and the court's decision. They help guide your reading of the full opinion by alerting you to the case's main questions and the court's resolution of them. When you finish reading each case (which may require considerable re-reading of difficult passages), you should be able to state the issue(s) presented by the case and the court's ruling(s) on them.

This chapter has laid a foundation for an understanding of the law affecting the working journalist. But before we get into the cases that have helped to create today's law, let's also lay some groundwork in the ethics of journalism, coming in the next chapter.

Questions for Discussion

1. Is a general assignment reporter more likely to encounter a criminal case or a civil case? In federal court or state court? Why?
2. If a court proceeding is not clear, how could a reporter better understand the proceeding?
3. Are federal courts limited to adjudicating disputes arising under federal law? Why?

4. Does a ruling of the U.S. Supreme Court bind future rulings of state courts as well as federal?
5. What does it mean if the U.S. Supreme Court *grants* a *writ of certiorari*? If the Court *denies* a *writ of certiorari*, does that mean the lower court's ruling is affirmed?

References

Bush v. Gore, 531 U.S. 98 (2000). http://www.law.cornell.edu/supct/html/00–949. ZPC.html/.

Citizens United v. Federal Election Commission, 558 U.S. 310, 130 S.Ct. 876 (2010). http://www.law.cornell.edu/supct/html/08–205.ZX1.html.

Gore v. Harris, 772 So.2d 1243 (Fla. 2000). http://scholar.google.com/scholar_case? case=744598102315694837&q=+gore+v.+harris&hl=en&as_sdt=2,14&as_ vis=1.

Masson v. New Yorker Magazine, 85 F.3d 1394 (9th Cir. 1996). http://caselaw.findlaw. com/us-9th-circuit/1264860.html.

New York Times Co. v. Sullivan, 376 U.S. 24 (1964). http://law2.umkc.edu/faculty/ projects/ftrials/conlaw/sullivan.html.

2

Ethics, Root and Branch

"I'd rather be right than president."
—Senator Henry Clay (1777–1852)

Opportunities Forfeited

Jayson Blair had a golden opportunity. Just twenty-three years old and without a college degree, he was promoted by the august *New York Times* from intern to reporter. He wrote fast and furiously, making many mistakes in his stories, but nevertheless rose from the metropolitan desk to a prime spot on a team of eight *Times* reporters covering a mesmerizing national story: a murder spree of two elusive snipers terrorizing the Washington, D.C., suburbs.

Blair promptly wrote an exclusive page-one story with gripping details about the arrest of John Muhammad, one of the suspects. Blair attributed his inside story to five unidentified law-enforcement officers. Both the U.S. attorney for Maryland and a senior FBI official immediately denied certain details, and veteran law-enforcement reporters in the *Times* Washington bureau expressed dismay. A few days later Blair wrote another front-page exclusive, again attributed to anonymous sources, asserting that "all the evidence" pointed to Muhammad's teenage accomplice, Lee Malvo, as the actual shooter. A prosecutor promptly called a news conference to slam the story.

It was discovered that Blair wrote a number of reports "from Washington" with false datelines when he was actually in Brooklyn. He even listed on one expense account an expenditure at a Starbucks clearly identified on the receipt as being in Brooklyn, while representing to the newsroom that he—and the Starbucks—were in Washington. A few months later Blair, by then suspected of numerous fabrications, was confronted by *Times* editors and resigned. A team of *Times* reporters painstakingly assembled a lengthy, detailed, and sorry tale of wanton deception and malfeasance. They wrote:

> Every newspaper, like every bank and every police department, trusts its
> employees to uphold central principles, and the inquiry found that Mr.

Blair repeatedly violated the cardinal tenet of journalism, which is simply truth. His tools of deceit were a cellphone and a laptop computer—which allowed him to blur his true whereabouts—as well as round-the-clock access to databases of news articles from which he stole.

Mr. Blair's deceptive techniques flouted long-followed rules at *The Times*. The paper, concerned about maintaining its integrity among readers, tells its journalists to follow many guidelines as described in a memo on the newsroom's internal Web site. Among those guidelines: "When we use facts gathered by any other organization, we attribute them"; "writers at *The Times* are their own principal fact checkers and often their only ones"; "we should distinguish in print between personal interviews and telephone or e-mail interviews." (Barry et al., 2003)

Soon, *Times* executive editor, Howell Raines, bearing ultimate responsibility for the newsroom and its work, also was forced to resign.

Another young journalist, Janet Cooke, went farther with her deceptions—to a Pulitzer Prize. She wrote movingly in the *Washington Post* about the agonies of an eight-year-old, third-generation drug addict. But "Jimmy" didn't exist. Cooke was dismissed, and the *Post* returned her prize.

Sadly, in recent years other fabricators and plagiarists, most of them experienced journalists, have been fired or suspended at other major news organizations, such as the *Boston Globe, USA Today,* ESPN, the *Village Voice,* the *Chicago Sun-Times,* the *New Yorker, Newsweek,* and CNN. These last two, simultaneous suspensions by *Newsweek* and CNN, represented a "twofer" by commentator Fareed Zakaria, who admitted his deceit and was quickly reinstated.

Success Under a Cloud

Happily, on the other hand, two young reporters for the *Chicago Sun-Times* made the most of their opportunity, though it raised an ethical question. To expose widespread graft, shakedowns, and bribe-taking in City Hall, the newspaper quietly rented a dilapidated storefront at Superior and Wells on Chicago's Near North Side and began remodeling it as a tavern. They named it, appropriately, The Mirage. Reporters Pam Zekman and Zay Smith partnered with Bill Recktenwald and Mindy Trossman of the Better Government Association, a local investigative organization, to apply for various health and building permits—and to deal with the "helpful" city inspectors who began to visit. Many of them offered to overlook obvious electrical, plumbing, and other code violations in return for cash—sometimes as little as ten dollars—which the tavern staff readily paid. Under Illinois law these conversations couldn't be secretly recorded, but photographers in a small space above the bar memorialized them all, and a CBS *Sixty Minutes* crew was there at times, too.

Shortly after The Mirage opened, it closed, and the *Sun-Times* spilled the engrossing story—in great detail, naming names, showing faces—over a period of weeks. Chicagoans devoured it, and so did City Hall. In CBS's story, correspondent Mike Wallace confronted a very surprised accountant who had offered to help The Mirage crew evade taxes; he admitted it. The inspectors didn't deny the stories. How could they? Some were chastised and disciplined, some fired, and then the Feds moved in, indicting one-third of the city's electrical inspectors and numerous others. Things changed at City Hall.

This story seems like the perfect candidate for the Pulitzer Prize for investigative journalism. However, the Pulitzer committee turned its back, without explanation at the time, because some of its members objected to the deception employed by the paper. The reporters had not revealed the fact that they were reporters, not tavern operators. Could they have gotten this delicious story if they had identified themselves? Of course not. Small business operators wouldn't talk, at least not on the record, about the shakedowns they encountered and for which they paid, for fear of being put out of business. Now, thanks to the imagination and courage of the *Sun-Times* team—Pam Zekman, Zay Smith, Bill Recktenwald, and Mindy Trossman—the whole sordid story was finally out in the open for all to see.

As these tales indicate, journalists make many judgments, many decisions, some deliberate and calculated, others quite personal and quick, on the spot. These are some common questions facing all journalists: Which story should I pursue? Where's the bigger payoff for me and my company? Whom should I interview? Do I say I'm a reporter, or conceal it to get at the unvarnished truth? Should I promise confidentiality? Which parts of my reporting do I include or exclude in telling the story? Should I give some cover ("a confidential source revealed . . .") to a talkative insider who could be useful in the future? Does it matter if a source's job might be jeopardized by what I write?

Classical Ethics

Scholarly ethicists such as Clifford G. Christians and colleagues in *Media Ethics: Cases and Moral Reasoning* (Boston: Allyn & Bacon, 2011) offer constructs to analyze and decide such questions, though they're not always practical for the working journalist out on a breaking story. These scholars also tell us that the values, the societal standards, of Western civilization are founded on the writings of moral philosophers that invoke higher human traits such as virtue, love, rights, duty, and utility. To illustrate, let's look at quotations from Confucius, Aristotle, Kant, Bentham, Mill, Locke, Rawls, and the Bible. They call on the reader to lead an upstanding life, but there are lessons here for working journalists, too. We'll observe later that those lessons don't necessarily lead a journalist to the same conclusions that might be permitted by the law. There are differences. Let's take the philosophical concepts in chronological order.

Virtue

Confucius (551–479 B.C.E.) was a teacher, magistrate, and the minister of justice in the Chou state of ancient China. Among his many writings, Confucius devised a decision-making rationale that he called the Golden Mean, defined as a morally virtuous position between two extremes. To help find the Golden Mean he wrote these cautionary epigrams:

> Yan Hui is of no help to me. There is nothing that I say that he doesn't like.
> Allowing that a person is earnest in his words the question is: is he an exemplary person or is he just pretending to be serious?
> On learning something, act upon it.
> Where everyone despises a person, you must look into the matter carefully; where everyone celebrates a person, you must also look into it carefully. (Confucius 1999)

And, in another translation of Confucius:

> The object of the exemplary person is truth.
> When you know a thing, to hold that you know it, and when you do not know a thing, to acknowledge that you do not know it—this is knowledge.
> Learning without thought is labour lost; thought without learning is perilous. (Confucius 1915)

Note Confucius' emphasis on skepticism, inquiry, verification, and truth. These brief quotations offer pearls of wisdom and exemplify the probing curiosity that a journalist should bring to work every day. They also provide very practical advice about how to cover a story with more than one dimension. To help us update these ancient expressions of virtue, *Webster's Dictionary* defines virtue as "moral excellence," "integrity of character," and "uprightness of conduct." Confucius wouldn't disagree.

Aristotle, too, idealized virtue and defined it as a mean between extremes, according to W. D. Ross's *Aristotle: The Nicomachean Ethics* (Oxford University Press, 2009). Aristotle (384–322 B.C.E.) was a student of Plato, tutor to Alexander the Great, and the "first philosopher to create a comprehensive system of Western philosophy, encompassing morality and aesthetics, logic and science, politics and metaphysics," Ross states. He quotes Aristotle: "Moral virtue is a middle state determined by practical wisdom. . . . The wise person within whom there are well-integrated traits of character is the ultimate arbiter of right and wrong." Both good upbringing and good education were needed to make such judgments: "so the man who has been educated in a subject is a good judge of that subject, and the man who has received an all-round education is a good judge in general." In today's journalism, advantage goes to the person who has both a solid general education and special knowledge of a particular subject, upon which sound judgments can be based. These same twin foundations—broad education and particular education—Aristotle reasoned, will help a person determine "the human good," which "is generally agreed to be happiness."

Like Confucius, Aristotle emphasized individual judgment.

Love

The Judeo-Christian religious tradition elevates the ethics of love, kindness, and compassion, qualities not necessarily associated with contemporary journalism. However, in the Jewish Bible (the Old Testament) we read:

> Thou shalt not take vengeance, nor bear any grudge against the children of thy people; but thou shalt love thy neighbor as thyself: I am Jehovah. (Leviticus 19:8)

> Let not kindness and truth forsake thee: Bind them about thy neck; Write them upon the tablet of thy heart: So shalt thou find favor and good understanding in the sight of God and man. (Proverbs 3:3–4)

> That which maketh a man to be desired is his kindness. (Proverbs 19:22)

> He that followeth after righteousness and kindness Findeth life, righteousness, and honor. (Proverbs 21:21)

> And what doth Jehovah require of thee? To do justly and to love kindness and to walk humbly with thy God. (Micah 6:8)

> Thus has Jehovah of hosts spoken saying, Execute true judgment, and show kindness and compassion every man to his brother. (Zechariah 7:9)

This Biblical linkage of kindness and truth in each person is worth pondering. A journalist is hardly exempt. Accepting the wisdom of personally embracing both kindness and truth, certain persons should not be excluded because of their profession.

And in the Christian Bible (the New Testament):

> Ye have heard that it was said, Thou shalt love thy neighbor, and hate thine enemy: but I say unto you, love your enemies, and pray for them that persecute you. (Matthew 5:43)

> Honor thy father and mother; and, Thou shalt love thy neighbor as thyself. (Matthew 19:19)

> One of them, a lawyer, asked him a question, trying him: "Teacher, which is the great commandment in the law? And he said unto him, Thou shalt love the Lord thy God with all thy heart, and with all thy soul, and with all thy mind. This is the great and first commandment. And a second like [unto it] is this, Thou shalt love thy neighbor as thyself. On these two commandments the whole law hangeth, and the prophets." (Matthew 22:35–40)

Love and compassion may not appear to be fundamentals of good journalism. But everyone, including journalists, experiences such emotions. An important lesson of this book is that these emotions should not be ignored. It's sometimes said that journalists, like physicians, should "do no harm," but that might better be stated as "do no unintentional harm."

Rights

Leaping forward many centuries, a British physician-philosopher, John Locke (1632–1704), remembered now as the "father of liberalism" and author of the theory of the Social Contract, articulated ethics based on individual rights. He wrote in "A Letter Concerning Toleration":

> It is the duty of the civil magistrate, by the impartial execution of equal laws, to secure unto all the people in general and to every one of his subjects in particular the just possession of these things belonging to this life. If anyone presume to violate the laws of public justice and equity, established for the preservation of those things, his presumption is to be checked by the fear of punishment, consisting of the deprivation or diminution of those civil interests, or goods, which otherwise he might and ought to enjoy. But seeing no man does willingly suffer himself to be punished by the deprivation of

any part of his goods, and much less of his liberty or life, therefore, is the magistrate armed with the force and strength of all his subjects, in order to the punishment of those that violate any other man's rights. (Locke 2010)

Locke saw recognition of rights as leading to decisions for "the greater good" and "the removing of pain, as long as we have any left, as the first and necessary step towards happiness."

Echoing Locke's emphasis on individual rights in the context of community or society, a latter-day Harvard philosopher, John Rawls (1921–2002), wrote in *A Theory of Justice* that the "most reasonable principles of justice are those everyone would accept and agree to from a fair position." To assume that "fair position," Rawls stated, a person should imagine himself without all social, educational, and economic advantages, adopting what he called a "veil of ignorance," so that "everyone is impartially situated as equals" in order to relate fairly to each other. Fairness and allegiance to society are necessary aspects of good journalism. Journalists are observers, true, but they are also inhabitants of the world they write about.

Duty

A century after Locke, an influential German philosopher, Immanuel Kant (1724–1804), set forth his Categorical Imperative: "Act so that the maxim of thy will can always at the same time hold good as a principle of universal legislation." In other words, what's good for the goose is good for the gander. Kant said "pure reason" provides "a universal law which we call the moral law," and morality, in turn, is "the formal supreme determining principle of the will." Kant's thinking is called deontological ethics, from the Greek word for duty, *deon* (Kant 2010).

Utility

A Kant contemporary, British philosopher and jurist Jeremy Bentham (1748–1832), was a man before his time. He espoused individual legal rights, economic freedom, separation of church and state, decriminalization of homosexual acts, and abolition of slavery and capital punishment. He also articulated a social philosophy called utilitarianism, meaning that the proper course of action is one that maximizes human happiness, thus sounding a bit like Locke and Aristotle, but with a difference. Unlike Confucius, Aristotle and Kant, who cherished virtue or duty in the decision-making process, to Bentham the quality of a decision would be measured later, by its results (Bentham 2010).

This philosophy of "utility" was further developed by Bentham's student John Stuart Mill (1806–1873), who wrote in his book, titled simply, *Utilitarianism:*

> The creed which accepts as the foundation of morals, Utility or the Greatest Happiness. Principle, holds that actions are right in proportion as they tend to promote happiness, wrong as they tend to produce the reverse of happiness. By happiness is intended pleasure, and the absence of pain; by unhappiness, pain, and the privation of pleasure . . . [P]leasure, and freedom from pain, are the only things desirable as ends; and . . . all desirable things (which are as numerous in the utilitarian as in any other scheme) are desirable either for the pleasure inherent in themselves, or as means to the promotion of pleasure and the prevention of pain. . . .
>
> This, being, according to the utilitarian opinion, the end of human action, is necessarily also the standard of morality; which may accordingly be defined, the rules and precepts for human conduct, by the observance of which an existence such as has been described might be to the greatest extent possible, secured to all mankind; and not to them only, but, so far as the nature of things admits, to the whole sentient creation. (Mill 2010)

Mill summarized his utilitarian philosophy in Biblical terms: "In the golden rule of Jesus of Nazareth, we read the complete spirit of the ethics of utility. To do as one would be done by, and to love one's neighbour as oneself, constitute the ideal perfection of utilitarian morality."

Journalists need to ask themselves whether only results matter, or if ethical judgments need to be rendered (as most of the philosophers quoted above would have it) at the time an action is taken, deciding whether the action is in itself right or wrong, regardless of ultimate results.

These various philosophies of ethics require some time to digest, both as guides to everyday living and as worthy considerations in journalism. There are some common threads running through at least some of them, such as truth, fairness, goodness, happiness, and the consideration of others. However, the overriding message is that there are few fixed rules here; determinations of what's ethical, in life and in journalism, are in the end your own. Your upbringing, education, life experience, reading, personal interests, values, and priorities—all are relevant in helping you determine what's ethical, in both thinking and acting.

Professional Codes of Conduct

On top of this ethical heritage in our Western society, journalism also requires a clear sense of social responsibility and a genuine concern for the citizenry.

These concepts are imbedded in the codes of ethics and codes of professional responsibility set forth by various news organizations. The Society of Professional Journalists' (SPJ) Code of Ethics begins:

> Members of the Society of Professional Journalists believe that public enlightenment is the forerunner of justice and the foundation of democracy. The duty of the journalist is to further those ends by seeking truth and providing a fair and comprehensive account of events and issues. Conscientious journalists from all media and specialties strive to serve the public with thoroughness and honesty. Professional integrity is the cornerstone of a journalist's credibility. Members of the Society share a dedication to ethical behavior and adopt this code to declare the Society's principles and standards of practice.

Sounding a bit like the Bible, the SPJ Code goes on:

> Ethical journalists treat sources, subjects and colleagues as human beings deserving of respect. Journalists should: Show compassion for those who may be affected adversely by news coverage. Use special sensitivity when dealing with children and inexperienced sources or subjects. Be sensitive when seeking or using interviews or photographs of those affected by tragedy or grief. (SPJ 1996)

The *New York Times* Policy on Ethics in Journalism states:

> Companywide, our goal is to cover the news impartially and to treat readers, news sources, advertisers and all parts of our society fairly and openly, and to be seen as doing so. The reputation of our company rests upon that perception, and so do the professional reputations of its staff members. Thus the company, its separate business units and members of its newsrooms and editorial pages share an interest in avoiding conflicts of interest or any appearance of conflict. (New York Times Company 2005)

And, the Radio Television Digital News Association Code of Ethics and Professional Conduct declares that:

> Professional electronic journalists should:
>
> • Understand that any commitment other than service to the public undermines trust and credibility.

- Recognize that service in the public interest creates an obligation to reflect the diversity of the community and guard against oversimplification of issues or events.
- Provide a full range of information to enable the public to make enlightened decisions.
- Fight to ensure that the public's business is conducted in public (Radio Television Digital News Association 2012).

It's essential that journalists observe professional codes of ethics. They invoke considerations that are compatible with the law, but go beyond it. Not everything that's legal is ethical. We will see court opinions in which judges, sometimes contrary to their own rulings on the law, implore journalists to recognize their responsibilities to society and to observe higher standards than the law imposes. Journalism ethics are not decreed by judges.

Concealment and Confidentiality

Even without a comprehensive personal philosophy of right and wrong, there will be occasions in journalism when ethical judgments will need to be made. Sometimes the luxury of carefully examining an ethical question—planning an investigation, perhaps—with the help of an editor or other colleagues will be available. Your company's code of ethics may provide useful guidance. At other times, out on a story, you'll need to make a snap judgment, a decision that you'll live with both personally and professionally.

Fabrication, Jayson Blair-style, is clearly wrong. So is plagiarism, which is lifting verbatim or paraphrasing someone else's recorded work and presenting it, deliberately or not, as your own work. Neither facts nor ideas are proprietary, either in law or in ethics, but a person's expression of facts or of an idea, whether in writing or another art form, clearly is. That includes blogging and all other forms of expression found on the Internet. When you become a successful blogger or website manager, commanding an audience big enough to attract advertising and thus generate a living wage, will you countenance another blogger's stealing your words and pictures and presenting them as his own?

However, beyond these clear rules, there are gray areas. Two of the most difficult decisions are whether to hide the fact that you're a journalist in order to get your story, as Pam Zekman and Zay Smith did at The Mirage tavern, and whether to divulge the name of a source to whom you've promised confidentiality. On deception, the SPJ Code says this: "Avoid undercover or other surreptitious methods of gathering information except when traditional open methods will not yield information vital to the public." On confidentiality, in one famous case, the federal prosecutor's search for the government source who leaked the name of covert CIA agent Valerie Plame to the press, *Time* reporter Matthew Cooper opted to reveal the identity of his source and thus avoided incarceration for contempt of court, while Judith Miller of the *New York Times* kept her promise to her anonymous source and went to jail. (More on confidentiality later when we get to anonymous sources and the journalist's privilege.)

Concealing your identity can take many forms, from the carefully planned deception of The Mirage to hiding your identity from a crime victim. One possible way of making this call is to evaluate, as the SPJ Code suggests, whether the public good of a better story outweighs the harm of concealment. Of course, that can be a difficult decision when you may not have a very good fix on either the harm or the good, both prospective at the moment you need to decide.

We'll revisit this recurring dilemma as we go through court cases in the chapters ahead. For instance, was it ethical for a television cameraman, without identifying himself to an auto accident victim, to photograph and record her conversation with a nurse as she was airlifted in pain to a hospital? Was it ethical for TV reporters to hide tiny cameras in their hair while posing as patients in a clinic, or as employees of a grocery chain? Was it ethical to help plan and then video a police raid that caused a terrified homeowner to commit suicide? Was it ethical to take advantage of a police slipup and print the name of a rape victim in the face of a state law prohibiting that? The law rendered a judgment in each of these cases, but that doesn't necessarily answer the ethical questions raised.

Conflict of Interest

One particular ethical concern, particularly of the business press, is avoidance of any conflict of interest, or even the appearance of a conflict. Reporters who cover business, finance, and markets inevitably obtain information that may affect stock prices. For instance, a comment from a corporate chief financial officer could cast doubt on the company's prevailing forecast of sales and profit in the coming quarter or year. Such insights are legitimate news, but they also could offer a dishonest journalist an opportunity to make some illicit money by immediately buying or selling the company's stock before filing the story. This is not only unethical journalistically, it's also illegal and is considered insider trading.

Another potential conflict of interest for a business reporter is a publicly held company (i.e., listed on a stock exchange or market) in which they or their family own stock or have a personal connection. It would be ethically wrong for that reporter to write about the company. But because such opportunities, call them temptations, might arise any day, and might taint the credibility of the publication as well as the individual journalist, business journalists are clearly admonished by their employers to avoid any possible hint of conflict of interest.

For instance, Dow Jones & Co., publisher of the *Wall Street Journal* and *Barron's* magazine, forbids its journalists to speculate in securities, or to buy futures or options on commodities or stocks. Furthermore:

> News personnel assigned to report on a specific industry may not buy or sell any tradable instruments in any company engaged in a whole or significant part in that industry or in any pooled investments (such as exchange traded funds and mutual funds) primarily invested in that industry, nor may the spouse, significant other, or dependents of any such employee do so. Editors are considered to be assigned to the industries for which their reporters have substantial responsibilities.
>
> News personnel not assigned to report on a specific industry or those covering an area outside of their assigned industry who own individual securities in a company or have a spouse, significant other, or dependent who owns any such securities must recuse themselves from working on any content that relates to that company. News personnel should note that owning securities in individual companies may prevent them from taking on additional assignments, moving to different coverage areas, or assuming other responsibilities. (Dow Jones & Company 2012)

Dow Jones also insists on avoiding any appearance of conflict in political matters, ruling out even personal political contributions: "All news personnel and members of senior management with any responsibility for news should refrain from partisan political activity. Partisan political activity includes passing out buttons, posting partisan comments on social-networking sites, blogging, soliciting campaign contributions, hosting a fundraiser for a partisan candidate, as well as making a financial contribution to a candidate's campaign."

And, there's also enforcement: "all Dow Jones employees shall be required each year to provide a written attestation that they have read and abided by this code during the previous calendar year. The matters addressed by this code are sufficiently important that any lapse in judgment within the areas covered here may be considered serious enough to warrant discipline up to and including dismissal."

Similarly, the *New York Times* Policy on Ethics in Journalism declares:

> Journalists who regularly cover business and financial news may not play the market: that is, they may not conduct in-and-out trading, speculate in options or futures or sell securities short. . . .

To avoid an appearance of conflict, business editors and their superiors in each news operation must affirm annually to their unit's chief financial officer that they have no financial holdings in violation of this set of rules. (New York Times Company 2005)

It's not possible in a single chapter or even an entire book to flag all the potential ethical dilemmas a journalist might encounter, much less to prescribe answers for them. Some ethical questions can be anticipated and resolved, or at least decided, in advance. But when you're covering the story of an accident and suddenly you see that the crash victim is still lying there on the road, do you photograph the body? Or when the gatekeeper at a "private" political fund-raiser doesn't recognize you as a journalist, do you ask whether the event is open to the press? When a vital source won't tell you anything unless you promise her absolute secrecy, are you prepared to go to jail to honor your pledge? The SPJ Code says "keep promises." Questions like these will be yours to answer, often right on the spot.

Questions for Discussion

1. Why is it difficult for a journalist to adhere to a personal code of ethics?
2. If you feel that your personal ethics impair your ability to cover a story, should you cover it anyway to please your editor? What if you're assigned a story that will question the practices of your brother's employer?
3. If you're aware that your grandparents own stock in a certain company, is it ethical for you to cover that company? What if the company isn't on your beat?
4. Is "happiness" a sufficient basis for making ethical decisions?
5. Is it fair to apply different ethical standards to different groups of people, say farmers or immigrants or the rich or the poor?
6. When might this disparity occur? Would it be fair?
7. Why do you think there is relatively low public regard for journalists? How might ethics figure into this feeling?

References

Barry, Dan, David Barstow, Jonathan D. Glater, Adam Liptak, and Jacques Steinberg. 2003. CORRECTING THE RECORD; Times Reporter Who Resigned Leaves Long Trail of Deception." *The New York Times,* May 11. http://www.nytimes.com/2003/05/11/us/correcting-the-record-times-reporter-who-resigned-leaves-long-trail-of-deception.html?pagewanted=all&src=pm (accessed December 1, 2012).

Bentham, Jeremy, *The Principles of Morals and Legislation* (Charleston: Nabu Press, 2010).

Christians, Clifford G., Mark Fackler, Kathy Brittain Richardson, and Peggy J. Kreshel, *Media Ethics: Cases and Moral Reasoning* (Boston: Allyn & Bacon, 2011).

Confucius, *The Analects of Confucius: A Philosophical Translation,* trans. Roger T. Ames and Henry Rosemont, Jr. (New York: Ballantine Books, 1999).

Confucius, *The Ethics of Confucius,* trans. Miles Menander Dawson (New York: G. P. Putnam's Sons, 1915).

Dow Jones & Company, Code of Conduct, 2012. http://www.dowjones.com/code-conduct.asp (accessed December 1, 2012).

Kant, Immanuel, *The Works of Immanuel Kant,* trans. T.K. Abbott (Hustonville, KY: Golgotha) 2010. Kindle edition.

Locke, John. "A Letter Concerning Toleration." In *The Work of John Locke* (Seattle: Amazon Digital Services) 2010. Kindle edition.

Mill, John Stuart, *Utilitarianism* (Seattle: Amazon Digital Services) 2012. Kindle edition.

New York Times Company Policy on Ethics in Journalism, The New York Times Company, October 2005. http://www.nytimes.com/nytco/press/ethics.html (accessed December 1, 2012).

Radio Television Digital News Association, Code of Ethics, 2012. http://rtdna.org/article/rtdna_code_of_ethics (accessed December 1, 2012).

Rawls, John, *A Theory of Justice* (Cambridge: Harvard, 1971).

Ross, W.D., *Aristotle: The Nicomachean Ethics* (Oxford: Oxford University Press, 2009).

SPJ Code of Ethics, Society of Professional Journalists (SPJ), 1996. http://www.spj.org/ethicscode.asp (accessed March 15, 2013).

3

Prior Restraint

"It is a newspaper's duty to print the news and raise hell."
—Wilbur F. Storey, editor and publisher, the *Chicago Times*, 1861

Now that everyone has the ability to publish worldwide on the Internet, are we really free to do so? The American answer to this question is probably yes, but it's hedged with so many qualifications and limitations that we need to understand how different the world was three hundred years ago and how we have gotten to where we are now. The answers are largely traceable to the advent of democracy, and in particular, to twentieth-century rulings of the U.S. Supreme Court as a manifestation of that democracy.

Seditious Libel

When printing began in England there was no freedom of the press. On the contrary, a printer needed a license from the crown to publish anything, and if he dared print anything derogatory of the royal government, he was likely to be jailed for an offense called seditious libel, meaning criticism of a public official. Truth was no defense. This was the common law at work, and royal governors of American colonies attempted to transplant these fierce restrictions into the new land. One of the earliest printers, James Franklin, was imprisoned for publishing articles that questioned the actions of the governor of the Massachusetts Bay Colony. (He had a teenage brother named Benjamin who kept the newspaper going during his incarceration, thus launching one of the most auspicious publishing careers in American history.) But in a later instance a Massachusetts grand jury declined to indict, or charge, an obstreperous printer with seditious libel. Benjamin Gray had published a pamphlet critical of the lack of credit available in the colony, and even had the effrontery to advertise how it could be obtained. His offensive behavior was referred to the grand jury in 1721; it simply refused to act (Dunway 1994).

The whole idea of governmental control of printing came crashing down in the 1732 New York case of immigrant printer John Peter Zenger. He had published newspaper articles critical of the royal governor, one William Cosby, who retaliated by hauling Zenger into court. But Zenger was defended by a persuasive advocate from Philadelphia named Andrew Hamilton (thus the origin of the complimentary phrase, "a Philadelphia lawyer"), who, in defiance of the judge's instructions, urged the jury to acquit Zenger because his criticisms were true. And the jury did. That verdict didn't end seditious libel, but it was the beginning of the end.

Declarations of Press Freedom

The notion that newspapers were free to publish took affirmative legal form in the 1770s, as "independence fever," openly nourished by newspapers, was running high throughout the American colonies. Virginians wrote a state constitution in 1776, even before the War of Independence began, and included in it a Declaration of Rights proclaiming that "Freedom of the Press is one of the great bulwarks of Liberty and can never be restrained but by Despotick governments" (Virginia Declarations of Rights, Section 12). It was the first governmental declaration of freedom of the press in human history.

Virginia's lead soon was followed during the War of Independence by eight more of the original thirteen states. The Massachusetts constitution, drafted by John Adams, contained language that was subsequently mimicked by other states: "The liberty of the press is essential to the security of freedom in a state: it ought not, therefore, to be restrained in this Commonwealth" (Massachusetts Constitution, Art. XVI). Only two of the original state constitutions omitted such a guarantee; two other states did not immediately adopt new constitutions. Subsequent constitutions adopted by new states as they joined the union often embraced the phrase "freedom to publish," extending that affirmative right.

Following the lead of the states, after independence was won, the new federal government and the states adopted the first ten amendments to the nation's new Constitution in 1791. (Approval by three-fourths of the states is required to amend it.) These historical amendments, called the Bill of Rights, guaranteed a multitude of individual rights and freedoms for the people of the new nation, among them the freedom of speech and freedom of the press. But the press clause, contained in the First Amendment, wasn't the forthright declaration of freedom to publish that many states adopted. It simply declared that "Congress shall make no law . . . abridging . . . the freedom of the press. . . ."

Although scholars today still may disagree on whether the press clause was intended to abolish the criminal offense of seditious libel, there's no disagreement that it was meant to abolish governmental censorship, or what lawyers call prior restraint of the press. However, ending prior restraint did not mean absolute freedom to publish offensive articles, for an aggrieved target, a government official or a private person, could still file a civil lawsuit for defamation, or libel (and later, invasion of privacy). So a newspaper might be required to pay money, what lawyers call "damages," if found guilty. Indeed, it was relatively easy to prove defamation. All the criticized person needed to prove was that he was clearly identified, and that derogatory information about him was published. Despite the Zenger acquittal, the First Amendment, and state guarantees of the freedom to publish, for many years libel still could be proved even if the offensive facts were demonstrably true. And criminal seditious libel, as we'll see in the next chapter, persisted into the early nineteenth century, faded out, and then recurred in World War I (1917–18). In other words, the impact of the constitutional promises of press freedom was not as exciting as the words themselves.

Two twentieth-century decisions of the U.S. Supreme Court cast a glaring light on that shortfall. Both involved newspapers that dared to criticize state court judges. The guilty party in a 1907 case, *Patterson v. Colorado*, 205 U.S. 454 (1907), was a former United States senator, who obviously obtained no deference from the justices. Thomas M. Patterson was the publisher of a Colorado newspaper that questioned the legitimacy of the election of judges of the state supreme court. They responded by holding him in contempt of court. At the U.S. Supreme Court, Justice Oliver Wendell Holmes, one of the most distinguished jurists in the Court's entire history, made short shrift of Patterson's First Amendment defense, summarily dismissing it.

A few years later, in 1918, the editor of an Ohio newspaper found himself in similar hot water. In that case, *Toledo Newspaper Company v. United States*, 247 U.S. 402 (1918), the Supreme Court at least acknowledged "the assuredly secured freedom of the press," if only to dismiss it as "subject to the restraints which separate right from wrong-doing."

Press Freedom Sustained

Near v. Minnesota

Finally, in 1931, a full 140 years after the adoption of the First Amendment, freedom of the press prevailed, though narrowly, in an historic case called *Near v. Minnesota*, 283 U.S. 697 (1931). Jay Near was the publisher of a Minnesota weekly newspaper that accused the Minneapolis mayor and police chief of taking payoffs from a crime syndicate. Acting under a Minnesota statute, the county prosecutor obtained a court order, an injunction, shutting the paper down. It was affirmed by the Minnesota Supreme Court.

Near appealed to Col. Robert R. McCormick, the haughty, conservative publisher of the *Chicago Tribune,* for funds to finance an appeal to the U.S. Supreme Court. Although Near was an unsavory character—anti-Semitic, anti-black, anti-labor, and anti-Catholic—his cause caught the aristocratic McCormick's attention, and he provided funds and his own lawyer, Weymouth Kirkland, to pursue the appeal. Kirkland pleaded freedom of the press and won a stunning 5–4 victory at the Supreme Court.

However, although Chief Justice Hughes acknowledged freedom of the press in his majority opinion, he based the ruling not so much on the First Amendment as on the Fourteenth Amendment's guarantee of due process under law. It was a curious rationale, perhaps needed to obtain the five votes needed. Nevertheless, *Near v. Minnesota* went down as the press's first big win at the Supreme Court. Hughes pointedly embraced "the immunity of the press from previous restraint in dealing with official misconduct."

The Pentagon Papers

It took the Supreme Court another four decades to dispatch prior restraint as a violation of the First Amendment, which was surely the Founders' intention. The case was *New York Times Co. v. United States*, 403 U.S. 713 (1971). Even then the Court remained divided.

The Vietnam War had been raging since 1965. Its illegitimacy (no Congressional declaration of war was even requested by President Lyndon Johnson) and its costs in dollars, materials, and human life, were tearing the nation apart. So was military conscription. Young men and their supporters demonstrated frequently and noisily against the draft. Many were imprisoned for resisting it, others fled to Canada.

Daniel Ellsberg, a Harvard economics Ph.D. then in his late thirties, had already served, in the Marines as a platoon leader. He had also worked as a civilian in the Pentagon and with the State Department in Vietnam during the war. In the late 1960s he was employed as a strategic analyst at an influential think tank, the RAND Corporation, in California. He was not a pacifist.

Because of the dubious history of the war, Defense Secretary Robert McNamara commissioned a study of its origins and decision-making processes, and the Defense Department contracted with RAND to do the study. Ellsberg was assigned to the project. He was given top-secret security clearance that provided access to the most sensitive, highly confidential government documents.

Ellsberg and his colleagues completed the study, also classified as top secret, in 1968. Their work later became known as the Pentagon Papers. The documents revealed that government leaders had acknowledged privately for some time that the United States couldn't win the war and that future casualties would be heavy. They also revealed that the Johnson administration had lied repeatedly to the public and to Congress.

The year after delivering the study, 1969, Ellsberg, though still at RAND, began attending anti-war rallies. One speaker proudly announced that he wouldn't be drafted and was going to jail. Ellsberg was quoted later by Marlo Thomas as being deeply moved by that testament:

> It wasn't what he said exactly that changed my worldview. It was the example he was setting with his life. How his words in general showed that he was a stellar American, and that he was going to jail as a very deliberate choice—because he thought it was the right thing to do. There was no question in my mind that my government was involved in an unjust war that was going to continue and get larger. Thousands of young men were dying each year. I left the auditorium and found a deserted men's room. I sat on the floor and cried for over an hour, just sobbing. The only time in my life I've reacted to something like that. (Thomas 2002)

Ellsberg secretly copied the Pentagon Papers and in 1970 quietly tried to persuade sympathetic U.S. senators to release them on the floor of the Senate, where a senator is immune from prosecution. He wasn't successful. So he leaked them to reporters at the *New York Times* and the *Washington Post*. After considerable study and deliberation, in mid-1971 they began to publish the Pentagon Papers—long excerpts and interpretative commentaries to help understand them. Ellsberg went into hiding for a time, fearing the papers' source would become known. He subsequently surrendered to a U.S. attorney and was tried, along with a colleague, for violating the Espionage Act of 1917, but the charges ultimately were dismissed because of evidence that the government had tapped his phone without a warrant.

President Richard Nixon's attorney general, John Mitchell, demanded that the two newspapers immediately cease publication of the Pentagon Papers, citing no statutory authority but asserting the president's constitutional powers to conduct the nation's military and foreign affairs. Nevertheless, the papers went ahead. So the government sued, in both New York and Washington, seeking preliminary injunctions to prohibit any further publication of the documents, alleging but not delineating, a threat to national security. As the nation, sick of the war, watched and waited, the courts responded with remarkable alacrity.

In Washington, the U.S. District Court judge asked the government to specify which documents would endanger national security. Upon examining them, the judge ruled that the government had failed to make its case and thus denied the requested injunction. The government appealed to the Circuit Court of Appeals for the District of Columbia, and a panel of that court, by a divided vote, reversed the District Court's order and directed it to hold a hearing on whether the threatened publication would impair national defense. Then the Court of Appeals had second thoughts and convened an *en banc* hearing of all nine judges to reconsider the question. Immediately after the hearing, on the same day, the court affirmed the decision of the District Court. In *United States of America v. Washington Post Company*, 446 F.2d 1327 (D.C. Cir. June 23, 1971), the court stated *per curiam* (by the court): "Our conclusion to affirm the denial of injunctive relief is fortified by the consideration that the massive character of the 'leak' which has occurred, and the disclosures already made by several newspapers, raise substantial doubt that effective relief of the kind sought by the government can be provided by the judiciary."

Meanwhile, the District Court for the Southern District of New York, in Manhattan, also denied the government's request for a preliminary injunction. But the Second Circuit Court of Appeals wasn't so sure. It also heard the case *en banc,* and a day later ruled, 5–3, in *United States of America v. New York Times Company*, 444 F.2d 544 (2d Cir. June 23, 1971), to remand the case to the District Court for a hearing on whether the publication of the documents would "pose such grave and immediate danger to the security of the United States as to warrant their publication being enjoined."

With the Courts of Appeals divided, the dispute was promptly laid before the Supreme Court. The justices heard oral argument on June 26 and rendered their decision just four days later. They divided, 6–3, for the newspapers and against prior restraint, but a reading of the individual justices' opinions made it clear that the Supreme Court wasn't totally rejecting the idea of prior restraint in some extreme situation.

There was little time to write the usual lengthy opinion of the Court, so the majority produced a remarkably brief but historic *per curiam* opinion. In *New York Times v. United States*, 403 U.S. 713 (June 30, 1971), they cited *Near v. Minnesota* and other precedents to postulate that the government has a "heavy burden" to prove the need for a prior restraint, concluding: "The District Court for the Southern District of New York in the *New York Times* case and the District Court for the District of Columbia and the Court of Appeals for the District of Columbia Circuit in the *Washington Post* case held that the Government had not met that burden. We agree." The government's requested injunctions were denied.

However, in contrast to the succinct *per curiam* opinion, all nine justices wrote separately, some at great length, to explain their votes. Each had something different to say about this unprecedented constitutional challenge by the federal government.

Justices Hugo Black and William O. Douglas voiced in separate concurring opinions an "absolutist" position that the First Amendment allows no restraints on the press, under any circumstances. Black declared, "The Government's power to censor the press was abolished so that the press would remain forever free to censure the Government. Only a free and independent press can effectively expose deception in government." Douglas noted that there is "no statute barring the publication by the press of the material which the Times and the Post seek to use," and saw the Pentagon Papers as contributing to the already-fervent public debate about the Vietnam war: "A debate of large proportions goes on in the Nation over our posture in Vietnam. That debate antedated the disclosure of the contents of the present documents. The latter are highly relevant to the debate in progress. Secrecy in government is fundamentally anti-democratic, perpetuating bureaucratic errors. Open debate and discussion of public issues are vital to our national health." (*New York Times v. United States*, 403 U.S. 720)

In his concurring opinion, Justice William Brennan, always sensitive to freedom of the press and usually aligned with Black and Douglas, wasn't quite ready to rule out all possibilities of prior restraint. Referring to restrictions imposed by the Espionage Act of 1917 on disclosing sensitive military information in times of war, he wrote: "only governmental allegation and proof that publication must inevitably, directly, and immediately cause the occurrence of an event kindred to imperiling the safety of a transport already at sea can support even the issuance of an interim restraining order. . . . Unless and until the Government has clearly made out its case, the First Amendment commands that no injunction may issue."

In a more measured concurrence, Justice Potter Stewart also questioned the sufficiency of the government's case:

> In the cases before us we are asked neither to construe specific regulations nor to apply specific laws. We are asked, instead, to perform a function that the Constitution gave to the Executive, not the Judiciary. We are asked, quite simply, to prevent the publication by two newspapers of material that the Executive Branch insists should not, in the national interest, be published. I am convinced that the Executive is correct with respect to some of the documents involved. But I cannot say that disclosure of any of them will surely result in direct, immediate, and irreparable damage to our Nation or its people. That being so, there can under the First Amendment be but one judicial resolution of the issues before us. I join the judgments of the Court." (*New York Times v. United States*, 403, U.S. 727)

Justice Byron White, also concurring, pointed out:

> When the Espionage Act was under consideration in 1917, Congress eliminated from the bill a provision that would have given the President

broad powers in time of war to proscribe, under threat of criminal penalty, the publication of various categories of information related to the national defense. Congress at that time was unwilling to clothe the President with such far-reaching powers to monitor the press. . . . The Criminal Code contains numerous provisions potentially relevant to these cases. Section 797 makes it a crime to publish certain photographs or drawings of military installations. Section 798, also in precise language, proscribes knowing and willful publication of any classified information concerning the cryptographic systems or communication intelligence activities of the United States as well as any information obtained from communication intelligence operations. . . . [Congress] has apparently been satisfied to rely on criminal sanctions and their deterrent effect on the responsible as well as the irresponsible press. (*New York Times v. United States,* 733–34, 735–36, 740)

Justice Thurgood Marshall's concurrence extended Justice White's line of thinking. He wrote that

it would be utterly inconsistent with the concept of separation of powers for this Court to use its power of contempt to prevent behavior that Congress has specifically declined to prohibit. . . .

It may be more convenient for the Executive Branch if it need only convince a judge to prohibit conduct rather than ask the Congress to pass a law, and it may be more convenient to enforce a contempt order than to seek a criminal conviction in a jury trial. Moreover, it may be considered politically wise to get a court to share the responsibility for arresting those who the Executive Branch has probable cause to believe are violating the law. But convenience and political considerations of the moment do not justify a basic departure from the principles of our system of government. (*New York Times v. United States,* 742–43)

Dissenting, Chief Justice Warren Burger and Justices John Marshall Harlan and Harry Blackmun fretted more about the haste with which the courts considered the sensitive case than its actual outcome. It had taken only sixteen days from start to finish. The always-prudent chief justice first took a shot at Black and Douglas, the absolutists: "Only those who view the First Amendment as an absolute in all circumstances—a view I respect, but reject—can find such cases as these to be simple or easy." He continued: "These cases are not simple for another and more immediate reason. We do not know the facts of the cases. No District Judge knew all the facts. No Court of Appeals judge knew all the facts. No member of this Court knows all the facts." Burger faulted *The Times* for precipitating unnecessary "frenetic haste" based on a claim of "the public 'right to know'" and posited this alternative scenario:

Would it have been unreasonable, since the newspaper could anticipate the Government's objections to release of secret material, to give the Government an opportunity to review the entire collection and determine whether agreement could be reached on publication? Stolen or not, if security was not in fact jeopardized, much of the material could no doubt have been declassified, since it spans a period ending in 1968. With such an approach—one that great newspapers have in the past practiced and stated editorially to be the duty of an honorable press—the newspapers and Government might well have narrowed the area of disagreement as to what was and was not publishable, leaving the remainder to be resolved in orderly litigation, if necessary. To me it is hardly believable that a newspaper long regarded as a great institution in American life would fail to perform one of the basic and simple duties of every citizen with respect to the discovery or possession of stolen property or secret government documents. That duty, I had thought—perhaps naively— was to report forthwith, to responsible public officers. This duty rests on taxi drivers, Justices, and the New York Times. The course followed by the Times, whether so calculated or not, removed any possibility of orderly litigation of the issues. (*New York Times v. United States,* 750–51)

In despair, Burger concluded: "The consequence of all this melancholy series of events is that we literally do not know what we are acting on. As I see it, we have been forced to deal with litigation concerning rights of great magnitude without an adequate record, and surely without time for adequate treatment either in the prior proceedings or in this Court."

Justice Harlan echoed with a lamentation that "the Court has been almost irresponsibly feverish in dealing with these cases." Justice Blackmun, like Burger, criticized the *Times'* hurry-up handling of the case:

[E]very deferral or delay, by restraint or otherwise, was abhorrent and was to be deemed violative of the First Amendment and of the public's 'right immediately to know.' Yet that newspaper stood before us at oral argument and professed criticism of the Government for not lodging its protest earlier than by a Monday telegram following the initial Sunday publication." The District of Columbia case is much the same with the *Washington Post* "on the excuse that it was trying to protect its source of information, initially refusing to reveal what material it actually possessed, and with the District Court forced to make assumptions as to that possession. (*New York Times v. United States,* 760)

Exasperated, Blackmun wrote that if untoward consequences should result from publication, "I strongly urge, and sincerely hope, that these two newspapers will be fully aware of their ultimate responsibilities to the United States of America" (*New York Times v. United States,* 762.

In sum, despite the justices' hedging about the law of prior restraint, for the press it was a sweet victory, based explicitly on the First Amendment at last.

Although the Pentagon Papers opinion didn't proclaim the same "freedom to publish" guaranteed by many state constitutions, Justice Potter Stewart, dissenting later in *Branzburg v. Hayes,* 408 U.S. 665 (1972), used that phrase to characterize the Court's holding in the Pentagon Papers case and one other, *Grosjean v. American Press Co.,* 297 U.S. 233 (1936), which held that a Louisiana tax on the state's largest newspapers but not other publications was discriminatory and therefore violated the First Amendment.

Prior Restraint Isn't Totally Gone

No one objected to Stewart's formulation "freedom to publish," and the Pentagon Papers ruling still stands as a powerful constitutional bar to government prior restraint of publication. However, that's not to say that courts never issue orders restraining publication.

In 1979 a federal district court in Wisconsin issued a temporary restraining order blocking the publication of a magazine article about how to construct a hydrogen bomb. The court based its order on the Atomic Energy Act (42 U.S.C. § 2280), holding that publication likely would cause direct, immediate, and irreparable injury to the nation, even though the statute did not specifically authorize such a prior restraint. After a hearing the court granted a preliminary injunction affirming the prior ruling, declaring that "First Amendment rights are not absolute" (*United States of America v. the Progressive, Inc.,* 486 F. Supp. 5 (W.D. Wis. 1979), the publisher did not appeal.

In another unusual case, a U.S. District Court judge in Miami ordered CNN not to broadcast recorded jailhouse conversations between a very high-profile prisoner, former Panama President Manuel Noriega, awaiting U.S. trial for drug trafficking, and his lawyer. The judge said he wanted first to hear the tapes to determine whether broadcasting them would prejudice Noriega's trial. CNN appealed the order to the Eleventh Circuit Court of Appeals, and while the matter was pending there, went ahead and broadcast eleven of the tapes. Soon, in *United States of America v. Noriega and Cable News Network,* 917 F.2d 1543 (11th Cir. 1990), the appellate court affirmed the restraining order, and the Supreme Court, over written objections by two justices who saw prior restraint, denied *certiorari,* letting the order stand. At that point the government dropped its objections, and CNN let the judge review the tapes. He found nothing offensive and so vacated his order.

In another instance, a U.S. District Court in Ohio ordered *Business Week* magazine not to publish corporate documents relating to an alleged securities fraud by Bankers Trust Company against Procter & Gamble Company. But that prior restraint was very short-lived. In *Procter & Gamble Company v. Bankers Trust Company*, 78 F.3d 219 (6th Cir. 1996), the U.S. Circuit Court of Appeals for the Sixth Circuit promptly set aside the order.

In recent years U.S. District Court Judge James Zagel, in Chicago, ordered the news media not to publish the names of the jurors trying fraud charges against a former Illinois governor, Rod Blagojevich. The press remonstrated, claiming prior restraint, but obeyed. Another high-profile Chicago criminal trial, for the murders of actress Jennifer Hudson's mother, sister, and nephew, brought a similar order from a state judge.

In sum, you may publish, but publish responsibly, or else it may be subject to serious penalties, as we shall see in the chapters to come.

Questions for Discussion

1. Is censorship the same as prior restraint? Why or why not?
2. Did *United States v. New York Times* absolutely preclude prior restraint in any and all circumstances? Should the justices have read the entire Pentagon Papers before ruling?
3. Do you consider Daniel Ellsberg courageous? Disloyal? Unethical? (His trial was derailed by the government's warrantless tapping of his phone conversations.)
4. How did the early declarations of press freedom by several states differ from the First Amendment adopted later?
5. Does the First Amendment bar even a modest prior restraint of the press? Should it?

References

Atomic Energy Act, 42 U.S.C. § 2280. *http://codes.lp.findlaw.com/uscode/42/23/A/XVII/2280.*

Branzburg v. Hayes, 408 U.S. 665 (1972). https://supreme.justia.com/cases/federal/us/408/665/case.html.

Dunway, Clyde Augustus, 1994. *The Development of Freedom of the Press in Massachusetts,* Google, http://books.google.com/books?id=Y6EyAAAAIAAJ&pg=PA197&dq=benjamin+gray+massachusetts+libel&hl=en&sa=X&ei=26FZUZXXDcfW0QGJooCoBw&ved=0CDcQ6AEwAA#v=onepage&q=benjamin%20gray%20massachusetts%20libel&f=false.

Grosjean v. American Press Co., 297 U.S. 233 (1936). http://www.law.cornell.edu/supct/html/historics/USSC_CR_0297_0233_ZO.html.

Massachusetts Constitution, Article XVI. https://malegislature.gov/laws/constitution#cart077.htm.

Near v. Minnesota, 283 U.S. 697 (1931). http://www.law.cornell.edu/supct/html/ historics/ USSC_CR_0283_0697_ZO.html.

New York Times Co. v. United States, 403 U.S. 713 (1971). http://www.gwu. edu/~nsarchiv/NSAEBB/NSAEBB48/decision.pdf.

Patterson v. Colorado, 205 U.S. 454 (1907). http://caselaw.lp.findlaw.com/cgi-bin/ getcase.pl?court=us&vol=205&invol=454.

Procter & Gamble Company v. Bankers Trust Company, 78 F.3d 219 (6th Cir. 1996). http://caselaw.lp.findlaw.com/scripts/getcase.pl?navby=search& case=/data2/ circs/6th/960076p.html.

Thomas, Marlo, *The Right Words at the Right Time* (New York: Altria Books, 2002).

Toledo Newspaper Company v. United States, 247 U.S. 402 (1918). http://www.law. cornell.edu/supremecourt/text/247/402.

United States of America v. New York Times Company, 444 F.2d 544 (2d Cir. June 23, 1971). http://www.law.cornell.edu/supct/html/historics/USSC_CR_0403_0713_ ZS.html.

United States of America v. Noriega, 917 F.2d 1543 (11 Cir. 1990).http://www.firsta-mendmentcoalition.org/handbook/cases/US_v_Noriega.pdf.

United States of America v. Progressive, Inc., 486 F. Supp. 5 (W.D. Wis. 1990). http:// www.bc.edu/bc_org/avp/cas/comm/free_speech/progressive.html.

United States of America v. Washington Post Company, 446 F.2d 1327 (D.C. Circ. June 23, 1971).

Virginia Declaration of Rights, section 12. http://www.archives.gov/exhibits/charters/ virginia_declaration_of_rights.html.

4

Libel

"Debate on public issues should be
uninhibited, robust, and wide-open."
—Justice William Brennan, *New York Times v. Sullivan*, 1964

As we noted earlier, the law of libel has posed a serious legal restraint on the freedom to publish, and thus on the discussion of public affairs. Libel is now much less an obstacle than it once was, thanks to the Supreme Court, but it's still real and deserves respect. Over the years it's been the most prevalent legal downside to careless journalism.

In our common-law system, libel is a tort, the French word for "wrong," and defined by *Black's Law Dictionary* as "[a]n injury or wrong committed, either with or without force, to the person or property of another."

The tort of libel is also called defamation. According to the authoritative legal reference *American Jurisprudence*, second edition, "Defamation is an impairment of a relational interest; it denigrates the opinion which others in the community have of the plaintiff and invades the plaintiff's interest in his or her reputation and good name. A cause of action for defamation is based on the transmission of derogatory statements, not on any physical or emotional distress to the plaintiff which may result." Libel originally had a twin in the defamation category, called slander. It referred to oral defamation, impairing a reputation through spoken words. But nowadays even broadcast defamatory speech is considered libel.

Seditious Libel and Civil Libel

A type of libel mentioned in historical terms was called seditious libel, or criticism of government officials, which carried the threat of criminal penalties including imprisonment. Although the First Amendment wasn't seen as abolishing seditious libel, the John Peter Zenger not-guilty verdict in 1732 already had punctured a big hole in seditious libel. But it made a brief, statutory comeback in the Sedition Act of 1798, signed by President John Adams. Under the Sedition Act, a number of journalists, and one congressman, were jailed for criticizing Adams and his government (the congressman won re-election from his jail cell in Vermont), but President Thomas Jefferson let the law expire in 1801 and pardoned all those convicted under the statute. With that, seditious libel under state law nearly died out. The Supreme Court's 1931 ruling in *Near v. Minnesota,* although it's seen as a test of prior restraint, reaffirmed that seditious libel has no place in modern American law.

However, civil libel continues in important ways. The American Law Institute's *Restatement of the Law, Second, Torts* describes this cause of action (section 558):

To create liability for defamation there must be:

a. a false and defamatory statement concerning another;
b. an unprivileged publication to a third party;
c. fault amounting at least to negligence on the part of the publisher; and
d. either actionability of the statement irrespective of special harm or the existence of special harm caused by the publication.

The *Restatement* (in section 559) goes on to define a defamatory communication as one that "tends so to harm the reputation of another as to lower him in the estimation of the community or to deter third persons from associating or dealing with him."

Today's libel cases are brought by individuals or even businesses who contend that a publication (which includes a broadcast) has maligned them, impairing their reputation to the point of causing financial loss (the meaning of subparagraph d above). The maligned party, of course, seeks to recover this amount from the allegedly offending news organization and likely from its individual journalists as well.

It is important to note that a company's libel insurance may not totally protect its staff. In the 1980s, Walter Jacobson, a prominent and respected investigative journalist at CBS television station WBBM-TV in Chicago, was found by a jury to have acted with actual malice. He was ordered to personally pay punitive damages of fifty thousand dollars for falsely accusing a tobacco company of luring teens to Viceroy cigarettes by likening smoking to alcohol, marijuana, and sex, all characterized by Jacobson as part of growing up. (CBS paid one million dollars in compensatory damages and two million dollars in punitive damages.) CBS and Jacobson had contended that his story was "commentary" or opinion, which can be a valid defense to a libel allegation if the opinion is based on fact, but the court rejected that argument. The Seventh Circuit Court of Appeals affirmed the jury's verdict (but adjusted the damages) in *Brown & Williamson Tobacco Corporation v. Walter Jacobson and CBS, Inc.,* 14 Media L. Rep. 1497 (7th Cir. 1987).

As inherited from England, common-law libel was relatively easy to demonstrate. A plaintiff had to prove only that he was identified and that derogatory things were printed about him. The truth, although it worked as John Peter Zenger's defense, was ordinarily not considered material in determining a libel verdict. Nor did the plaintiff need to prove that the offending article actually impaired his reputation or caused him any financial loss. He could claim and collect money damages anyway.

New York Times v. Sullivan

All of that changed very suddenly in 1964. The case was *New York Times Co. v. Sullivan*, 376 U.S. 24 (1964). The stage had been set several years earlier by a courageous woman named Rosa Parks, who defied a driver's order to move to the back of a bus in Montgomery, Alabama, as the state's racial segregation law required. That act of defiance marked the beginning of a civil rights revolution that swept the entire country, not just the South, for years to come. An eloquent young Montgomery preacher named Dr. Martin Luther King, Jr., soon emerged as the leading voice of the movement. He advocated non-violent resistance to the "Jim Crow" laws that segregated southern trains, buses, and other public accommodations, and to the *de facto* discrimination that existed in housing, jobs, and much of the life of the entire country. The appalling unfairness of segregation moved President Lyndon Johnson and Congress to take remedial action. The Civil Rights Act of 1964, barring discrimination in elements of interstate commerce such as transportation and public accommodations, was in the works.

In the midst of this political and social turmoil, the *New York Times* published an advertisement signed by Eleanor Roosevelt, actors Marlon Brando and Sidney Poitier, baseball hero Jackie Robinson, writer Nat Hentoff, and a number of other prominent citizens soliciting donations for the legal defense of Dr. King. The ad related that King, previously arrested seven times and accused of various crimes, was now facing felony charges growing out of his leadership of a black boycott of the Montgomery bus system, and that demonstrating black college students had been surrounded by shotgun-toting police and confined to their campus in Montgomery, their dining hall locked in an effort to starve them into submission, and that they were "being met by an unprecedented wave of terror."

Commissioner L.B. Sullivan, one member of the three-man Montgomery city commission who was responsible for public safety including the police force, demanded that the *Times* publicly retract the statements in the advertisement. Alabama law provided that a public official suing for libel on account of a publication concerning his official conduct could not seek punitive damages unless he first demanded a retraction and the publication failed or refused to comply. (Other states have similar retraction provisions.) The *Times* did not retract the statements, but sent Commissioner Sullivan a letter expressing puzzlement that he felt the advertisement applied to him and asking him to explain why he thought so. (Some time later the *Times* acquiesced to a retraction demand from Alabama Governor John Patterson, but it had no significance in this case.)

Commissioner Sullivan did not reply to the *Times* question and a few days later sued for libel, claiming that he was personally defamed because the ad described the police in pejorative terms. He asked for five hundred thousand dollars in damages. Significantly, Sullivan was not named in the ad, nor did he claim any financial loss, but a jury nevertheless upheld his claim and awarded him the full amount. The judgment was affirmed by the Alabama Supreme Court. The *Times* successfully petitioned the U.S. Supreme Court for a *writ of certiorari*.

The Court's ruling was truly electrifying. Justice William Brennan, writing for a unanimous court, overturned the Alabama judgment and its award of damages. For the first time the Court applied the First Amendment (which the Court in 1925 had interpreted to apply, by virtue of the Fourteenth Amendment's guarantee of "due process of law," to the states as well as to the federal government) to a state law of libel, finding it constitutionally deficient. In fact, the Court wrote new rules to govern libel actions remaining in effect today, to the benefit of the news media and to the disadvantage of public officials who might feel maligned by them.

The Court declared that for a public official to prevail in a libel suit, he must prove "actual malice" by the news organization, a new standard defined as the publication of a known falsehood or publishing with reckless disregard for the truth. While noting that Commissioner Sullivan wasn't named or clearly identified in the *Times* advertisement, and that he hadn't offered any proof of financial loss, the Court acknowledged his claim that not everything in the ad was entirely true: King had been arrested only four times, not seven; the police were deployed *near* the campus but didn't surround it; and the students were not locked out of their dining hall. But Justice Brennan brushed these inconsequential errors aside.

One practical reason for not insisting on the absolute truth, Brennan wrote, was that otherwise "would-be critics of official conduct may be deterred from voicing their criticism, even though it is believed to be true and even if it is in fact true, because of doubt whether it can be proved in court or fear of the expense of having to do so." Another reason, noted by Justice Arthur Goldberg in a concurring opinion: public officials have "equal if not greater access than most private citizens to media of communication" and thus can defend themselves against public criticism.

This sweeping opinion, in addition to giving the press some wiggle room for minor mistakes, extended the tough, new anti-libel protection to newspaper advertising as well as news stories. Moreover, Justice Brennan wrote passionately about the need for free press in a democracy: "we consider this case against the background of a profound national commitment to the principle that debate on public issues should be uninhibited, robust and wide-open, and that it may well include sometimes vehement, caustic and sometimes unpleasantly sharp attacks on government and public officials."

It should be noted that three of the justices, Hugo Black, William O. Douglas, and Arthur Goldberg, felt the Court didn't go far enough to protect the press. Black contended in a concurring opinion, which Douglas joined, that the promise of the First Amendment was "at the very least" the freedom to "criticize officials and discuss public affairs with impunity," meaning without fear of libel suits. He went on: "The Nation, I suspect, can live in peace without libel suits based on public discussions of public affairs and public officials. But I doubt that a country can live in freedom where its people can be made to suffer physically or financially for criticizing their government, its actions, or its officials." Justice Arthur Goldberg wrote a similar concurring opinion. This strict view became known as the "absolutist" interpretation of the First Amendment. The absolutists read the phrase "Congress shall make no law . . . impairing . . . the freedom of the press" to mean just that. However, although Justices Black and Douglas reiterated this view in subsequent opinions, it has never been adopted by the Court as a whole.

Public Figures, Too

The Supreme Court didn't stop there, either. In a pair of later cases it extended the "actual malice" proof requirement to "public figures," prominent people with no government office. The protagonists were a famous football coach and an ex-Army general who opposed racial desegregation. The two decisions were combined as *Curtis Publishing Co. v. Butts* and *Associated Press v. Walker*, 388 U.S. 130 (1967).

General Walker and Coach Butts

Major General Edwin Walker had commanded army troops dispatched by President Dwight Eisenhower to enforce a court order desegregating public schools in Little Rock, Arkansas, in 1957. But Walker felt such a use of federal troops was improper, so he resigned from the army "to engage in political activity," as the Supreme Court put it. In 1962, he joined a protest against another court desegregation order, this one to admit the first black student to the University of Mississippi. He addressed a group of white student demonstrators, and soon thereafter some of them charged federal marshals assigned to enforce the court order. Van Savell, an Associated Press reporter at the scene, filed a dispatch stating that Walker had taken command of a violent crowd of protestors, encouraged them to use violence, instructed them how to cope with tear gas, and led the charge against the marshals. Disputing the story, Walker sued the AP for libel in a Texas court and won a jury verdict of five hundred thousand dollars in compensatory damages. The trial judge rejected an additional award of three hundred thousand dollars in punitive damages, finding no malice on the part of the AP. Texas appellate courts affirmed the decision.

In the companion case, Wally Butts, famed as the very successful football coach at the University of Georgia and then the university's athletic director, was accused by the widely read and reputable weekly magazine *Saturday Evening Post* of fixing a game with arch-rival Alabama. The article, based on a phone conversation overheard by an insurance salesman, alleged that Butts provided detailed information about his team's plays and defenses to Alabama coach Paul (Bear) Bryant shortly before the game, which Alabama won. The magazine made no effort to confirm the tip. Butts forcefully denied the entire story and won a libel judgment of four hundred sixty thousand dollars in federal court against the *Post*'s publisher, Curtis Publishing Co.

The Supreme Court affirmed Butts's judgment but reversed Walker's, describing them both as "public figures" required to meet the *Times v. Sullivan* standard of "actual malice" in order to overcome the publications' First Amendment protection. In ruling against Walker, the justices pointed to the professionalism they attributed to Van Savell, the AP reporter. Justice John Marshall Harlan wrote approvingly:

> [T]he dispatch which concerns us in *Walker* was news which required immediate dissemination. The Associated Press received the information from a correspondent who was present at the scene of the events and gave every indication of being trustworthy and competent. His dispatches in this instance, with one minor exception, were internally consistent and would not have seem unreasonable to one familiar with General Walker's prior publicized statements on the underlying controversy. Considering the necessity for rapid dissemination, nothing in this series of events gives the slightest hint of a severe departure from accepted publishing standards. (*Curtis Publishing Co. v. Butts*, 158–59)

By contrast, in affirming Butts's judgment, the Court was highly critical of the *Post's* handling of the story:

> The evidence showed that the Butts story was in no sense "hot news" and the editors of the magazine recognized the need for a thorough investigation of the serious charges. Elementary precautions were, nevertheless, ignored. *The Saturday Evening Post* knew that Burnett [George Burnett, the tipster] had been placed on probation in connection with bad check charges, but proceeded to publish the story on the basis of his affidavit without substantial independent support. Burnett's notes were not even viewed by any of the magazine's personnel prior to publication.
>
> The Post writer assigned to the story was not a football expert and no attempt was made to check the story with someone knowledgeable in the sport. . . . In short, the evidence is ample to support a finding of highly unreasonable conduct constituting an extreme departure from the standards of investigation and reporting ordinarily adhered to by responsible publishers. (*Curtis Publishing Co. v. Butts* 157, 158)

On balance, of course, the two rulings were decidedly pro-press, erecting a higher barrier against libel suits by prominent people with no public office, while deservedly faulting the *Saturday Evening Post* for deplorable journalism.

Misquotation Allowed

Further enlarging its libel protections for the press, the Supreme Court ruled in 1991 that deliberate misquotation in derogatory magazine articles "does not equate with knowledge of falsity . . . unless the alteration results in a material change in the meaning conveyed by the statement." This surprising ruling came in a case called *Masson v. New Yorker Magazine*, 501 U.S. 496 (1991). It was initiated by a prominent psychoanalyst alleging that the writer, Janet Malcolm, who had interviewed him on tape for more than forty hours, had simply made up quotations attributed to him that were false and defamatory. She wrote, for instance, that he said, "I was like an intellectual gigolo" in the minds of senior psychoanalysts, that the London home of the Sigmund Freud Archives at which he worked should become a place of "sex, women, fun," and that other analysts would regard him as "the greatest analyst who ever lived" after reading his new book. Masson protested that he had never made the statements, and Malcolm was unable to produce notes or recordings to support the quotations. The courts considered Masson a public figure and thus required to prove actual malice.

The Supreme Court, by a vote of 7–2, ruled that the misquotations didn't demonstrate conclusively that Malcolm was knowingly peddling falsity, so sent the case back for trial, leaving the final call up to a jury. Bolstered by the Court's generous tolerance of derogatory misquotation, Malcolm and the *New Yorker* eventually won at trial, and that was affirmed on appeal (*Masson v. New Yorker Magazine*, 85 F.3d 1394, 9th Cir. 1996). The Supreme Court's tolerance of calculated misquotation is troubling in that it conflicts with journalism's professed insistence on telling the truth. But in legal terms, the case was another victory for the press, providing further protection against libel suits.

Private Plaintiffs

So, does all this protection mean that journalists are free to write critical stories without fear of legal consequences? Hardly.

A threshold question in the newsroom should be: is the subject of our story a public official, a public figure, or neither? A public official, elected or appointed, is clearly defined, but a public figure is not. And if the person is neither, the exposure to a possible libel finding is much greater, as a private citizen doesn't need to prove actual malice. So, what does a private citizen need to prove?

A case that helps answer that question is *Gertz v. Robert Welch, Inc.*, 418 U.S. 323 (1974), decided by the Supreme Court in 1974. Elmer Gertz was a prominent Chicago lawyer, a successful advocate for civil rights and labor and a writer on legal matters, who became a libel plaintiff himself. When he agreed to represent the family of a black youngster killed by a policeman, a publication of the ultra-conservative John Birch Society was outraged, calling him a Communist, an officer of a Marxist organization, and an officer of a lawyers' organization that "probably did more than any other outfit to plan the Communist attack on the Chicago police during the 1968 Democratic convention." Gertz sued for libel in U.S. District Court in Chicago, alleging several errors in the article. Both the trial court and the appellate court held that discussion of a public issue warranted application of the actual malice test, regardless of the public or private status of the people involved. They found no actual malice and so ruled for the defendant magazine.

But the Supreme Court disagreed with this analysis. In a close call, 5–4, Justice Lewis Powell focused on the plaintiff, Gertz, rather than on the public-issue question. Powell wrote for the majority that Gertz:

> had achieved no general fame or notoriety in the community. None of the
> prospective jurors called at the trial had ever heard of petitioner [Gertz]

prior to this litigation. . . . Absent clear evidence of general fame or notoriety in the community, and pervasive involvement in the affairs of society, an individual should not be deemed a public personality for all aspects of his life. (*Gertz v. Robert Welch* 352)

So, if Gertz was not a public figure for the purpose of this litigation, what did he need to prove to win his libel suit? "[T]he states may define for themselves," Powell wrote, "the appropriate standard of liability for a publisher or broadcaster of defamatory falsehood injuries to a private individual," but to win *punitive* damages the private citizen, too, must prove actual malice. The Court did not elaborate further on the appropriate standards in private-citizen libel cases, but in most states the standard is negligence, or a failure to observe the accepted professional standards of responsible journalism. The Supreme Court sent the case back to Chicago for a new trial. Gertz proved actual malice and was awarded one hundred thousand dollars in compensatory damages and three hundred thousand dollars in punitive damages. The jury verdict was affirmed by the Seventh Circuit Court of Appeals in *Gertz v. Robert Welch, Inc.*, 680 F.2d 527 (7th Cir. 1982). Gertz and his wife took a long trip to Asia on his award.

If Gertz, hardly an unknown in Chicago, was not deemed a public figure, what about a divorcing wife with a famous family name? That was the question in *Time, Inc. v. Firestone*, 424 U.S. 448 (1976). Mary Alice Firestone married into the wealthy, prominent manufacturing family in 1961. Three years later she sued in Palm Beach, Florida, for separate maintenance, but her husband, Russell Firestone, counterclaimed for divorce on grounds of extreme cruelty and adultery. When the court ruled, *Time* magazine reported briefly that Mr. Firestone divorced his wife "on grounds of extreme cruelty and adultery," adding: "The 17-month intermittent trial produced enough testimony of extramarital adventures on both sides, said the judge, 'to make Dr. Freud's hair curl.'" Mary Alice Firestone sued for libel, alleging that a portion of the article was "false, malicious and defamatory," and won a judgment of one hundred thousand dollars. The Florida Supreme Court affirmed, and *Time* petitioned the U.S. Supreme Court to review on the grounds that she was a public figure and thus obliged to prove actual malice. *Time* also claimed that its story was an accurate report of a public proceeding, a libel defense called "fair report."

The Supreme Court rejected both claims. Mary Alice Firestone was not a public figure because she "did not assume any role of especial prominence in the affairs of society, other than perhaps Palm Beach society, and she did not thrust herself to the forefront of any particular public controversy in order to influence the resolution of the issues involved in it." As to the claimed accuracy of *Time*'s story, the Court noted that the article stated the divorce was granted in part on grounds of adultery, which her husband had claimed, but that was not mentioned in the court's divorce decree. Nevertheless, because the lower courts had not made an explicit finding of fault by the magazine, the Court vacated the libel judgment and sent the case back for further proceedings.

Actual Malice Proved

As if to underscore the *Butts* ruling that a public figure can vault the high barrier of actual malice, the Supreme Court found similarly sloppy journalism in an Ohio lawsuit brought by a politician. The case was *Harte-Hanks Communications, Inc. v. Connaughton*, 491 U.S. 657 (1989). The Court stretched a bit to unanimously uphold a ruling by the U.S. Sixth Circuit Court of Appeals that a newspaper's departures from accepted standards were sufficient to justify the jury's verdict of actual malice. The plaintiff, Daniel Connaughton, was an unsuccessful candidate for a municipal judgeship in Hamilton, Ohio, and thus clearly a public figure. He had tape-recorded interviews with two sisters, one a witness before a grand jury investigating bribery allegations against the incumbent judge's assistant. Shortly before the election a local newspaper, the *Journal News,* which supported the incumbent for reelection, quoted the grand jury witness as saying that Connaughton had used "dirty tricks" and offered her and her sister jobs and a trip to Florida "in appreciation" for their help in the investigation.

Connaughton sued for libel, alleging that the article was false, had damaged his personal and professional reputation, and was published with actual malice. A U.S. District Court jury awarded him five thousand dollars in compensatory damages and one hundred ninety-five thousand in punitive damages, and the Sixth Circuit Court of Appeals affirmed, as did the Supreme Court. It faulted the newspaper for disregarding denials it had heard from six witnesses that Connaughton had made the alleged offers to the sisters, and especially for declining to interview the other sister, whom both Connaughton and the accusing sister contended would corroborate their conflicting accounts of the events. Justice John Paul Stevens wrote for the Court: "When these findings are considered alongside the undisputed evidence, the conclusion that the newspaper acted with actual malice inexorably follows."

The *Wall Street Journal* in Error

Another libel case that's instructive for journalists, although the case was ultimately dismissed, surprisingly involved that most authoritative and trustworthy newspaper, the *Wall Street Journal.* In 1993, it published an article by reporter Laura Jereski alleging that a ninety-four-person Houston investment firm, MMAR Group, Inc., had spent two million dollars on limousines in the previous year; its two flamboyant founders had siphoned off one hundred million dollars over three years; it caused losses of fifty million dollars by the Louisiana state pension fund; and that as a result, the National Association of Securities Dealers had issued a formal complaint accusing the firm of fraudulent practices. The result, as the *American Lawyer* later reported, "was devastating." Brokers and customers backed away from MMAR and in just three weeks the firm collapsed.

MMAR howled that the accusations were false and sued the *Journal's* parent, Dow Jones & Co., and Laura Jereski for libel. Despite its substantial business, the firm was deemed a private figure needing to prove only negligence, which it did to the satisfaction of a seven-person Houston jury in U.S. District Court. It awarded MMAR 22.7 million dollars in compensatory damages. But the jury also found actual malice, and adjudged punitive damages of twenty thousand dollars against Jereski and a staggering two hundred million against Dow Jones. It was by far the largest libel verdict in history.

Although it did not stand, it's worth asking what triggered the jury's harsh judgment against a great newspaper. According to the *American Lawyer* of June 1997, in an article by Susan Beck, the *Journal* made several critical mistakes:

1. Laura Jereski's written questions to the CEO (he wouldn't agree to an interview) failed to ask him about her principal accusations: the limousines, the personal compensation, the amount of the Louisiana pension fund's losses, and whether the NASD had filed a formal complaint. In fact, there was no such complaint at the time, though one was filed several months later.

2. The newspaper's editor on the story, who had already substantially rewritten the article, went on vacation feeling that the article was "pretty much ready to go," according to her later testimony. She turned it over to a reporter filling in for her, who later "claimed in his deposition that he didn't remember much about his editing of the piece."

3. Laura Jereski's notes "only made matters worse. Consisting mostly of undated, sketchy sentence fragments that were often illegible, they didn't always support what she wrote."

4. On the witness stand, "she quickly alienated the jurors. Not only did Jereski's defiant attitude come off badly, even her posture left a poor impression. . . . Even when her notes failed to support what she'd written, the reporter continued to insist that she hadn't made a mistake," while other evidence showed that all four of her accusations were incorrect.

5. As for the story's editor, Gay Miller, "it was Miller's imperious attitude on the stand that stood out to the jurors." She "challenged the plaintiff's lawyers at every turn" and at one point "flared in annoyance" when the lawyer moved on to another question.
6. Another *Journal* witness, Deputy Managing Editor Byron Calame, "didn't recall if he had reviewed Jereski's story even though he did maintain that his job required him to 'pay special attention to sensitive stories, sensitive situations.'" Calame "stood by the article."

So, exactly how did the *Journal* get away with such sloppy work? It turned out later that MMAR had withheld, contrary to legal requirements, telephone conversation recordings that clearly indicated the firm had regularly overstated to clients the current value of securities that MMAR had purchased for them, apparently trying to cover up a declining financial condition of the firm. So the judge granted the *Journal* a new trial (*MMAR Group, Inc. v. Dow, Jones & Co., Inc. and Laura Jereski*, 187 F.R.D. 282, S.D. Tex. April 8, 1999), whereupon MMAR dropped its suit without having recovered anything.

Proof of Libel

Out of these and other cases, the *Restatement of the Law, Second, Torts*, and state statutes, a libel plaintiff ordinarily must prove the following facts in order to win his case:

1. The story was published or broadcast (an audience of one suffices).
2. The plaintiff was clearly identified, preferably by name.
3. The story was defamatory; it impaired the plaintiff's reputation.
4. The publisher was at fault, guilty of negligence, or of actual malice.
5. The amount of damages, stated in dollars.

Defenses to Libel

So how does a journalist defend against an allegation of libel? Because the proof of libel requires a showing of fault by the journalist, the perfect defense is truth. Even if it's critical, a story that is correct and accurate cannot give rise to a libel judgment. As stipulated in the *Restatement* (section 581A): "One who publishes a defamatory statement of fact is not subject to liability for defamation if the statement is true."

Another solid defense is "fair report," the defense claimed by Time, Inc. when Mary Alice Firestone sued for libel, although it turned out that *Time's* story was not accurate, and so the defense failed. Fair report, meaning a correct story about a government meeting or official action, developed as a defense during libel's common-law origins, but now most states have codified it, i.e., written it into law, though not necessarily using the term "fair report." It may instead call such a story "privileged." The *Restatement* says (section 611): "The publication of defamatory matter concerning another in a report of an official action or proceeding or of a meeting open to the public that deals with a matter of public concern is privileged if the report is accurate and complete or a fair abridgement of the occurrence reported." Section 47 of the California Civil Code defines a "privileged publication or broadcast" as one "In any (1) legislative proceeding, (2) judicial proceeding, (3) in any other official proceeding authorized by law, or (4) in the initiation or course of any other proceeding authorized by law. . . ." (California Civil Code §47)

Another useful libel defense, the one advanced unsuccessfully by Walter Jacobson and CBS, is "fair comment," meaning opinion such as an editorial or op-ed piece, though it must be based on fact. In one case, the courts wrestled with this defense over a period of fifteen years. Poetically, it involved a wrestling match.

The match was between Maple Heights High School, in Maple Heights, Ohio, and a visiting team from Mentor High School. At one point a fight (off the mat) broke out between the wrestlers, then the home crowd jumped in, and four Mentor wrestlers were injured. The Ohio High School Athletic Association held a hearing, then censured Maple Heights coach Michael Milkovich for his actions during the altercation, put his team on probation, and barred it from the state tournament. Defying the association, wrestlers and their parents went to court and won a temporary injunction blocking the probation and ineligibility orders, on the grounds that the athletic association had failed to afford due process to the coach and the school. The next day a sportswriter for the *Lorain Journal*, J. Theodore Diadiun, implied in his "TD Says" column that Milkovich and the school superintendent, H. Don Scott, had lied in court. Diadiun wrote:

> a lesson was learned (or relearned) yesterday by the student body of Maple Heights High School, and by anyone who attended the Maple-Mentor wrestling meet of last Feb. 8. A lesson which, sadly, in view of the events of the past year, is well they learned early. It is simply this: If you get in a jam, lie your way out.
>
> . . .
>
> Anyone who attended the meet, whether he be from Maple Heights, Mentor, or impartial observer, knows in his heart that Milkovich and Scott lied at the hearing after each having given his solemn oath to tell the truth.

. . .
But they got away with it. (*Milkovich v. Lorain Journal,* 497 U.S. 1,
4–5 (1990).

Milkovich sued for libel. (Scott filed a separate suit, not relevant here.) The
lawsuit went up and down in the Ohio courts, including two separate decisions
by the Ohio Supreme Court, always turning on the question of whether the
column was "fair comment." In the last go-around the Ohio courts granted
summary judgment, a decision without a trial, for the newspaper and Diadiun
on the grounds of fair comment. But in *Milkovich v. Lorain Journal,* the U.S.
Supreme Court reversed by a vote of 7–2 and sent the case back for trial.
Writing for the majority, Chief Justice William Rehnquist stated that whether
Milkovich committed perjury "is sufficiently factual to be susceptible of being proved true or false. A determination whether petitioner [Milkovich] lied
in this instance can be made on a core of objective evidence by comparing,
inter alia, petitioner's testimony before the OHSAA board with his subsequent
testimony before the trial court."

But Justice William Brennan, ever supportive of freedom of the press, saw
the column quite differently. He noted an occasional "probably" and "apparently" and the fact that Diadiun didn't claim any first-hand knowledge of the
court hearing, because he wasn't there. Brennan argued in a dissent joined
by Justice Thurgood Marshall:

> Diadiun's assumption that Milkovich must have lied at the court hearing
> is patently conjecture. The majority finds Diadiun's statements actionable,
> however, because it concludes that these statements imply a factual asser-
> tion that Milkovich perjured himself at the judicial proceeding. I disagree.
> Diadiun not only reveals the facts upon which he is relying but he makes
> it clear at which point he runs out of facts and is simply guessing. Read in
> context, the statements cannot reasonably be interpreted as implying such
> an assertion as fact. . . . No reasonable reader could understand Diadiun to
> be impliedly asserting—as fact—that Milkovich had perjured himself. Nor
> could such a reader infer that Diadiun had further information about Milk-
> ovich's court testimony on which his belief was based. It is plain from the
> column that Diadiun did not attend the court hearing. Diadiun also clearly
> had no detailed secondhand information about what Milkovich had said in
> court. (*Milkovich v. Lorain Journal,* 28–30)

This case hardly provides a helpful understanding of what constitutes fair
comment. But one thing is clear in *Milkovich:* it's up to the jury. The case has
been cited in more than a thousand subsequent court opinions. For instance,

in *Veilleux v. National Broadcasting Company*, 206 F.3d 92 (lst Cir. 2000), a truck driver agreed to be videotaped by an NBC *Dateline* crew as he crossed the country, but then sued for defamation when the program aired. He objected to a statement by the reporter, Fred Francis, that long-distance drivers' "stay awake and on the road at all costs mentality" led to many accidents and deaths on the highway. However, a jury accepted the statement as opinion, and a federal appellate court affirmed.

Two other libel defenses, available only in some states, are called "neutral reportage," meaning a fair, unbiased story, and "wire service," meaning the story was provided by the Associated Press, Reuters, Dow Jones or another wire service and was published as received.

So these are the journalist's defenses that can defeat a libel claim:

1. Truth. The perfect, absolute defense.
2. Fair report, of a government meeting or document.
3. Fair comment, opinion based on facts.
4. Neutral reportage (not available in all states).
5. Wire service (also not available in all states).

In short, journalists may publish critical articles so long as they are true, which of course implies all the care, prudence, and accuracy—not to mention good conscience—that truth demands.

Product Disparagement

While we're thinking defamation, let's look at a somewhat similar tort available in some states. The difference is that it concerns the reputation of things rather than people. It's generally called product disparagement, and often it's meant to safeguard the reputation of an important product of the state.

For instance, a Texas statute prohibits false disparagement of perishable food products, and it gave rise to the most famous case of this genre when it was turned by Texas beef producers against Oprah Winfrey. One day in April 1996 her daily TV talk show was titled "Dangerous Food" and included a segment on Bovine Spongiform Encephalopathy, or Mad Cow Disease, a degenerative and deadly disease of cattle. The disease was linked by British researchers to a new variant, also fatal, of a human disorder called Creutzfeldt-Jakob Disease, and consumption of beef was identified as the most likely cause.

Although neither Mad Cow Disease nor the Creutzfeldt-Jakob variant had been detected in the United States, the report set off a flurry of American media attention and public interest. Oprah asked her expert guests, "could it happen here?" Two said no, but one said yes. The broadcast did not mention Texas or name any ranchers there.

Nevertheless, several of them, and the Texas Beef Group, sued Oprah and her pessimistic guest, Howard Lyman (who previously had been a cattle rancher himself), for product disparagement and other alleged wrongs. The plaintiffs claimed that the Oprah show had caused beef markets to collapse, damaging their business. When the case went to trial, Oprah moved her entire television production to Amarillo, Texas, where she split her time each day between the federal courtroom and a local television studio.

After the plaintiffs presented their evidence and witnesses, instead of offering a defense, Oprah's lawyers moved for judgment as a matter of law, in other words, a favorable verdict on the grounds that the plaintiffs had not presented evidence sufficient to persuade a jury to rule in their favor. U.S. District Court Judge Mary Lou Robinson agreed. She questioned whether cattle on the hoof would qualify as a perishable food product, but even if it could, she ruled, the plaintiffs had not satisfied the statute's requirement that the disparagement be carried out with actual knowledge of falsity. "Plaintiffs have wholly failed in this burden," she declared in *Texas Beef Group v. Oprah Winfrey*, 11 F.Supp.2d 858 (N.D. Tex. 1998). "There is no evidence by which a reasonable juror could conclude that the Defendants had actual knowledge of the falsity, if any, of the statements made." The ruling was affirmed by the Fifth Circuit Court of Appeals (212 F.3d 597, 2000).

An earlier product disparagement case of great interest, one oft-cited in subsequent court opinions, was *Bose Corp. v. Consumers Union of United States, Inc.*, 466 U.S. 485 (1984). Evaluating various medium-priced loudspeakers, *Consumer Reports* stated that the Bose 901 system was "unique and unconventional" and that a listener "could pinpoint the location of various instruments much more easily with a standard speaker than with the *Bose* system."

The article went on:

> Worse, individual instruments heard through the *Bose* system seemed to grow to gigantic proportions and tended to wander about the room. For instance, a violin appeared to be 10 feet wide and a piano stretched from wall to wall. With orchestral music, such effects seemed inconsequential. But we think they might become annoying when listening to soloists. . . .
>
> We think the *Bose* system is so unusual that a prospective buyer must listen to it and judge it for himself. We would suggest delaying so big an investment until you were sure the system would please you after the novelty value had worn off. (*Bose Corp. v. Consumers Union of United States, Inc.*, 488)

The case, tried in the U.S. District Court in Massachusetts under diversity jurisdiction, applied the product disparagement laws of both Massachusetts and New York, which were deemed virtually identical. It was a bench trial, by a judge alone without a jury. The judge ruled, after long questioning of the *Consumer Reports* engineer who wrote the evaluation from which the article was drawn, that instruments heard through the speakers tended to wander "along the wall"—the engineer's own characterization at trial of his finding—rather than "about the room" and that the statement was disparaging. Deeming Bose a "public figure," the judge applied the *New York Times v. Sullivan* standard and found *Consumer Reports* guilty of actual malice, that it published a falsehood knowingly or with reckless disregard of the truth. But the First Circuit Court of Appeals reversed and the U.S. Supreme Court affirmed that judgment, though by a divided vote of 6–3. For the majority, Justice John Paul Stevens, quoting from previous opinions, wrote:

> [A]doption of the language chosen was "one of a number of possible rational interpretations" of an event "that bristled with ambiguities" and descriptive challenges for the writer. The choice of such language, though reflecting a misconception, does not place the speech beyond the outer limits of the First Amendment's broad protective umbrella. Under the District Court's analysis, any individual using a malapropism might be liable, simply because an intelligent speaker would have to know that the term was inaccurate in context, even though he did not realize his folly at the time. . . . The statement in this case represents the sort of inaccuracy that is commonplace in the forum of robust debate to which the *New York Times* rule applies. (*Bose Corp. v. Consumers Union of United States, Inc.,* 512–13)

Justice William Rehnquist, in a dissent joined by Justice Sandra Day O'Connor, doubted the ability of appellate courts to determine the state of mind required for a finding of actual malice. Noting that the trial judge had questioned the engineer for hours, Rehnquist declared, "surely such determinations are best left to the trial judge."

Internet Libel

Though the cases in this chapter may not give final answers to all questions of defamation that might arise in your work, they do provide considerable guidance, and should at least help you spot possible problems and get the necessary editorial or legal advice to make a sound decision about what to publish. Bear in mind that the laws of defamation and product disparagement apply on the Internet as well as in print and on the air. Furthermore, just as a newspaper or a TV station may be held liable for the mistakes of an errant reporter, so, too, is the owner of a blog or website liable for defamatory material posted there by others (although an Internet service provider, or ISP, is not, by virtue of special legislation).

Needless to say, lots of derogatory comments are posted online anonymously, and state and federal courts are struggling with whether to require authors to disclose their names. In *Doe v. Cahill*, 884 A.2d 451 (Del. 2005), the Delaware Supreme Court declined to require disclosure of the writer of criticisms of a Smyrna city councilman. The court described the remarks as opinion and stated that "a reasonable person would not interpret Doe's statements as stating facts about [Councilman] Cahill. The statements are, therefore, incapable of a defamatory meaning."

However, in a commercial dispute not involving political opinion, *In re Anonymous Online Speakers*, 661 F.3d 1168 (9th Cir. 2011), the U.S. Ninth Circuit Court of Appeals held that anonymous writers' names could be revealed. Quixtar, Inc., successor to Amway Corporation and a distributor of cosmetics and other consumer products, filed suit in U.S. District Court in Nevada alleging tortious interference with contracts and business relations by a competitor, Signature Management TEAM, LLC. Quixtar claimed that TEAM orchestrated an Internet smear campaign via anonymous postings and videos disparaging Quixtar and its business practices. Companies enjoy a limited right of free speech, called "commercial speech," but it doesn't warrant the same high level of First Amendment protection that political speech enjoys. In this case, however, the district court applied the higher First Amendment standard for *political* speech and still held that Quixtar could obtain the names of the anonymous writers. Taking note of that higher level of scrutiny and citing its application in the Delaware *Cahill* case, the circuit court rejected a challenge to the district court order. "We leave to the district court the details of fashioning the appropriate scope and procedures for disclosure of the identity of the anonymous speakers," the appellate court stated. It is possible this ruling could influence future cases where the targets of anonymous *political* speech on the Internet want to know the speakers' names.

At the very least, operators of blogs and websites must be aware that publishing defamatory remarks or photos submitted by anonymous users could give rise to this sort of discovery demand and perhaps even to personal liability as a publisher. The same caution applies to Internet violations of personal privacy; of an accused person's right to a fair trial; of copyright protection of articles, photos or other created works, and to everything else that you or others may post on your own or someone else's site.

Questions for Discussion

1. Do you think your Internet postings might potentially defame someone? How do you decide? How can you guard against libelous postings on your site by someone else?
2. Is an individual (as opposed to a company employee) more or less likely to encounter a libel problem by a posting on the Internet?
3. What legal protection does the Internet provide?
4. Is it possible to defame a person who already has an unsavory public reputation?
5. In light of occasional disagreement over versions of the truth, is that still a reliable standard as a libel defense?

References

American Jurisprudence, second edition (AmJur 2d), Lawyers Cooperative Publishing/Bancroft Whitney (Thomson Reuters).

Anonymous Online Speakers, In re, 661 F.3d 1168 (9th Cir. 2011). http://networkmarketinglaw.com/free-speech/anonymous-online-speakers-9th-cir-jan-7-2011/.

Beck, Susan, "Trial and Errors," *The American Lawyer*, p. 24, June 1997.

Black's Law Dictionary Free 2d edition. http://thelawdictionary.org/tort/.

Bose Corp. v. Consumers Union of United States, Inc., 466 U.S. 485 (1984). http://caselaw.lp.findlaw.com/scripts/getcase.pl?court=US&vol=466&invol=485.

Brown & Williamson Tobacco Corporation v. Walter Jacobson and CBS, Inc., 14 Media L. Rep. 1497 (7th Cir. 1987). http://scholar.google.com/scholar_case?case=6498914364025308015&q=brown+%26+williamson+tobacco+corp.+v+jacobson&hl=en&as_sdt=2,14&as_vis=1.

California Civil Code § 47. http://law.onecde.com/california/civil/47.html.

Curtis Publishing Co. v. Butts and *Associated Press v. Walker*, 388 U.S. 130 (1967). https://bulk.resource.org/courts.gov/c/US/388/388.US.130.37.150.html.

Doe v. Cahill, 884 A.2d 451 (Del. 2005).

Gertz v. Robert Welch, Inc., 418 U.S. 323 (1974). http://scholar.google.com/scholar_case?case=7102507483896624202&q=Gertz+v.+Robert+Welch,+Inc.,+418+U.S.+323+(1974)+&hl=en&as_sdt=2,14&as_vis=1.

Gertz v. Robert Welch, Inc., 680 F.2d 527 (7th Cir. 1982). http://scholar.google.com/scholar_case?case=16994790679424813388&q=Gertz+v.+Robert+Welch,+Inc.,+418+U.S.+323+(1974)+&hl=en&as_sdt=2,14&as_vis=1.

Harte-Hanks Communications, Inc. v. Connaughton, 491 U.S. 657 (1989). http://caselaw.lp.findlaw.com/scripts/getcase.pl?court=us&vol=491&invol=657.

Masson v. New Yorker Magazine, 501 U.S. 496 (1991). http://www.law.cornell.edu/supct/html/89-1799.ZS.html.

Masson v. New Yorker Magazine, 85 F.3d 1394 (9th Cir. 1996). http://caselaw.findlaw.com/us-9th-circuit/1264860.html.

Milkovich v. Lorain Journal, 497 U.S. 1 (1990). http://www.supremeobserver.com/case-document/?doc=5383.

MMAR Group, Inc. v. Dow, Jones & Co., Inc. and Laura Jereski, 187 F.R.D. 282

(S.D. Tex. April 8, 1999). http://scholar.google.com/scholar_case?case=14473026 345757540881&q=MMAR+Group,+Inc.+v.+Dow,+Jones+%26+Co.,+Inc.+and+ Laura+Jereski,&hl=en&as_sdt=2,14&as_vis=1.

New York Times Co. v. Sullivan, 376 U.S. 24 (1964). http://law2.umkc.edu/faculty/projects/ftrials/conlaw/sullivan.html.

Restatement of the Law, Second, Torts (Philadelphia: American Law Institute, 1977).

Texas Beef Group v. Oprah Winfrey, 11 F.Supp.2d 858 (N.D. Tex. 1998). http://www.cspinet.org/foodspeak/oprah/court.htm.

Time, Inc. v. Firestone, 424 U.S. 448 (1976). http://www.law.cornell.edu/supct/html/historics/USSC_CR_0424_0448_ZS.html.

Veilleux v. National Broadcasting Company, 206 F.3d 92 (1st Cir. 2000). http://caselaw.findlaw.com/us-1st-circuit/1438704.html.

5

Invasion of Privacy

> *"A man's home is his castle."*
> —English common law, adapted from Rome

American Origins

The right of personal privacy is second only to libel in legally circumscribing American journalism. Though it has cultural roots in England and as far back as ancient Rome, as law in the United States it dates from an 1890 *Harvard Law Review* article by two Boston lawyers, Samuel D. Warren and Louis D. Brandeis. (Brandeis later became a distinguished justice of the U.S. Supreme Court.) They were indignant about what they deemed intrusive press coverage of men and women prominent in Boston society. "Instantaneous photographs and newspaper enterprise," they averred, "have invaded the sacred precincts of private and domestic life," such that "the details of sexual relations are spread broadcast in the columns of the daily papers." So they proposed that the law should recognize "a general right of the individual to be let alone." Significantly, they contended that neither truth nor the absence of malice should be recognized as a defense to a violation of personal privacy. (Warren and Brandeis 1890.)

States responded to Warren and Brandeis (and we'll look at some examples shortly), but it wasn't until 1965 that the federal government recognized a right of privacy. It came through Supreme Court action rather than legislation. In a case challenging a hoary state statute that prohibited the use of contraceptives even by married couples, *Griswold v. Connecticut*, 381 U.S. 479 (1965), the Supreme Court unanimously found a hitherto undiscovered right of privacy in the "penumbras formed by emanations from [other constitutional] guarantees that help give them life and substance." Writing for the Court, Justice William O. Douglas went on, "Various guarantees create zones of privacy," and he cited five:

1. The "right of association" (First Amendment; actually it's "the right of the people peaceably to assemble")
2. The prohibition against forced quartering of soldiers "in any house" (Third Amendment)
3. The "right of the people to be secure in their persons, houses, papers, and effects, against unreasonable searches and seizures" (Fourth)
4. The bar against self-incrimination (Fifth) and
5. "The enumeration in the Constitution, of certain rights, shall not be construed to deny or disparage others retained by the people." (Ninth).

In the wake of that historic privacy decision flowed another, just a few years later. Deciding *Roe v. Wade*, 410 U.S. 113 (1973), the Supreme Court ruled, 7–2, that a state law prohibiting all abortions except to save the life of the mother was unconstitutional, a violation of the due-process guarantee of the Fourteenth Amendment. For the majority, Justice Harry Blackmun wrote a scholarly opinion, stating, we "conclude that the right of personal privacy includes the abortion decision, but that this right is . . . subject to some limitations; and that, at some point, the state interests as to protection of health, medical standards, and prenatal life, become dominant." The Court set that point at the end of the first trimester of pregnancy, after which limitations might be imposed by the state.

As important as these Supreme Court decisions were, and still are, of more particular professional interest to journalists are state privacy-protection statutes and cases testing them. A number of these cases were decided in favor of the press, but some of these victories also connote troublesome issues of ethics in journalism. In some cases the judges go beyond the law to question journalists' ethics; in others we will do so.

Five Privacy Torts

State statutes, all of them bolstering privacy guarantees of state constitutions, generally prohibit the following types of invasion of privacy. Note that this tort is not tied to falsity. In other words, as Warren and Brandeis originally proposed, truth is not (ordinarily) a defense. Here are the five categories of invasion of privacy:

1. Intrusion upon seclusion, a cautionary tale for news-gathering, notably photography. It may be triggered without actually printing, broadcasting, or posting anything.
2. Disclosure of embarrassing private facts.

3. False light, sometimes called "libel without defamation," a misleading depiction of someone that would be highly offensive or embarrassing to a reasonable person. This is meant to safeguard a person's feelings or emotions rather than his reputation (not available in all states).
4. Intentional infliction of emotional distress (not available in all states).
5. Appropriation, designed to prevent unauthorized commercial exploitation of someone else's (usually a celebrity's) name, picture, voice, or other personal attributes.

In this chapter we'll look at the first two, which are available in all states and thus more likely to be encountered by journalists.

Intrusion upon Seclusion

This tort relates only to the gathering of news, not to publication, and as such is of particular importance to photographers and videographers. The authoritative legal treatise, *Restatement of the Law, Second, Torts*, published by the American Law Institute, defines the tort: "One who intentionally intrudes, physically or otherwise, upon the solitude or seclusion of another or his private affairs or concerns, is subject to liability to the other for invasion of his privacy, if the intrusion would be highly offensive to a reasonable person."

In one of the earliest such cases, *Dietemann v. Time, Inc.*, 449 F.2d 245 (9th Cir. 1971), *Life* magazine, published by Time, Inc., carried an article, "Crackdown on Quackery," describing a Los Angeles man as a quack doctor and included a photo of him taken in his home by a *Life* photographer with a hidden camera. The photographer, William Ray, accompanied by a reporter, Jackie Metcalf, had rung the doorbell of A.A. Dietemann, a disabled veteran and licensed plumber with little education who—in his home—practiced healing with clay, minerals, and herbs, though he didn't advertise or charge for his treatments or accept contributions. Working in collaboration with the Los Angeles district attorney, who suspected Dietemann of practicing medicine without a license, the journalists told Dietemann they had been sent by a "Mr. Johnson" and were admitted to his home. Metcalf, who had a radio transmitter hidden in her purse that conveyed the conversation to another *Life* reporter and law enforcement officers in a nearby automobile, represented that she had a lump in her breast.

The U.S. District Court's opinion, finding an invasion of privacy by the journalists, stated that one of Ray's photos "appeared in Life Magazine showing plaintiff with his hand on the upper portion of Mrs. Metcalf's breast while he was looking at some gadgets and holding what appeared to be a wand in his right hand. . . . Plaintiff concluded that she had eaten some rancid butter 11 years, 9 months, and 7 days prior to that time. Other persons were seated in the room during this time." Three weeks later the district attorney, after tipping off the press, went to Dietemann's home and arrested him on a charge of practicing medicine without a license. The *Life* article included a picture of the arrest.

Fined one thousand dollars for injury to Dietemann's "feelings and peace of mind," Time, Inc. appealed on First Amendment grounds to the U.S. Court of Appeals for the Ninth Circuit, based in San Francisco. It affirmed the judgment:

> Plaintiff's den was a sphere from which he could reasonably expect to be free of eavesdropping newsmen. . . . The First Amendment has never been construed to accord newsmen immunity from torts or crimes committed during the course of newsgathering. The First Amendment is not a license to trespass, steal, or intrude by electronic means into the precincts of another's home or office. It does not become such a license simply because the person subjected to the intrusion is reasonably suspected of committing a crime. . . . Assessing damages for the additional emotional distress suffered by a plaintiff when the wrongfully acquired data are purveyed to the multitude chills intrusive acts. It does not chill freedom of expression guaranteed by the First Amendment. (*Dietemann v. Time, Inc.*, 249, 250)

However, a finding of intrusion need not be based on secrecy or malicious intent. A TV videographer seeking a graphic report of a public event, in other words, just doing his job, may stumble over this line.

A California woman named Ruth Shulman and her son were severely injured when her car left a highway in Riverside County, tumbled down an embankment, and came to rest upside-down. Mrs. Shulman was pinned under the car; both she and her son had to be cut free. A rescue helicopter was dispatched, carrying a flight nurse, Laura Carnahan, and a TV cameraman, Joel Cooke, who was shooting a documentary on emergency services. At his request the nurse wore a microphone. Cooke filmed the rescue and the flight to a hospital, recording conversations between the nurse and the injured Mrs. Shulman. The video ran for nine minutes in the ensuing documentary.

In *Shulman v. Group W Productions, Inc.*, 18 Cal. 4th 200 (1998), Mrs. Shulman sued for invasion of privacy, including alleged intrusion upon seclusion, arguing that she was entitled to privacy during her rescue. The Supreme Court of California, evaluating whether her claims warranted a jury trial, said they did. The court held that "a reasonable jury could find highly offensive the placement of a microphone on a medical rescuer in order to intercept what would otherwise be private conversations with an injured patient," and also could "believe that fundamental respect for human dignity requires the patients' anxious journey be taken only with those whose care is solely for them and out of sight of the prying eyes (or cameras) of others." (As with a number of the cases we'll consider, there's no public record of any further legal proceedings in this case; it was assumed that, in light of the California Supreme Court's favorable view of Mrs. Shulman's prospects at trial, the broadcaster settled the matter out of court by paying an amount of money to her.)

The result was similar in still another California case, this involving a television investigation, *Sanders v. American Broadcasting Companies, Inc.*, 20 Cal. 4th 907 (1999). A reporter named Stacy Lescht was part of an ABC probe of the "telepsychic" industry, in which employees gave readings to customers who called in on a 900 number, paying a per-minute charge. She obtained a job as a telepsychic in the Los Angeles office of a company called Psychic Marketing Group, and worked there in a large room with about 100 individual cubicles. She wore a tiny camera concealed in her hat, clipped a microphone to her brassiere, and videotaped a number of conversations with her coworkers, including one Mark Sanders. He talked with her about his personal aspirations and beliefs and gave her a psychic reading. A brief clip of that conversation found its way into ABC's resulting *Prime Time Live* broadcast.

Sanders sued Lescht and ABC for intrusion upon seclusion, contending that he had a reasonable expectation of privacy in his workplace, although other employees walked close by and even chatted in passing as he was being videotaped. The Supreme Court of California agreed, declaring, "In an office or other workplace to which the general public does not have unfettered access, employees may enjoy a limited, but legitimate, expectation that their conversations and other interactions will not be secretly videotaped by undercover television reporters, even though those conversations may not have been completely private from the participants' coworkers."

Significantly, however, the court added this:

> Although we reverse, for these reasons, the Court of Appeal's judgment for defendants, we do not hold or imply that investigative journalists necessarily commit a tort by secretly recording events and conversations in offices, stores or other workplaces. Whether a reasonable expectation of privacy is violated by such recording depends on the exact nature of the conduct and all the surrounding circumstances. In addition, liability under the intrusion tort requires that the invasion be highly offensive to a reasonable person, considering, among other factors, the motive of the alleged intruder. (*Sanders v. American Broadcasting Companies, Inc.*, 911)

Perhaps newsworthiness could be a defense. In some intrusion cases the courts have, in fact, accorded some leeway to surreptitious videotaping, typically based on the First Amendment.

In one such case, *Desnick v. American Broadcasting Companies, Inc.*, 233 F.3d 514 (7th Cir. 2000), an eye clinic owned by a Chicago ophthalmologist sued for intrusion after ABC "star reporter" Sam Donaldson and colleagues produced a program describing Medicare fraud and unnecessary cataract surgeries. The journalists gained entrance by misrepresenting their planned story as a "fair and balanced" report about cataracts, and seven of them posed as patients in Desnick clinics. Four were told they needed cataract surgery. The journalists took pictures with hidden cameras. Donaldson also interviewed Desnick patients and former employees who were critical of the clinics' work, and an outside ophthalmologist who separately examined the test patients' eyes and found no need of surgery.

The clinic and two of its doctors sued for invasion of privacy, as well as trespass, defamation, and other alleged violations, but the U.S. District Court in Chicago dismissed their claims. That ruling was affirmed by the U.S. Seventh Circuit Court of Appeals, also located in Chicago. Chief Judge Richard Posner, one of the nation's most influential and most quoted appellate jurists, wrote that "no intimate personal facts concerning the two individual plaintiffs (remember that Dr. Desnick himself is not a plaintiff) were revealed; and the only conversations that were recorded were conversations with the testers themselves." Briskly defending investigative journalism, Posner also rejected the clinic's claim of fraud for ABC's deceptions:

> Investigative journalists well known for ruthlessness promise to wear kid gloves. They break their promise, as any person of normal sophistication would expect. If that is "fraud," it is the kind against which potential victims can easily arm themselves by maintaining a minimum of skepticism about journalistic goals and methods. Desnick, needless to say, was no child, or otherwise a member of a vulnerable group. He is a successful professional and entrepreneur; no legal remedies to protect him from what happened are required by Illinois. An elaborate artifice of fraud is the central meaning of a scheme to defraud through false promises. The only scheme here was a scheme to expose publicly any bad practices that the investigative team discovered, which is nothing fraudulent. (*Desnick v. American Broadcasting Companies, Inc.*, 1354–55)

TV news obtained similar support in a case involving an American Airlines flight attendant who was on O.J. Simpson's flight from Los Angeles to Chicago immediately after the 1994 murders of his ex-wife Nicole Simpson and her friend Ronald Goldman. The attendant's name was Beverly Deteresa, and her case was *Deteresa v. American Broadcasting Companies, Inc.*, 121 F.3d 460 (9th Cir. 1997). A week after Simpson's flight, an ABC producer, Anthony Radziwill, called at Deteresa's condominium in Irvine, California, and asked to interview her on camera. She declined, but said, as the Ninth Circuit Court of Appeals stated in its opinion, she was "'frustrated' to hear news reports about the flight that she knew were false. She informed Radziwill, for instance, that contrary to the reports she had heard, Simpson had not kept his hand in a bag during the flight. She also told Radziwill how many passengers had sat in first class and in which seat Simpson had sat." The next day Radziwill told Deteresa that he had secretly recorded their conversation, and that his cameraperson had videotaped it from the street. She asked him not to use her name or the recordings, but ABC showed a silent five-second clip of the video, not identifying her, with a voice-over summarizing what she had told Radziwill. She sued ABC, alleging intrusion upon seclusion and other violations.

A U.S. District Court dismissed her suit and the Ninth Circuit affirmed, rather simply: "With no dispute that ABC videotaped Deteresa in public view from a public place, broadcast only a five-second clip of the tape, and did not broadcast either her name or her address, no intrusion into seclusion privacy claim lies as a matter of law." The message, not a new one, is clear: photographing from a public street does not constitute an invasion of privacy.

Adding to ABC's string of victories, the Ninth Circuit Court of Appeals ruled in its favor in *Medical Laboratory Management Consultants v. American Broadcasting Companies, Inc., Diane Sawyer, et al.*, 306 F.3d 806 (9th Cir. 2002). The plaintiff, in Phoenix, was one of several laboratories included in a *Prime Time Live* broadcast alleging hurried analysis and inaccurate results from women's pap smears. Again, ABC used subterfuges to gain entrance. One producer, Rhondi Charleston, posing as a representative of a Michigan women's health clinic, called to have 623 slides processed over a weekend. Previously another producer, Robbie Gordon, claiming to be a Georgia cytotechnologist, a technician who analyzes pap smear slides, had called to say she was traveling to Phoenix soon and asked whether she could visit Medical Laboratory to help her learn how to start her own laboratory. The Medical Laboratory's founder and co-owner, John Devaraj, agreed to see her, and she scheduled her visit for the same day the 623 slides would arrive. She showed up with two colleagues, introducing them as a computer expert and an administrator. The "computer expert" was Jeff Cooke, an undercover photography specialist, who hid a camera in his wig. He videotaped the visit, including a conversation with Deveraj and a tour of the facility; fifty-two seconds was used in ABC's broadcast, showing Devaraj seated, stating that the cytotechnologists who work at Medical Laboratory also work at other laboratories. The broadcast did not name Deveraj or the laboratory but referred to it simply as a "lab in Arizona." Devaraj sued for intrusion upon seclusion and other alleged violations.

A U.S. District Court granted ABC's motion for summary judgment in its favor, meaning that the judge, Roslyn O. Silver, determined that she could rule on the case without a trial because there was no disagreement as to the facts. The U.S. Court of Appeals for the Ninth Circuit affirmed her ruling. "Devaraj's willingness to invite these strangers into the administrative offices for a meeting and then on a tour of the premises," the court declared, "indicates that Devaraj did not have an objectively reasonable expectation of solitude or seclusion in the parts of Medical Lab that he showed the ABC representatives." It added: "Devaraj did not reveal any information about his personal life or affairs, but only generally discussed Medical Lab's business operations, the pap smear testing industry, and Gordon's supposed plans to open her own laboratory."

Food Lion v. ABC

Another case of deceptive entry and concealed cameras, perhaps the best known, should be mentioned here, though the target, a grocery chain called Food Lion, Inc., claimed neither an invasion of privacy nor defamation. In effect, it acknowledged that the story was true. But it found several other reasons to sue. Like some of the plaintiffs mentioned above, Food Lion alleged trespass. It claimed breach of a duty of loyalty owed by employees who turned out be phony. And the company alleged a violation of a North Carolina statute called the Unfair and Deceptive Trade Practices Act, which prohibits "unfair or deceptive acts or practices" affecting commerce. The case is *Food Lion v. Capital Cities/ABC, Inc.,* 194 F.3d 505 (4th Cir. 1999). Again, ABC's *Prime Time Live* was investigating, this time pursuing allegations that outdated meat was being repackaged and sold as fresh.

ABC reporters Lynne Dale (then Lynne Litt) and Susan Barnett applied for jobs with Food Lion, using false identities, references, local addresses, and work experience. Dale was hired as a meat wrapper trainee at a North Carolina store, and a South Carolina store hired Barnett as a deli clerk. Dale worked for a week, Barnett for two. In the meat cutting room, the deli counter, the employee break room, and a manager's office, they used concealed cameras (one described as a "lipstick" camera) and microphones to record forty-five hours of employees treating, wrapping, and labeling meat; cleaning machinery; and discussing the practices of the meat department. Portions of the recordings used in the broadcast, according to the appellate court opinion, "appeared to show Food Lion employees repackaging and redating fish that had passed the expiration date, grinding expired beef with fresh beef, and applying barbecue sauce to chicken past its expiration date in order to mask the small and sell it as fresh in the gourmet food section."

Food Lion sued in a U.S. District Court in North Carolina and won a staggering verdict. The jury found ABC guilty of fraud and awarded Food Lion fourteen hundred dollars in compensatory damages and a stunning $5,545,750 in punitive damages. It found Dale and Barnett guilty of trespass and breaching the loyalty owed to their employer, but awarded Food Lion only a token two dollars each on those counts. The jury also decided that ABC violated the North Carolina deceptive trade practices act. Reviewing the verdict, a district court judge ruled that the punitive award was excessive, and Food Lion agreed to a total award of $315,000.

On appeal, the Fourth Circuit of Appeals reversed the fraud judgment and the deceptive trade practices judgment (on the grounds that ABC's actions hadn't hurt consumers), but affirmed the trespass and breach of duty of loyalty verdicts and the two-dollar awards against Dale and Barnett. The court pointed out, as others had, that the First Amendment does not excuse the press from complying with generally applicable laws. Applying them in this case, the court commented, would not "have more than an 'incidental effect' on newsgathering. . . . We are convinced that the media can do its important job effectively without resorting to the commission of run-of-the-mill torts." The court, like the others that gave the media a wide berth in these intrusion cases, seemed to be saying that the truth uncovered by their endeavors was a mitigating consideration in the innocence findings and the modest penalties adjudged for violations.

Paparazzo Restricted

One prominent privacy case produced a different sort of remedy. The dispute is famous because it was between Jacqueline Kennedy Onassis and an obnoxious freelance "paparazzo" photographer, Donald Galella, who made a living photographing Onassis and her still-young children, John Jr. and Caroline. On one occasion he became so obtrusive that the former First Lady's Secret Service agents arrested Galella, who proceeded to sue them and Mrs. Onassis for false arrest. She claimed harassment and invasion of privacy, even though his antics occurred out in the open, mostly in public places. In *Galella v. Onassis*, 487 F.2d 986 (2d Cir. 1973), the U.S. Court of Appeals for the Second Circuit described the photographer's aggressive tactics:

Galella took pictures of John Kennedy riding his bicycle in Central Park across the way from his home. He jumped out into the boy's path, causing the agents concern for John's safety. The agents' reaction and interrogation of Galella led to Galella's arrest and his action against the agents; Galella on other occasions interrupted Caroline at tennis, and invaded the children's private schools. At one time he came uncomfortably close in a power boat to Mrs. Onassis swimming. He often jumped and postured around while taking pictures of her party notably at a theater opening but also on numerous other occasions. He followed a practice of bribing apartment house, restaurant and nightclub doormen as well as romancing a family servant to keep him advised of the movements of the family. (*Galella v. Onassis,* 992)

Moreover, the court went on, evidence presented by Mrs. Onassis "showed that Galella had on occasion intentionally physically touched Mrs. Onassis and her daughter, caused fear of physical contact in his frenzied attempts to get their pictures, followed [her] and her children too closely in an automobile, endangered the safety of the children while they were swimming, water skiing and horseback riding." Sweeping aside Galella's First Amendment defense to point out, as in the case with Food Lion, that general laws apply to journalists, too, the appellate court declared:

Galella's action went far beyond the reasonable bounds of news gathering. When weighed against the *de minimis* public importance of the daily activities of the defendant, Galella's constant surveillance, his obtrusive and intruding presence, was unwarranted and unreasonable. If there were any doubt in our minds, Galella's inexcusable conduct toward defendant's minor children would resolve it. . . . There is no threat to a free press in requiring its agents to act within the law. (*Galella v. Onassis,* 995)

The appellate court actually relaxed certain restrictions imposed by the trial court against Galella, prohibiting him from approaching within twenty-five feet of Mrs. Onassis and within thirty feet of the children, blocking her movement in public places, entering the children's schools or play areas, and generally from taking any action that could reasonably be foreseen to harass or frighten any of them. Acknowledging that its order might be deemed a prior restraint, the court stated, "the relief granted fully allows Galella the opportunity to photograph and report on Mrs. Onassis' public activities. Any prior restraint on news gathering is miniscule and fully supported by the findings."

Disclosure of Embarrassing Private Facts

We turn now to the invasion of privacy torts that relate to publication, which of course includes broadcasting and Internet posting. In these areas, even more than in intrusion upon seclusion, newsworthiness may be a defense. Some of these cases raise questions of journalism ethics that may point to different answers than the courts of law provided.

The *Restatement of the Law, Second, Torts* defines the tort this way: "One who gives publicity to a matter concerning the private life of another is subject to liability to the other for invasion of his privacy, if the matter published is of a kind that (a) would be highly offensive to a reasonable person, and (b) is not of legitimate concern to the public."

Highly Offensive

Take, for instance, a man secretly ill with AIDS, identified in the court opinion only by his last name, Kubach, who agreed to participate in a TV call-in show in Macon, Georgia, about the disease only on condition that his image by digitized to prevent recognition. The case was *Multimedia WMAZ, Inc. v. Kubach*, 212 Ga. App. 707 (1994). Kubach had formerly operated a popular Macon restaurant, but had given up his business and was working part-time at the front counter of a local cleaning establishment. When he appeared on camera, the station's electronic fuzzing for the first several seconds was insufficient and he was recognized. He suffered considerably as a consequence. After the broadcast, in the words of the appellate court:

> [P]laintiff became withdrawn, extremely depressed and almost suicidal. He refused to leave his home for fear of being recognized and pointed out as an AIDS patient, and this situation was exacerbated when his sister convinced him to go out to a fast food place and he was in fact recognized and harassed by several young people. Plaintiff was unable to continue working at the cleaners because he no longer felt he could deal with the public at the front counter. . . . (*Multimedia WMAZ, Inc. v. Kubach*, 708)

Kubach sued the station for disclosure of embarrassing private facts and won a jury award of five hundred thousand dollars in general damages and $100 in punitive damages. A Georgia appellate court affirmed the verdict, except for the modest punitive damages award. It declared that although Kubach was earning the equivalent of only $3.35 an hour for twenty to twenty-five hours a week, "This evidence provided a sufficient basis for an award of lost wages."

State Privacy Statutes

This ruling was based on common law, but more frequently in recent cases of disclosure of embarrassing private facts we're dealing with statutes enacted by state legislatures to guard against publishing or broadcasting such specific facts as the names of juvenile offenders and the names of victims of sexual crimes. These statutes sometimes pose challenges of judgment for reporters and their editors, on both legal and ethical levels.

One especially important case, *Cox Broadcasting Corp. v. Cohn*, 420 U.S. 469 (1975), grew out of a vicious attack on a seventeen-year-old Georgia girl. Six high school students were indicted for rape and murder. Despite great publicity, her name was not disclosed pending trial, in keeping with a Georgia criminal statute that prohibited publication or broadcast of the name of a rape victim. But when the six defendants appeared in court, an experienced reporter for Atlanta television station WSB-TV perused the indictment documents available for public inspection in the courtroom, found the victim's name, and reported on the air: "Six youths went on trial today for the murder-rape of a teenaged girl. The six Sandy Springs high school boys were charged with murder and rape in the death of seventeen year old Cynthia Cohn following a drinking party last August 18. The tragic death of the high school girl shocked the entire Sandy Springs community."

Cynthia's father sued the station for money damages, contending that *his* right to privacy was violated by the disclosure, and won a summary judgment (meaning, without a trial) in the trial court, with the amount of damages to be determined later by a jury. The Georgia Supreme Court affirmed, holding that the statute was a legitimate limitation on the freedom of expression guaranteed by the First Amendment. The TV station's parent company challenged that determination in a petition to the U.S. Supreme Court.

The Supreme Court, by a vote of 8–1, reversed. In the majority opinion by Justice Byron White, the Court described the Georgia common-law right of privacy as the individual's "right to be free from unwanted publicity about his private affairs, which, although wholly true, would be offensive to a person of ordinary sensibilities . . . the publication . . . of which is embarrassing or otherwise painful to an individual. . . ." Nevertheless, while recognizing the growing importance of the right of privacy in modern society, Justice White went on:

> We are reluctant to embark on a course that would make public records generally available to the media but forbid their publication if offensive to the sensibilities of the supposed reasonable man. . . . Once true information is disclosed in public court documents open to public inspection, the press cannot be sanctioned for publishing it. In this instance as in others

reliance must rest upon the judgment of those who decide what to publish or broadcast. (Cox Broadcasting v. Cohn, 496)

Justice White was saying that, even when the First Amendment protects publication, there's still an ethical call to be made by journalists about whether to publish embarrassing private facts.

Oklahoma City reporters attended a juvenile court proceeding in which an eleven-year-old boy, present in the courtroom, was named as a suspect in the fatal shooting of a railroad switchman as he stood on the platform of a moving switch engine. Photographers took the boy's picture as he left the courtroom. Radio stations broadcast the boy's name, Larry Donnell Brewer; television stations ran film of him and identified him by name; and the *Daily Oklahoman* and other newspapers printed his name and photograph, and identified his parents. The judge subsequently issued a pre-trial order directing the news media not to state the boy's name or use his photo. But the papers and broadcasters briefly defied the order and for two more days ran additional stories naming the boy.

The Oklahoma Supreme Court affirmed the judge's order under a state statute requiring that juvenile proceedings be kept confidential. But the U.S. Supreme Court, in *Oklahoma Publishing Co. v. Oklahoma County District Court*, 430 U.S. 308 (1977), unanimously reversed, citing *Cox Broadcasting v. Cohn*. In a brief *per curiam* (by the court) opinion, the Supreme Court noted simply that "members of the press were in fact present at the hearing with the full knowledge of the presiding judge, the prosecutor, and the defense counsel. No objection was made to the presence of the press in the courtroom or to the photographing of the juvenile as he left the courthouse. There is no evidence that petitioner acquired the information unlawfully or even without the State's implicit approval."

The Supreme Court again upheld the First Amendment in a very different context: the publication of the name of a judge facing possible disciplinary action in a confidential proceeding. The case was *Landmark Communications, Inc. v. Virginia*, 435 U.S. 829 (1978). The Norfolk *Virginian Pilot* correctly identified the judge, whose conduct was being investigated by the Virginia Judicial Inquiry and Review Commission; most states have a similar secrecy requirement regarding judicial disciplinary proceedings. The article stated that "[no] formal complaint has been filed by the commission against [the judge], indicating either that the five-man panel found insufficient cause for action or that the case is still under review."

A grand jury soon indicted the paper's publisher, Landmark Communications, Inc., for violating a state law prohibiting publication of the name of a judge under investigation. At trial, the only witness, *Virginian Pilot* managing editor Joseph W. Dunn, Jr., testified that the matter was of public importance and merited reporting to the paper's readers. Nevertheless, the judge, trying the case without a jury, found the company guilty and fined it a modest five hundred dollars plus the costs of prosecution. The Virginia Supreme Court affirmed. However, the U.S. Supreme Court, by unanimous vote of seven justices (two did not participate), set aside the conviction, in effect agreeing with Mr. Dunn. Citing *New York Times Co. v. Sullivan,* Chief Justice Warren Burger wrote: "The article published by Landmark provided accurate factual information about a legislatively authorized inquiry pending before the Judicial Inquiry and Review Commission, and in so doing clearly served those interests in public scrutiny and discussion of governmental affairs which the First Amendment was adopted to protect."

Alert reporting was again protected by the Supreme Court in *Smith v. Daily Mail Publishing Co.*, 443 U.S. 97 (1979). Monitoring a police band radio frequency, reporters for two West Virginia newspapers, the *Charleston Daily Mail* and the *Charleston Gazette,* heard that a fifteen-year-old student was shot and killed at Hayes Junior High School in St. Albans, West Virginia, near Charleston. A fourteen-year-old classmate was identified as the shooter by seven eyewitnesses and was arrested by the police. The newspapers sent photographers and reporters Leslie Milam and Mary Schnack to the school, where they learned the name of the alleged perpetrator by questioning witnesses, the police, and an assistant prosecutor. *Daily Mail* editors, aware that a West Virginia statute prohibited newspapers from publishing the name of a juvenile suspect without court permission, omitted his name from the paper's story published that same afternoon. But the *Gazette* used it, and it was promptly repeated by local radio stations. The next day the *Daily Mail,* too, printed his name. Both newspapers, their editors, and the two reporters were indicted, but they challenged the indictment on First Amendment grounds. The West Virginia Supreme Court of Appeals saw a prior restraint and ruled for the papers. However, in an unusual step, the trial judge, Robert K. Smith, sought review from the U.S. Supreme Court.

Once again Chief Justice Warren Burger wrote for a unanimous Court (this time, eight justices participating), upholding the state Supreme Court of Appeals. He declared that "state action to punish the publication of truthful information seldom can satisfy constitutional standards," and that "if a newspaper lawfully obtains truthful information about a matter of public significance then state officials may not constitutionally punish publication of the information, absent a need . . . of the highest order." Burger found fault with the state statute on two grounds, very simply stated:

> The magnitude of the State's interest in this statute is not sufficient to justify application of a criminal penalty to respondents. Moreover, the statute's approach does not satisfy constitutional requirements. The statute does not

restrict the electronic media or any form of publication, except "newspapers," from printing the names of youths charged in a juvenile proceeding. In this very case, three radio stations announced the alleged assailant's name before the Daily Mail decided to publish it. Thus, even assuming the statute served a state interest of the highest order, it does not accomplish its stated purpose. (*Smith v. Daily Mail Publishing Co.,* 104–5)

Indicating some sympathy with the desire to keep juvenile suspects' names secret, Burger noted that "all 50 states have statutes that provide in some way for confidentiality, but only 5, including West Virginia, impose criminal penalties on nonparties for publication of the identity of the juvenile. . . . [A]ll but a handful have found other ways of accomplishing the objective."

When a similar First Amendment question came before the Supreme Court a decade later, the case was redolent with ineptness by both the press and a police agency. The result was an important but troubling decision. A Florida woman reported to the Duval County, Florida, Sheriff's Department that she had been robbed and raped at knifepoint as she crossed a park on the way to her bus stop. Sheriff's personnel prepared a report stating the victim's full name and posted it in the pressroom, despite a Florida statute that prohibited publication and broadcast of the name of a victim of a sexual offense. A reporter-trainee for the *Florida Star,* a weekly with a circulation of eighteen thousand in the Jacksonville area, copied the police report verbatim, including the victim's name. Based entirely on this report, a *Florida Star* reporter wrote a one-paragraph story about the crime, using the name, in the face of both the law and the newspaper's own policy of not publishing the names of sexual offense victims. (It's not stated in the court opinions, but it would not be unreasonable to assume that a *Florida Star* copy editor was a third person at the paper who had a hand in the story.)

The victim, known as B.J.F., filed suit against the newspaper and the Sheriff's Department alleging that they negligently violated the statutory prohibition. Before the trial the sheriff settled the case against his department, paying her twenty-five hundred dollars to be dismissed from her complaint. But the case continued against the newspaper. B.J.F. testified at the trial that the article had caused her emotional distress, that her mother had received phone calls from a man who threatened to rape B.J.F. again, that she felt compelled to change her residence and her phone number, and that she had sought police protection and mental health counseling. The judge found the newspaper guilty, and the jury awarded B.J.F. seventy-five thousand dollars in compensatory damages (which the judge reduced by the twenty-five hundred dollars from the Sheriff's Department) plus twenty-five thousand dollars in punitive damages. A District Court of Appeal affirmed the judgment, and the

Florida Supreme Court declined to review it. But the newspaper persisted and appealed to the U.S. Supreme Court.

Unlike previous First Amendment cases, this vexing confrontation yielded no unanimous opinion at the U.S. Supreme Court. In *Florida Star v. B.J.F.*, 491 U.S. 524 (1989) the vote was 6–3 to reverse the Florida courts. Justice Thurgood Marshall, writing for the majority, distinguished the case from *Cox Broadcasting v. Cohn,* which involved court records, and relied especially on *Smith v. Daily Mail,* where reporters got the suspect's name through their own questioning of witnesses. "It is undisputed," Marshall declared, "that the news article describing the assault on B.J.F. was accurate. In addition, appellant [the newspaper] lawfully obtained B.J.F.'s name." He also faulted the statute for prohibiting publication only in an "instrument of mass communication," ignoring the possibility that a victim's name could become known in other ways. "Without more careful and inclusive precautions against alternative forms of dissemination, we cannot conclude that Florida's selective ban on publication by the mass media satisfactorily accomplishes its stated purpose."

The dissenters saw the case as different from *Smith v. Daily Mail.* Justice Byron White, writing for himself, Chief Justice William Rehnquist, and Justice Sandra Day O'Connor, pointed out that the *Florida Star*'s trainee-reporter acknowledged at trial that a sign in the sheriff's pressroom prohibited publication of a rape victim's name and that she was "not supposed to take the information from the police department." White went on:

> As I see it, it is not too much to ask the press, in instances such as this, to respect simple standards of decency and refrain from publishing a victim's name, address, and/or phone number. . . . If the First Amendment prohibits wholly private persons (such as B.J.F.) from recovering for the publication of the fact that she was raped, I doubt that there remain any "private facts" which persons may assume will be not be published in the newspaper or broadcast on television. . . . Today, we hit the bottom of the slippery slope. I would find a place to draw the line higher on the hillside: a spot high enough to protect B.J.F.'s desire for privacy and peace-of-mind in the wake of a horrible personal tragedy. There is no public interest in publishing the names, addresses, and phone numbers of persons who are the victims of crime—and no public interest in immunizing the press from liability in the rare cases where a State's efforts to protect a victim's privacy have failed. (*Florida Star v. B.J.F.*, 547, 550–51, 553)

Newsworthiness Defense

In 2000, the U.S. Court of Appeals for the First Circuit, in Boston, addressed a different disclosure of private facts question in *Veilleux v. National Broadcasting Company*, 206 F.3d 92 (1st Cir. 2000). It involved a *Dateline*

NBC broadcast stimulated by a tragic highway accident in Maine in which four teenagers were killed when their car was struck by a truck driven by Robert Hornbarger, who later pleaded guilty to falsifying his driving hours in his logbook. NBC, its reporter Fred Francis, and freelance producer Alan Handel obtained the cooperation of an over-the-road driver, Peter Kennedy, and his boss, Raymond Veilleux, to interview and film Kennedy on a cross-country trip. Kennedy maintained he never used drugs, but during the trip was required to take a Department of Transportation drug test; it registered positive for marijuana and amphetamines. The broadcast, as described in the appellate court's opinion, "emphasized the pressures on long-distance truckers, the danger posed by truck-driver fatigue to others on the nation's highways, and the disregard of federal 'hours of service' and other regulations that govern the industry." Veilleux and Kennedy sued NBC, reporter Francis, and producer Handel for defamation, invasion of privacy, and other alleged violations of law, and won jury verdicts totaling $525,000 in the U.S. District Court in Maine.

On appeal, the First Circuit Court of Appeals reversed most of the jury verdict. In regard to a ruling of "unreasonable publication" of private facts, the court asked whether the unsavory personal revelations about Kennedy were in the public interest, and concluded they were. The court stated:

> We believe that Kennedy's drug test results reasonably tend to illustrate the report's newsworthy themes of interstate truck driving, highway safety and relevant government regulation. Because the public may be legitimately concerned with federally-mandated drug testing of truckers, Kennedy's test results, and the consequences of the results with regard to his driving career, defendants cannot be liable for invasion of privacy as a matter of law. . . . We think defendants [NBC and Francis] were entitled to illustrate their messages about highway safety and regulation with new information about the individual subject of their report. Simply reporting statistics about truckers who use drugs, or discussing the details of Kennedy's case without mentioning him by name, would have substantially less impact. (*Veilleux v. National Broadcasting Company*, 132, 133)

For a journalist, the message is clear: a defense of newsworthiness (which is questionable against intrusion upon seclusion) may be effective against an accusation of disclosure of embarrassing private facts.

Intercepted Communications

The case of *Bartnicki v. Vopper*, 532 U.S. 514 (2001) covers the alleged unlawful disclosure by a journalist of information from an illegal wiretap.

A long and difficult negotiation over a teachers' contract was the subject of great public interest in the Wyoming West School District in Kingston, Pennsylvania. A radio talk-show host, Fred Williams, of WILK in Wilkes Barre, expressed sympathy with the school board and against the teachers' union. One day, Jack Yocum, head of a local taxpayers' group formed to oppose the union's demand for a six percent pay increase (the school board offered three percent), sent Williams an audio tape of a dicey conversation between Gloria Bartnicki, the teachers' chief negotiator, and Anthony F. Kane, Jr., president of the union local. Kane told Bartnicki, who was on her car phone: "If they're not going to move for three percent, we're gonna have to go to their, their homes . . . to blow off their front porches, we'll have to do some work on some of those guys. . . . Really, uh, really and truthfully, because this is, you know, this is bad news."

Yocum said an unknown person had dropped the audio tape into his mailbox. He played the tape, recognized the voices as Bartnicki's and Kane's, made copies of the tape, and delivered them to Williams and another radio reporter, Rob Neyhard of WARM in Scranton. Williams, whose real name was Frederick Vopper, repeatedly played parts of the tape on his Fred Williams Show. TV stations picked it up, and some local newspapers printed transcripts. Bartnicki and Kane sued Vopper (Williams) and his station in U.S. District Court for violating federal and state anti-wiretapping statutes. The District Court posed questions about the statutes to the U.S. Third Circuit Court of Appeals in Philadelphia. It responded that Vopper had not violated the wiretapping prohibitions, and the First Amendment permitted him to air the tapes of a private conversation inasmuch as they concerned a significant public issue.

The U.S. Supreme Court agreed with the appellate court, but not unanimously. The vote was 6–3. For the majority, Justice John Paul Stevens invoked the Court's decision in *Smith v. Daily Mail,* as well as those in *Florida Star v. B.J.F.,* U.S. 524 (1989) and *Landmark Communications v. Virginia,* 435, U.S. 829 (1978). Noting that "one of the costs associated with participation in public affairs is an attendant loss of privacy," Stevens declared that "a stranger's illegal conduct does not suffice to remove the First Amendment shield from speech about a matter of public concern. The months of negotiations over the proper level of compensation for teachers at the Wyoming Valley West High School were unquestionably a matter of public concern, and respondents were clearly engaged in debate about that concern."

But Chief Justice William Rehnquist, in a dissent joined by Justices Antonin Scalia and Clarence Thomas, took issue with the Court's reliance on public interest. He stated that protection of individual privacy:

at its narrowest must embrace the right to be free from surreptitious eavesdropping on, and involuntary broadcast of, our cellular telephone conversations. The Court subordinates that right, not to the claims of those who themselves wish to speak, but to the claims of those who wish to publish the intercepted conversations of others. Congress' effort to balance the above claim to privacy against a marginal claim to speak freely is thereby set at naught. (*Bartnicki v. Vopper,* 555–56)

The majority opinion, though disputed, stands as still another reminder to journalists that newsworthiness may justify disclosure of embarrassing private facts.

However, note that in a later case, *Peavy v. WFAA-TV,* 221 F.3d 158 (5th Cir. 2000), the U.S. Fifth Circuit Court of Appeals, in New Orleans, made it clear that *Bartnicki v. Vopper* applies only if the journalist had no role in the illicit recording. Robert Riggs, an investigative reporter for WFAA-TV in Dallas, was informed by one of the station's news producers that one Charles Harman had called to say he was recording the cellphone conversations of a neighbor, Dan Peavy. Harman and Peavy were not friendly toward each other. Peavy was a trustee of the Dallas Independent School District, where he oversaw its insurance purchases. Harman suggested that there were improprieties in those purchases. Riggs, the reporter, contacted Harman, obtained the recordings from him, and encouraged him to continue his recording. Riggs received eighteen tapes in all, containing 188 conversations between Peavy and others. At the same time, Riggs and Ward, taking advantage of information obtained from the recorded cellphone calls, undertook an extensive investigation of Peavy's role at the school district, requesting records from the district and other government agencies, looking into the district's insurance providers and their political contributions, and interviewing a number of people.

WFAA-TV aired three stories alleging wrongdoing by Peavy in connection with the school district's insurance purchases. Peavy was indicted, but acquitted of all charges. The appellate court, reversing the trial court's judgment for the station and Riggs, framed the wiretap issue this way, an important *caveat* for journalists:

> [T]he Acts do *not* prohibit *disclosure* of information that might be contained in illegal interceptions, *so long as* such disclosed information is acquired by *other, non-prohibited means.* Therefore, if a jury finds defendants' television broadcasts reported information obtained from sources independent of the tapes, defendants would *not* be liable, under the Wiretap Acts, for *disclosing* such information in their television broadcasts, *even if* the infor-

mation so disclosed was also included in the contents of those intercepted communications. (*Peavy v. WFAA-TV,* 175)

However, the Court of Appeals noted that, unlike the broadcaster in *Bartnicki v. Vopper,* Riggs and WFAA-TV "had some participation concerning the interceptions" and therefore were covered by the statutes' prohibitions against use and disclosure of intercepted conversations, the First Amendment notwithstanding. The court explained, "Although intercepted conversations were *not* played in the broadcasts, the district court held that, in violation of the Federal and Texas Wiretap Acts, WFAA and Riggs 'disclosed' portions of the tapes' contents during them." So the appellate court remanded the case to the District Court for further proceedings.

The above invasion of privacy torts—intrusion upon seclusion and disclosure of embarrassing private facts—are available in all states and thus are the most likely privacy lawsuits a journalist might face. In the next chapter we'll look at less likely privacy claims.

Questions for Discussion

1. Is it only photographers who need to be concerned about intrusion upon seclusion?
2. In these days of massive disclosure of personal information on the Internet, how does a journalist decide what constitutes an embarrassing private fact?
3. How would you have decided *Florida Star v. B.J.F.?* Why?
4. From these cases, can you draw a clear line between acceptable journalistic newsgathering tactics and illicit invasions of privacy? Once you define what's acceptable under law, how can you apply the SPJ Code of Ethics to make ethical judgments about whether to proceed with the story?

References

Bartnicki v. Vopper, 532 U.S. 514 (2001). http://www.law.cornell.edu/supct/html/99-1687.ZS.html.
Cox Broadcasting Corp. v. Cohn, 420 U.S. 469 (1975). http://www.bc.edu/bc_org/avp/cas/comm/free_speech/cox.html.
Desnick v. American Broadcasting Companies, Inc., 233 F.3d 514 (7th Cir. 2000). http://caselaw.findlaw.com/us-7th-circuit/1203729.html.
Deteresa v. American Broadcasting Companies, Inc., 121 F.3d 460 (9th Cir. 1997). http://caselaw.findlaw.com/us-9th-circuit/1187883.html.
Dietemann v. Time, Inc., 449 F.2d 245 (9th Cir. 1971). http://www.bc.edu/bc_org/avp/cas/comm/free_speech/dietemann.html.

Florida Star v. B.J.F., 491 U.S. 524 (1989). http://www.bc.edu/bc_org/avp/cas/comm/free_speech/floridastar.html.

Food Lion v. Capital Cities/ABC, Inc., 194 F.3d 505 (4th Cir. 1999). http://www.ca4.uscourts.gov/Opinions/Published/972492.P.pdf.

Galella v. Onassis, 487 F.2d 986 (2d Cir.1973). http://www.bc.edu/bc_org/avp/cas/comm/free_speech/gallela.html.

Griswold v. Connecticut, 381 U.S. 479 (1965). http://www.law.cornell.edu/supct/html/historics/USSC_CR_0381_0479_ZO.html.

Landmark Communications, Inc. v. Virginia, 435 U.S. 829 (1978). http://caselaw.lp.findlaw.com/cgi-bin/getcase.pl?court=us&vol=435&invol=829.

Medical Laboratory Management Consultants v. American Broadcasting Companies, Inc., Diane Sawyer, et al., 306 F.3d 806 (9th Cir. 2002). http://caselaw.findlaw.com/us-9th-circuit/1003103.html.

Multimedia WMAZ, Inc. v. Kubach, 212 Ga. App. 707 (1994). http://georgia-court-appeals.vlex.com/vid/multimedia-wmaz-inc-v-kubach-20437432.

Oklahoma Publishing Co. v. Oklahoma County District Court, 430 U.S. 308 (1977). http://caselaw.lp.findlaw.com/scripts/getcase.pl?navby=case&court=us&vol=430&invol=308.

Peavy v. WFAA-TV, 221 F.3d 158 (5th Cir. 2000). http://caselaw.findlaw.com/us-5th-circuit/1297051.html.

Restatement of the Law, Second, Torts (Philadelphia: American Law Institute, 1977).

Roe v. Wade, 410 U.S. 113 (1973). http://www.law.cornell.edu/supct/html/historics/USSC_CR_0410_0113_ZS.html.

Sanders v. American Broadcasting Companies, Inc., 20 Cal. 4th 907 (1999). http://www.firstamendmentcoalition.org/handbook/cases/Sanders_V.pdf.

Shulman v. Group W Productions, Inc., 18 Cal. 4th 200 (1998). http://www.eejlaw.com/materials/Shulman_v_Group_W_T08.pdf.

Smith v. Daily Mail Publishing Co., 443 U.S. 97 (1979). http://caselaw.lp.findlaw.com/scripts/getcase.pl?court=us&vol=443&invol=97.

Veilleux v. National Broadcasting Company, 206 F.3d 92 (1st Cir. 2000). http://scholar.google.com/scholar_case?case=16314580346067045234&q=veilleux+v.+national+broadcasting+company&hl=en&as_sdt=2,14&as_vis=1.

Warren, Samuel D., and Louis D. Brandeis, "The Right to Privacy," IV *Harvard Law Review* 5, December 15, 1890.

6

Less Common Invasion of Privacy Torts

> *"The fantastic advances in the field of electronic communication constitute a greater danger to the privacy of the individual."*
> Chief Justice Earl Warren, *Lopez v. United States*, 373 U.S. 427 (1963)

False Light

The invasion of privacy tort called false light is not available in all states and can be a bit slippery. Though it's sometimes called "libel without defamation," there is an element of distortion, if not outright reputational damage, in false light. The *Restatement of the Law, Second, Torts* says this:

> One who gives publicity to a matter concerning another that places the other before the public in a false light is subject to liability to the other for invasion of his privacy, if
>
> a. the false light in which the other was placed would be highly offensive to a reasonable person, and
> b. the actor had knowledge of or acted in reckless disregard as to the falsity of the publicized matter and the false light in which the other would be placed.

However, as we will see, courts haven't always applied this definition scrupulously, sometimes opting for more subjective determinations of false light invasion of privacy.

New York's Privacy Statute

In the states that recognize false light, it is largely common law, i.e., law pronounced by judges rather than legislatures. However, much of the definition of false light grows out of two prominent cases during the 1960s based not on common law, but on a New York statute. It's labeled "Invasion of Privacy," but the statute is limited: It seeks merely to prohibit unauthorized use of a person's name or image for "trade purposes." On its face the statute seems to pertain more to another invasion of privacy tort, called appropriation. It forbids use of a celebrity's likeness or reputation for commercial gain, and we'll deal with it shortly. But in its interpretation and application, the New York statute gave considerable form to false light. The two cases were brought by a famous baseball player and by an inadvertently prominent victim of a sensational crime.

Warren Spahn was *Sports Illustrated*'s choice in 1991 as the left-handed pitcher on its all-time, major league all-star team. (The right hander was Christy Mathewson, good company indeed.) Although delayed three years by World War II, Spahn spent twenty-one years in the majors, mostly with the Boston and Milwaukee Braves. He had thirteen twenty-win seasons, including a 23–7 record at age forty-two. He also hit thirty-five home runs along the way. He was elected to the Baseball Hall of Fame in 1973, with 83 percent of the vote.

While Spahn was in mid-career and justly famous, without his permission or cooperation one Milton J. Shapiro wrote a children's biography of him, published by Julian Messner, Inc., called *The Warren Spahn Story*. It was full of inaccuracies, false and embarrassing descriptions of Spahn's private thoughts, and his personal relationships with his father and then his wife, and wholly concocted quotations of conversations that never happened. For instance, Shapiro wrote that Spahn won a Bronze Star in European combat; not true (though he had a distinguished war record, including a Purple Heart and a battlefield commission). Similarly, Spahn wasn't responsible for the "supervision of the repairs" of the bridge at Remagen, did not go "from man to man, urging them on," had not "raced out into the teeth of the enemy barrage." And so it went, throughout the book.

Spahn sued Shapiro and his publisher Messner under the New York privacy statute. At trial the writer admitted that he had never interviewed Spahn or any member of his family, or any baseball player who knew Spahn, hadn't even contacted the Braves. It was all based on unverified clippings and articles. "I created dialogue based upon a secondary source," Shapiro testified. The judge ruled for Spahn, awarded him ten thousand dollars and issued an injunction barring further distribution of the book. In *Spahn v. Messner*, 21 N.Y. 2d 124 (1967), New York's highest court, the Court of Appeals, affirmed the judgment, noting "gross errors of fact" and immense distortions and inaccuracies. "Fictionalization," the court declared, "is the heart of the cases in point," referring to several previous rulings of New York courts.

The second influential application of the New York statute, also involving some creative writing about actual people, turned out differently. Near Philadelphia, three escaped convicts invaded the home of James Hill, his wife and five children, and held them hostage. The grim news spread rapidly. After nineteen hours the convicts fled but were pursued by the police, who killed two of them. Hill told the press that the convicts had treated them courteously, hadn't harmed or molested them, and weren't violent. The family then moved away to Connecticut and turned down all efforts by the press to pursue their story further.

Nevertheless, capitalizing on the well-known story, a writer named Joseph Hayes produced a novel, *The Desperate Hours,* about a family taken hostage by convicts who treated them violently, and he later turned the book into a play (and a movie as well). *Life,* a hugely popular weekly magazine published by Time, Inc., took pictures of the play during its pre-Broadway run (in Philadelphia, no mere coincidence), transported actors to the Hills' former house and photographed re-enactments of scenes "on the site of the crime." One photo showed convicts roughing up one of the family's sons, another depicted a daughter biting a convict's hand to make him give up a gun, and another showed the father throwing his gun out the door after a "brave try" to save his family failed.

James Hill sued Time, Inc. under the privacy statute of New York (location of the company's headquarters), alleging that *Life* sought to capitalize commercially on his family's misfortune. The jury awarded him thirty thousand dollars in compensatory damages. Affirming the judgment, a New York appellate court stated, "Although the play was fictionalized, *Life's* article portrayed it as a re-enactment of the Hills' experience. It is an inescapable conclusion that this was done to advertise and attract further attention to the play, and to increase present and future magazine circulation as well. It is evident that the article cannot be characterized as a mere dissemination of news. . . ."

The New York Court of Appeals, the state's highest court, also upheld the trial court's ruling. However, the U.S. Supreme Court, in *Time, Inc. v. Hill,* 385 U.S. 374 (1967), reversed by a vote of 5–4. Although "false light" wasn't mentioned, the Court's majority opinion, by Justice William Brennan, recognized that in invasion of privacy cases, "the primary damage is the mental distress from having been exposed to public view," which is in fact the damage done by false light. Still, the Court majority determined that James Hill, by virtue of his prominence, however unwanted, was a public figure and therefore decided, "We hold that the constitutional protections for speech and press preclude the application of the New York statute to redress false reports of matters of public interest in the absence of proof that the defendant published the report with knowledge of its falsity or in reckless disregard of the truth." In other words, the Court applied the same "actual malice" standard that it had previously enunciated in libel cases brought by public figures. It noted that the New York trial judge's instructions to the jury had not included this specific requirement for a guilty verdict, and therefore the Court reversed the ruling and remanded the case for further proceedings, meaning a new trial.

Nevertheless, six of the justices diverged from the majority opinion. Two felt that the Court should have gone further, should have blocked any dilution of press freedom, even in the face of such a significant right as privacy. Justice Hugo Black, while concurring with setting aside the New York judgment, wrote in an opinion joined by Justice William O. Douglas, that the First Amendment's freedom of the press was not meant to be balanced, or weighed, against any other rights and freedoms:

> Finally, if the judicial balancing choice of constitutional changes is to be adopted by this Court, I could wish it had not started on the First Amendment. The freedoms guaranteed by that Amendment are essential freedoms in a government like ours. That Amendment was deliberately written in language designed to put its freedoms beyond the reach of government to change while it remained unrepealed. If judges have, however, by their own fiat today created a right of privacy equal to or superior to the right of a free press that the Constitution created, then tomorrow and the next day and the next, judges can create more rights that balance away other cherished Bill of Rights freedoms. If there is any one thing that could strongly indicate that the Founders were wrong in reposing so much trust in a free press, I would suggest that it would be for the press itself not to wake up to the grave danger to its freedom, inherent and certain in this "weighing process." (*Time, Inc. v. Hill,* 400)

On the other hand, four of the justices felt the "actual malice" test imposed on Hill was too stringent. Justice John Marshall Harlan, concurring in some part and dissenting in another, argued in support of the New York privacy statute that a state has a legitimate "interest in encouraging the publication of well researched materials more likely to be true." He noted that states may take land to build libraries, and that state universities include "professional schools of journalism." These manifestations of state interest in the publication of truth, Harlan contended, militate for a lesser standard of proof than "actual malice" in a state privacy law.

Three justices dissented outright, expressing sympathy for the plight of the Hills. Justice Abe Fortas, joined by Chief Justice Earl Warren and Justice Tom Clark, contended that the trial judge's jury instructions were quite adequate to justify the jury's verdict of a violation of the New York privacy law. They hoped openly that a new trial would enable Hill to "recover damages for the reckless and irresponsible assault upon himself and his family which this article represents." However, as Fortas noted, "he has litigated this case for 11 years." In fact, Hill threw in the towel at that point. After two trials, untold lawyers' bills, and winning the support of four justices of the U.S. Supreme Court, he and his family never received any compensation for *Life's* misleading treatment of their ordeal.

Indefensible Press Conduct

Despite the scattering of the justices in *Time v. Hill,* just a few years later eight of them ruled in favor of a false-light plaintiff, but it took an egregious case of press misconduct to warrant such near-unanimity.

Joseph Eszterhas, a reporter for the *Cleveland Plain Dealer,* covered the tragic collapse of an Ohio River bridge at Point Pleasant, West Virginia, in which a Point Pleasant resident named Melvin Cantrell, a forty-year-old father of seven children, ages one to sixteen, was killed along with forty-three others. Eszterhas wrote a story about Cantrell's funeral and the impact of his death on his family. His coverage won three press awards.

Five months later Eszterhas returned to Point Pleasant with a photographer, Richard Conway, for a follow-up story on the Cantrell family for the newspaper's Sunday magazine. Eszterhas and Conway called at the Cantrell home, and although Mrs. Cantrell was not at home, they talked with the children for over an hour and Conway took fifty pictures. Their article described the family's poverty, the children's worn clothing, and the dilapidated condition of their home, all misrepresented or exaggerated in the opinion of later appellate reviews, and baldly stated this: "Margaret Cantrell will talk neither about what happened nor about how they are doing. She wears the same mask of non-expression she wore at the funeral. She is a proud woman. Her world has changed. She says that after it happened, the people in town offered to help them out with money and they refused to take it."

Mrs. Cantrell and one of her teenage children, William, sued the newspaper and the two journalists in U.S. District Court for false-light invasion of privacy "causing them to suffer outrage, mental distress, shame, and humiliation." Although the trial judge did not explicitly define Mrs. Cantrell as a public figure, he instructed the jury that it could rule for the plaintiffs only if it found that the article contained known falsehoods or was published in reckless disregard of the truth. The jurors found the newspaper guilty and liable for compensatory damages. The judgment was set aside by the Sixth Circuit Court of Appeals on First Amendment grounds, but the U.S. Supreme Court reversed that ruling. In *Cantrell v. Forest City Publishing Co.,* 419 U.S. 245

(1974), a majority of eight ordered that the trial court's judgment be upheld. Justice Potter Stewart, writing for the Court, strongly affirmed the trial judge's handling of the case:

> [A]s his instructions to the jury made clear, the District Judge was fully aware that the *Time, Inc.* v. *Hill* meaning of the *New York Times* "actual malice" standard had to be satisfied for the Cantrells to recover actual damages. . . . Moreover, the District Judge was clearly correct in believing that the evidence introduced at trial was sufficient to support a jury finding that the respondents Joseph Eszterhas and Forest City Publishing Co. had published knowing or reckless falsehoods about the Cantrells. There was no dispute during the trial that Eszterhas, who did not testify, must have known that a number of the statements in the feature story were untrue. In particular, his article plainly implied that Mrs. Cantrell had been present during his visit to her home and Eszterhas had observed her "[wearing] the same mask of non-expression she wore [at her husband's] funeral." These were "calculated falsehoods," and the jury was plainly justified in finding that Eszterhas had portrayed the Cantrells in a false light through knowing or reckless untruth. (*Cantrell v. Forest City Publishing Co.*, 252–53)

The lone dissent was registered by Justice William O. Douglas, reiterating his absolutist view that the First Amendment allowed no restrictions on the press. "Those who write the current news," he declared, "seldom have the objective, dispassionate point of view—or the time—of scientific analysts. They deal in fast-moving events and the need for 'spot' reporting. The jury under today's formula sits as a censor with broad powers—not to impose a prior restraint, but to lay heavy damages on the press."

Thoughtless, misleading use of file photos has given rise to allegations of false light invasion of privacy. A West Virginia newspaper used a two-year-old photo of Sue S. Crump, a local coal miner, alongside a story on harassment of women in the industry. She brought suit in a state court for libel as well as false light, asserting that she never had been harassed but the article caused people to raise embarrassing questions about her experience at work. She said one newspaper reader asked whether she had ever been "stripped, greased and sent out of the mine," quoting the paper's description of another woman's experience. The Supreme Court of West Virginia reversed a trial judge's summary judgment for the newspaper publisher and sent the case back for trial. In *Crump v. Beckley Newspapers, Inc.*, 173 W.Va. 699 (1983), the court stated, "whether the statements in the article involved referred to the appellant with regards to her privacy cause of action is a question of fact for the jury."

Similarly, Nellie Mitchell, a ninety-seven-year-old resident of Mountain

Home, Arkansas, well known for selling and delivering newspapers for nearly fifty years, went to court when a supermarket tabloid publisher placed a ten-year-old file photo of her next to a fictitious story about a 101-year-old Australian who supposedly was forced to give up delivering newspapers when she became pregnant by a millionaire customer on her route. In *Peoples Bank and Trust Company of Mountain Home, as Conservator of the Estate of Nellie Mitchell, an Aged Person v. Globe International Publishing, Inc., doing business as "Sun"*, 978 F.2d 1065 (8th Cir. 1992), the U.S. Eighth Circuit Court of Appeals affirmed a jury verdict of six hundred fifty thousand dollars for false light invasion of privacy, describing the immediate impact of the article:

> Customers at supermarket checkout lines in Baxter County who scanned the cover page of the *Sun* saw only that Nellie Mitchell was featured next to a headline about a "granny" forced to quit work because of pregnancy. ... Word spread quickly in Mountain Home that Nellie Mitchell, "the paper lady," was featured in the offending edition of the *Sun*. This edition of the *Sun* was a "sell-out" in the northern region of Arkansas where Mitchell lives. (*Peoples Bank v. Globe International*, 1067).

The court concluded that the "Globe contends it made a simple mistake, and that it was not on notice that Mitchell was alive. The jury, however, had sufficient evidence to determine that Globe purposefully avoided the truth about Mitchell."

Intentional Infliction of Emotional Distress

The *Restatement of the Law, Second, Torts*:

> One who by extreme or outrageous conduct intentionally or recklessly causes severe emotional distress to another is subject to liability for such emotional distress, and if bodily harm to the other results from it, for such bodily harm.

Notice, as with false light and disclosure of embarrassing personal facts, that this tort, too, is measured by the extent of emotional damage rather than by any pecuniary loss.

Again, Actual Malice

We have seen allegations of intentional infliction of emotional distress, sometimes called outrage, in some of the above privacy cases. But the Supreme Court's definitive ruling on this little-known tort, which isn't recognized in all states, is *Hustler Magazine and Larry C. Flynt v. Jerry Falwell*, 485 U.S. 46 (1988). *Hustler* parodied a Campari Liqueur advertisement with an apocryphal interview with the Reverend Jerry Falwell, a well-known and outspoken evangelist, purporting to quote him as saying that his "first time" was during a drunken rendezvous with his mother in an outhouse. Small print at the bottom of the page stated, "ad parody—not to be taken seriously."

Nevertheless, Falwell brought an action in a federal district court in Virginia for libel, invasion of privacy, and intentional infliction of emotional distress. The first two claims fell, but the jury found *Hustler* and Larry Flynt, its publisher, guilty under Virginia's law of infliction of emotional distress, which required a plaintiff to show that the defendant's conduct was intentional or reckless, that it offended generally accepted standards of decency or morality, that it was a cause of the plaintiff's emotional distress, and that the distress caused was severe. The jury awarded Falwell one hundred thousand dollars in compensatory damages and fifty thousand dollars from each defendant in punitive damages.

Unanimously reversing the judgment in an opinion by Chief Justice William Rehnquist, the Supreme Court extolled the virtues of political cartooning. "Despite their sometimes caustic nature," Rehnquist wrote, "from the early cartoon portraying George Washington as an ass down to the present day, graphic depictions and satirical cartoons have played a prominent role in public and political debate." Recognizing, however, that the *Hustler* cartoon was "at best a distant cousin of the political cartoons described above," the Court dismissed Falwell's claim that the magazine's depiction of him was "outrageous," saying that such a subjective standard "would allow a jury to impose liability on the basis of the jurors' tastes or views, or perhaps on the basis of their dislike of a particular expression." Therefore, the Court held, to sustain a claim of intentional infliction of emotional distress, a public figure such as Falwell would have to prove that the publication contained a false statement of fact made with "actual malice," in other words, with "knowledge that the statement was false or with reckless disregard as to whether or not it was true." As it had in *Time, Inc. v. Hill*, the Court insisted that this was not merely a "blind application" of its *New York Times v. Sullivan* standard in libel cases, but was a reflection of "our considered judgment that such a standard is necessary to give adequate 'breathing space' to the freedoms protected by the First Amendment."

But Private Plaintiffs Can Win

However, courts have allowed private plaintiffs' claims of intentional infliction of emotional distress to proceed in a variety of unusual circumstances, generally involving cameras.

Ruben Norte, a TV news producer at KNBC in Los Angeles, wanted live footage for a "mini-documentary" on emergency services. He arranged with the Los Angeles Fire Department to alert him to emergency calls for medical help. One evening, Norte and a camera crew followed paramedics into the apartment of Dave Miller, who had suffered a heart attack in his bedroom, and filmed the efforts to resuscitate him. The paramedics were unsuccessful. KNBC used some footage on its nightly news and later included some portions of it in a commercial promoting its mini-documentary. Miller's wife, Brownie, who was in the apartment at the time of the incident, didn't see the film until weeks later when she stumbled across it while channel-surfing for a soap opera. In the words of a California appellate court reviewing her claim of intentional infliction of emotional distress, *Brownie Miller v. National Broadcasting Company*, 187 Cal. App.3d 1463 (1986), "She screamed and turned the television off. That was the only time she saw the film. Plaintiff Miller also received telephone calls from friends who had seen the sequence; the calls upset her."

The trial court granted NBC's motion for summary judgment, but the appellate court saw it differently, remanding the case for trial:

> [T]he NBC camera crew, the uninvited media guests, not only invaded the Millers' bedroom without Dave Miller's consent, they also invaded the home and privacy of his plaintiff wife, Brownie Miller, referred to by Norte in his deposition as "a woman in the hallway." Not only was the "woman in the hallway" Dave Miller's wife, the hallway was a part of her home, a place where NBC had no right to be without her consent. . . . [T]he record discloses that the NBC camera crew apparently devoted little or no thought whatsoever to its obvious transgression. "Little or no thought" constitutes, in this context, "reckless disregard" of the rights and sensitivities of others. . . . [W]e leave it to a reasonable jury whether the defendants' conduct was "outrageous." (*Brownie Miller v. National Broadcasting Company*, 1486)

Max Saxenmeyer, a reporter for KOVR-TV in Sacramento, accompanied by a cameraman, called at the home of seven-year-old Amanda Mehrkens, where she and two friends were playing. No adults were home. With the camera rolling at the front door, Saxenmeyer asked the youngsters about the neighboring Weber family and their children, six and three years old. Amanda and her friends knew them. In *KOVR-TV, Inc. v. Superior Court of Sacramento County*, 31 Cal. App. 4th 1023 (1995), the appellate court described the next moments: "At this point defendant [Saxenmeyer] states: 'Well, the mom has killed the two little kids and herself.' Amanda exclaims: 'Oh my God!' Defendant then inquires if the minors know of 'any problems' at the Webers. The minors state they do not. After a few more questions about the Webers, defendant thanks the minors, asks them their names and terminates the interview."

The court, determining whether the plaintiffs' lawsuit for intentional infliction of emotional distress should go to trial, characterized the event as "an uninvited, intrusive encounter by adult strangers with children of tender years not in a public place but in their home." It concluded:

> Even if defendant was innocently gathering news when he initiated the interview, it is a reasonable inference that when he discovered the minors were friends of the Weber children but unaware of their demise, he abruptly informed them "the mom has killed the two little kids and herself," in the hope it would elicit an emotional reaction that would be "newsworthy," e.g., suitable to redeem a promise of "film at eleven." We further conclude a jury could find that a television reporter who attempts deliberately to manipulate the emotions of young children for some perceived journalistic advantage has engaged in conduct "so outrageous in character, and so extreme in degree, as to go beyond all possible bounds of decency. . . ."
> [*Restatement, Second, of Torts*]
>
> If indeed defendant sought to elicit an emotional reaction from the minors for the voyeuristic titillation of KOVR-TV's viewing audience, this is shameless exploitation of defenseless children, pure and simple, not the gathering of news which the public has a right to know. A free press is not threatened by requiring its agents to operate within the bounds of basic decency. (*KOVR-TV, Inc. v. Superior Court of Sacramento County,* 1027, 1032)

The fact that the TV station decided not to use the videotape was of no significance, the court ruled, sending the case back for trial.

Orchestrating Police Raids

Two other cases, both involving NBC crews staging incidents for a *Dateline* series called "To Catch a Predator," demonstrate the downside of TV news producers' efforts to orchestrate police tactics on-camera to make them appear more dramatic and sensational. The NBC strategy, in collaboration with local police departments, was to lure men looking to meet "a young teenager" by inviting them online to a staked-out house, where they would be confronted by correspondent Chris Hansen and then arrested by the police, all on camera.

In one instance, Hansen teamed up with the police in the town of Terrell, Texas. Their sting succeeded in attracting several men to the designated house. They then went after another who had responded briefly to the online invitation but never appeared. Hansen and the police figured that he could be charged with trying to solicit a minor online. They apparently had no evidence of his actually abusing children. Furthermore, as a law enforcement target he was highly unusual: a well-known fifty-six-year-old assistant district attorney, a career prosecutor. His name was Louis William Conradt, Jr.

As NBC's cameras rolled, an overwhelming force of a dozen or more police officers, some carrying rifles, took up positions around Conradt's house. In *Patricia Conradt v. NBC Universal, Inc.*, 536 Fed.Supp.2d 380, S.D. N.Y. (2008), Judge Denny Chin of the U.S. District Court in Manhattan, where NBC was sued, picked up the narrative: "Members of the SWAT team opened a locked glass sliding door at the rear of the house and entered. The officers called out 'Terrell Police!' and 'Search Warrant.' They saw Conradt standing at the end of a hallway. He stepped into the room and said, 'I'm not gonna hurt anyone.' He then shot himself with a handgun."

The *Dateline* program, showing the removal of Conradt's body, aired on February 20, 2007. In the lawsuit that followed, Conradt's sister and administratrix of his estate, Patricia Conradt, lodged multiple claims against NBC, among them intentional infliction of emotional distress. The judge granted NBC's motion to dismiss much of Patricia Conradt's suit, but not the emotional distress claim, which he ordered tried. He noted the elements of proof under Texas law (the same as set forth above in *Hustler v. Falwell*): "a plaintiff must prove that: (1) the defendant acted intentionally or recklessly; (2) the defendant's conduct was extreme and outrageous; (3) the defendant's actions caused the plaintiff emotional distress; and (4) the resulting emotional distress was severe."

Relating these elements to the standards of the journalism profession, Judge Chin wrote:

> In considering whether NBC's conduct was outrageous, a jury could take note of the fact that, as alleged in the amended complaint, NBC failed to act "ethically" and violated "numerous journalistic standards." The reporter-subject relationship is not monitored by statute, but the profession is guided by self-enforced principles and standards of practice. Although unethical conduct, by itself, does not necessarily equate to outrageous conduct, the failure to abide by these journalistic standards may indeed be relevant to the jury's determination of whether Dateline acted in a reckless and outrageous manner. (*Patricia Conradt v. NBC Universal, Inc.*, 397)

Then, in a most unusual inclusion in a court opinion, Judge Chin in a long footnote quoted the Society of Professional Journalists' code of ethics as stating that journalists should:

- Avoid . . . staged news events.
- Distinguish between advocacy and news reporting.
- Recognize that gathering and reporting information may cause harm or discomfort.
- Recognize that private people have a greater right to control information about themselves than do public officials and others who seek power, influence or attention. Only an overriding public need can justify intrusion into anyone's privacy.
- Show good taste. Avoid pandering to lurid curiosity.
- Be judicious about naming criminal suspects before the formal filing of charges.
- Avoid conflicts of interest, real or perceived.
- Be wary of sources offering information for favors or money; avoid bidding for news. (*Patricia Conradt v. NBC Universal, Inc.,* 397–98)

The judge concluded:

a reasonable jury could find that Dateline violated some or all of these standards by failing to take steps to minimize the potential harm to Conradt, by pandering to lurid curiosity, by staging (or overly dramatizing) certain events, by . . . providing equipment and other consideration to law enforcement, by failing to be judicious about publicizing allegations before the filing of charges, by advocating a cause rather than independently examining a problem, and by manufacturing the news rather than merely reporting it. (*Patricia Conradt v. NBC Universal, Inc.,* 398)

The other *Dateline* case arose in Petaluma, California: A man named Anurag Tiwari took the bait. In *Tiwari v. NBC Universal, Inc.,* Number C-08–3988 EMC (N.D.Cal. 2011), U.S. District Court Judge Edward M. Chen picked up this description of the action, as set forth in Tiwari's complaint:

After being confronted by Mr. Hansen, Mr. Tiwari left the back yard and walked into the garage, at which point approximately half a dozen police officers rushed and shouted at [him] in a loud and dramatic manner. Although [Mr. Tiwari] was unarmed, several of the police officers had their guns drawn and aimed at [his] head. Police officers forcefully pushed [him] against the garage wall, yanked his arms behind his back, handcuffed him, and transported him down the driveway and away from the set. Mr. Tiwari was then taken to a "makeshift 'pre-booking' area at the Petaluma airport constructed by NBC and law enforcement personnel for the Catch episode." (*Tiwari v. NBC Universal, Inc.,* 4)

NBC filmed Mr. Tiwari arriving at the pre-booking facility and then his interrogation there. The police initially charged Tiwari with two felony offenses, but in the end settled for a guilty plea to a minor infraction and a thirty-dollar "court security fee."

> He sued NBC, asserting that it "instructed law enforcement 'to give special intensity to arrests—including rushing targets, surrounding them, hollering at them, throwing them to the ground or against walls, roughly handcuffing them, and drawing of weapons—so as to enhance the camera effect.' Finally, NBC paid or helped law enforcement in devising special booking and interrogation areas that allowed NBC to watch, listen in on, and record police interrogations with the individuals."

Tiwari alleged defamation, which Judge Chen agreed to strike at NBC's behest, and intentional infliction of emotional distress, which he did not strike. The judge wrote, "NBC has failed to cite any authority establishing that nightmares cannot constitute severe emotional distress. . . . Mr. Tiwari has sufficiently established a probability of success on the claim for intentional infliction of emotional distress, and therefore the motion to strike with respect to this claim is denied." A trial was ordered.

Appropriation

This invasion of privacy tort is for the protection of entertainers and other prominent people who can command a fee for the use of their name, face, or other aspects of their persona. The *Restatement of the Law, Second, Torts* provides: "One who appropriates to his own use or benefit the name or likeness of another is subject to liability to the other for invasion of his privacy."

In a notable case decided by the U.S. Supreme Court, a circus performer named Hugo Zacchini gained more lasting fame in the law than he ever did under the Big Top. Zacchini was a human cannonball and made his living by simply climbing into a cannon and being shot out some two hundred feet into a net. One day, in Burton, Ohio, at the Geauga County Fair, a freelance photographer for Scripps-Howard Broadcasting Co. watched Zacchini's one-shot performance, but at Zacchini's request did not videotape it. The next day, however, at the direction of his company, the photographer shot the entire act, all fifteen seconds of it, and it was on the eleven o'clock news that evening, with favorable commentary.

Zacchini sued in state court for appropriation, or violation of what's sometimes called the right of publicity. He argued that his act was his livelihood and that the TV station had usurped his right to sell his own performance. He won his trial, but the Ohio Supreme Court reversed on the grounds that the broadcast was a report of a matter of legitimate public interest and therefore was protected by the constitutional freedom of the press. The U.S. Supreme Court reversed again, restoring Zacchini's verdict, but it was a close call, just 5–4.

Justice Byron White wrote for the majority, in *Zacchini v. Scripps-Howard Broadcasting Co.*, 433 U.S. 562 (1977):

> [T]he First and Fourteenth Amendments do not immunize the media when they broadcast a performer's entire act without his consent. . . . [T]he broadcast of a film of petitioner's entire act poses a substantial threat to the economic value of that performance. . . . [I]f the public can see the act free on television, it will be less willing to pay to see it at the fair. . . . Petitioner does not seek to enjoin the broadcast of his performance; he simply wants to be paid for it. (578)

In a dissent joined by Justices William Brennan and Thurgood Marshall, Justice Lewis Powell wrote, "I would hold that the First Amendment protects the stations from a 'right of publicity' or 'appropriation' suit, absent a strong showing by the plaintiff that the news broadcast was a subterfuge or cover for private or commercial exploitation."

Several much more prominent celebrities also have proved appropriation. Boxing great Muhammad Ali sued *Playgirl* magazine's publisher over a "portrait" depicting, in the words of the trial court, "a nude black man seated in the corner of a boxing ring" whom Ali claimed was "unmistakably recognizable" as himself. The judge, in *Ali v. Playgirl, Inc.*, 447 F.Supp. 723 (S.D. N.Y., 1978), had to make a personal assessment to decide whether to grant a preliminary injunction barring further distribution of the magazine:

> Even a cursory inspection of the picture which is the subject of this action strongly suggests that the facial characteristics of the black male portrayed are those of Muhammad Ali. The cheekbones, broad nose and wide set brown eyes, together with the distinctive smile and close cropped black hair are recognizable as the features of the plaintiff, one of the most widely known athletes of our time. . . . [T]he identification of the individual as Ali is further implied by an accompanying verse which refers to the figure as "the Greatest." This court may take judicial notice that plaintiff Ali has regularly claimed that appellation for himself and that his efforts to identify himself in the public mind as "the Greatest" have been so successful that he is regularly identified as such in the news media. . . . The foregoing discussion also establishes the likelihood that plaintiff will prevail on his claim that his right of publicity has been violated by the publication of the offensive portrait. (*Ali v. Playgirl, Inc.*, 726–27, 728)

The judge granted the temporary injunction.

An Atlantic City radio talk-show host named Fred Robbins interviewed Cher, the entertainer, then wrote an article about his interview and sold it to the *Star* tabloid and pocket-sized *Forum* magazine. *The Star* promoted the interview story in published advertising that suggested Cher was *endorsing* the magazine. One ad read: "So take a tip from Cher and hundreds of thousands of other adventurous people and subscribe." Affirming a trial court's judgment against the publisher, a federal appellate court concluded in *Cher v. Forum International, Ltd.*, 692 F.2d 634 (9th Cir. 1982):

> We are satisfied that the trier could find, from the record as a whole, that no matter how carefully the editorial staff of *Forum* may have trod the border between the actionable and the protected, the advertising staff engaged in the kind of knowing falsity that strips away the protection of the First Amendment. (Cher v. Forun International, Ltd. 640)

The penalty was severe: $269,117, including one hundred thousand dollars in exemplary or punitive damages. Fred Robbins, the broadcaster-writer, was exonerated.

In a somewhat similar allegation of appropriation, actor Clint Eastwood sued the *National Enquirer* weekly over an article stating that he was involved in a "love triangle" with singer Tanya Tucker and actress Sondra Locke. Among other allegations, Eastwood said the *Enquirer* aired a TV commercial featuring his name and photograph, and that the TV ad and the magazine cover were calculated to promote sales of the *Enquirer.* A California appellate court, reviewing a trial court order blocking Eastwood's suit, held in *Eastwood v. Superior Court of Los Angeles County*, 198 Cal. Rptr. 342 (1983):

> To the extent their use attracted the readers' attention, the Enquirer gained a commercial advantage. Furthermore, the Enquirer used Eastwood's personality in the context of an alleged news account entitled "Clint Eastwood in Love Triangle with Tanya Tucker" to generate maximum curiosity and the necessary motivation to purchase the newspaper. Moreover, the use of Eastwood's personality in the context of a news account, allegedly false but presented as true, provided the Enquirer with a ready-made "scoop"—a commercial advantage over its competitors which it would otherwise not have. Absent a constitutional or statutory proscription, we find that Eastwood can show that such use is a subterfuge or coverup for commercial exploitation. We therefore conclude that Eastwood has sufficiently alleged that the Enquirer has commercially exploited his name, photograph, and likeness . . . (*Eastwood v. Superior Court of Los Angeles County,* 420–21)

Thus the court opened the door for Eastwood to pursue his complaint at trial.

However, celebrities don't always succeed in their claims of appropriation. San Francisco 49ers quarterback Joe Montana sued the *San Jose Mercury News* for distributing posters that reproduced an article previously printed on the front page celebrating the football team's fourth Super Bowl victory in one decade, calling them a "team of destiny." The article included an artist's rendering of Montana. He questioned whether the poster was entitled to First Amendment protection. "We conclude that it is," stated a California appellate court in *Montana v. San Jose Mercury News, Inc.*, 34 Cal. App. 4th 790 (1995). "This is because Montana's name and likeness appeared in the posters for *precisely* the same reason they appeared on the original newspaper front pages: because Montana was a major player in contemporaneous newsworthy sports events. Under these circumstances, Montana's claim that SJMN used his face and name solely to extract the commercial value from them fails."

Dustin Hoffman also lost out. The actor sued *Los Angeles Magazine* and its parent company over its use of an altered photograph (among several of other Hollywood personalities) from the movie *Tootsie,* in which he posed as a woman in order to get a job. The alteration kept Hoffman's head but replaced the body with a male model wearing "a spaghetti-strapped, cream-colored, silk evening dress and high-heeled sandals." The text read: "Dustin Hoffman isn't a drag in a butter-colored silk gown by Richard Tyler and Ralph Lauren heels." A federal trial court in California awarded Hoffman three million dollars in compensatory and punitive damages and $269,528.50 in attorney fees. But the U.S. Ninth Circuit Court of Appeals reversed.

Differentiating the case from the commercial pitches involved in the cases described above, the appellate court held in *Hoffman v. Capital Cities/ABC, Incorporated and L.A. Magazine, Inc.*, 255 F.3d 1180 (9th Cir. 2001) that "LAM did not use Hoffman's image in a traditional advertisement printed merely for the purpose of selling a particular product." Therefore, the court held, the magazine was entitled to First Amendment protection, and Hoffman, obviously a public figure, would have to prove actual malice. This he failed to do, the court ruled. It went on:

> Viewed in context, the article as a whole is a combination of fashion photography, humor, and visual and verbal editorial comment on classic films and famous actors. . . . We do not believe that the totality of LAM's presentation of the article and the "Tootsie" photograph provides clear and convincing evidence that the editors intended to suggest falsely to the ordinary reader that he or she was seeing Hoffman's body in the altered "Tootsie" photograph. All but one of the references to the article in the

magazine make it clear that digital techniques were used to substitute current fashions for the clothes worn in the original stills. (*Hoffman v. Capital Cities/ABC, Incorporated and L.A. Magazine, Inc.*, 1185, 1188)

Defenses to Invasion of Privacy Claims

The best defense to an appropriation claim by a celebrity is a signed contract giving you the right to use the interview or the photographs as you may determine. But for the other four privacy claims, it's apparent from the above cases that there is no defense as surefire as the truth defense to a defamation claim.

Newsworthiness

Truth is always a journalist's strength, and it will help support a defense of newsworthiness against allegations of intrusion upon seclusion or disclosure of embarrassing private facts, as we've seen earlier in *Desnick v. American Broadcasting Companies, Veilleux v. National Broadcasting Company, Landmark Communications v. Virginia,* and *Bartnicki v. Vopper.*

Fair Report

More reliable, when it's available, is the defense of fair report, which was the essence of the pro-press rulings in *Florida Star v. B.J.F.* and *Cox Broadcasting v. Cohn.* In effect, it's another version of truth.

The letter of the law says that fair report involves an official document, but consider this Oklahoma case. Lieutenant Tom Easley, spokesman for the Norman, Oklahoma Police Department, triggered an invasion of privacy lawsuit when he publicized the wrong security camera video of a woman using an automatic teller machine. The police were seeking public help in identifying a thief who stole a wallet, and the video was believed to show the culprit. It didn't. Linda Stewart, the woman in the video, sued the corporate owners of two local television stations, KFOR and KWTV, that had referred to her as a "thief," for false light as well as defamation. But the jury ruled for the media, and an appellate court affirmed in *Stewart v. NYT Broadcast Holdings, L.L.C., and Griffin Communications, L.L.C.,* 2010 Okla.Civ.App. 89, 240 P.3d 722 (2010). The court stated: "if accurate, the reports . . . by KFOR and KWTV fell within the scope of the fair report privilege," and it ruled that the jury had sufficient evidence to conclude that the reports were indeed accurate.

Fair report might work even when there's an error. Pete Dunan, a reporter for the *San Luis Obispo County (California) Telegram-Tribune,* woke up one morning to hear a radio report that a prominent local architect, Ethan A. Jennings, Jr., had pleaded no contest to federal charges of failing to report substantial taxable income. He checked it out (but couldn't reach Jennings), and wrote: "San Luis Obispo architect Ethan A. Jennings Jr. faces a possible sentence of up to two years in prison and a $20,000 fine for his failure to file federal income tax returns during 1970 and 1971. Jennings pleaded no contest in Los Angeles Federal Court Tuesday to charges he failed to report a total combined income during the two years of more than $436,000."

The story was entirely correct, but it ran under this headline: "Prominent SLO architect convicted of tax fraud." The *Telegram-Tribune* ran two more articles subsequently, one stating that Jennings had pled no contest to tax evasion, at which point Jennings' attorney sent a telegram to the newspaper labeling certain portions of each article libelous and demanding a retraction. The paper declined. Jennings sued for libel, invasion of privacy, and intentional infliction of emotional distress, noting that "tax fraud" and "tax evasion" are felonies, serious crimes that may warrant prison sentences of a year or more, while his acknowledged failure to file income tax returns was merely a misdemeanor. Despite the accuracy of Jennings' plea, a California trial court ruled that the defendants justifiably claimed the defense of fair report, and it granted their motion to terminate the action. That decision was affirmed by an appellate court in *Jennings v. Telegram-Tribune Company,* 164 Cal. App.3d 119 (1985). Trying to assess what readers might understand, the court stated:

> California does not hold the press to the precision in reporting that Jennings suggests should prevail. . . . The facts of the crimes were accurately described in the articles, as were the court proceedings and judgment. "Tax fraud" and "tax evasion" are harsh terms; but we cannot say that the average reader would have viewed the offenses differently, given the amount of gross income involved and the length of time it had gone unreported, had less colorful descriptions been chosen. In short, while perhaps overblown or exaggerated, the terms are easily within the literary license concept. . . . (*Jennings v. Telegram-Tribune Company,* 125, 127)

"Literary license," though hardly a precise legal concept, referred to the California Supreme Court's characterization of the U.S. Supreme Court opinion in the product-disparagement case of *Bose Corp. v. Consumers Union* that, in the California court's words, "clearly recognized the need for a certain degree of literary license when properly applying the *New York Times* standard to the facts of each case."

Libel Plus Invasion of Privacy

We've seen in a number of the cases above that the plaintiff alleges both invasion of privacy and libel or another tort in the same complaint. A trial court must consider each such allegation separately, applying the appropriate, different standards of proof and defenses. To get a glimpse of how truth can work to the journalist's advantage in confronting multiple counts, consider a Washington State case involving the *Seattle Post-Intelligencer* and reporter Andrea James.

James headed a team of eight reporters and was the principal writer of the lead follow-up story after the sudden collapse of a tower crane at a construction site in the Seattle suburb of Bellevue. It killed a young Microsoft lawyer in his apartment and caused significant property damage. But the operator of the crane, Warren Yeakey, survived, so in one of several second-day stories, the *Seattle Post-Intelligencer* understandably focused on him, although first James had to tease out Yeakey's name because it wasn't officially released.

At the top of page one was this headline: "Operator in crane wreck has history of drug abuse." An accompanying photo portrayed the wrecked crane and emergency crews on the scene. Another showed the deceased young man. The story contained these paragraphs, starting at the top:

> The man who was operating the massive tower construction crane at the time of its deadly collapse in downtown Bellevue Thursday night has a long criminal record, including at least six drug convictions.
>
> Crane operator Warren Taylor Yeakey, 34, of Tacoma, who survived the fall with minor injuries, went into a drug treatment program in 2000 after an arrest for methamphetamine possession in Pierce County, records show.
>
> . . . .
>
> L&I [Washington State Department of Labor and Industries] spokesman Charles Lennon said Yeakey is being tested for drug use, but he did not know the test results Friday evening. The state doesn't require drug testing of crane operators before they are hired, he said.
>
> . . . .
>
> Court records show that Yeakey has a history of drug abuse that includes a meth possession conviction in 2000, and three meth possession convictions and one cocaine possession conviction in 1994.
>
> . . . .
>
> In 2005, Yeakey was acquitted on two counts of child rape after a 15-year-old Seattle girl told police that she had sex with Yeakey on several occasions at her home in July 2004. Yeakey told a detective that he had sex with the girl two times, but that she'd told him she was 18 years old,

court papers say. A King County Superior Court jury found Yeakey not guilty on both counts.

. . . .

Yeakey also has convictions for domestic violence, marijuana posses-sion and soliciting a prostitute, according to records filed in King County Superior Court. He did not return calls seeking comment. (Seattle Post-Intelligencer, 2006)

The long, comprehensive story also dealt at length with safety and crane inspection requirements, and included this statement: "It doesn't appear as if the state had ever conducted a workplace-safety inspection at that job site before Thursday." Yeakey's wife, mother of their four children, was quoted, expressing her shock and relief. "It was really emotional for me; it's not a phone call everybody wants to get."

Two days later Yeakey's drug test came back negative, and a subsequent investigation by the state agency determined that the collapse was caused by a flawed engineering design. There was no operator error.

Not surprisingly, Yeakey's lawyer threw the book at Andrea James, the *Post-Intelligencer,* and its parent company, Hearst Communications, Inc. The lawsuit alleged defamation, false light invasion of privacy, negligent infliction of emotional distress, and outrage, contending that the page-one juxtaposition of articles and photos falsely implied that Yeakey's drug use and operator er-ror were factors in the collapse. However, Yeakey conceded in his complaint that all statements in the articles were true, and he also acknowledged that his claims were not based on a contention that facts were omitted from the articles. Nevertheless, responding to a *Post-Intelligencer* motion to dismiss, the trial judge kept the case alive, stating that Yeakey might be able to prove "defama-tion by implication" based simply on "juxtaposition of truthful statements."

The Washington appellate court disagreed. In *Yeakey v. Hearst Commu-nications, Inc.,* 156 Wn. App. 787 (2010), Judge Lisa Worswick declared, "we have held that a plaintiff may not base a defamation claim on the nega-tive implication of true statements." She acknowledged that a state supreme court opinion held the door open for action against a publication that "leaves a provably false impression contradicted by the inclusion of omitted facts," but concluded: "Nothing in this case suggests that the PI [*Post-Intelligencer*] omitted material facts in its articles." She added in a brief footnote: "Yeakey asserted a series of other claims below, including false light, negligent inflic-tion of emotional distress, and outrage, but conceded that those claims would rise and fall with his defamation claim. Because he has not prevailed on his defamation claim, we do not consider his other claims." The court remanded the case to the trial court for dismissal.

So truth prevailed against Yeakey's invasion-of-privacy claims as well as his libel claim, a victory for scrupulously accurate and thorough reporting (under deadline pressure) that left no room for criticism that the article was skewed by omission of relevant facts.

Truth may not always provide such an effective defense against multiple allegations, but *Yeakey* is a good lesson and a salubrious way to wind up our consideration of both libel and invasion of privacy.

Questions for Discussion

1. What's the difference between libel and false light invasion of privacy?
2. Could a story that's entirely truthful still constitute false light?
3. What are the best defenses against invasion of privacy allegations?
4. Looking at the invasion of privacy cases in Chapters 5 and 6, would you say the risk of privacy liability requires more *ethical* considerations by journalists than the risk of libel? Why or why not?
5. Does responsible, conscientious journalism have anything to fear from a story about the private life of a public figure? What tort might be claimed?

References

Ali v. Playgirl, Inc., 447 F.Supp. 723 (S.D. N.Y. 1978) http://www.leagle.com/xml-Result.aspx?xmldoc=19781170447FSupp723_11068.xml&docbase=CSLWAR1-1950-1985.

Cantrell v. Forest City Publishing Co., 419 U.S. 245 (1974). http:/caselaw.lp.findlaw.com/scripts/getcase.pl?court=us&vol=419&invol=245.

Cher v. Forum International, Ltd., 692 F.2d 634 (9th Cir. 1982). http://openjurist.org/692/f2d/634/cher-v-forum-international-ltd.

Conradt, Patricia v. NBC Universal, Inc., 536 F.Supp.2d 380 (S.D. N.Y. 2008). http://www.leagle.com/xmlResult.aspx?xmldoc=2008916536FSupp2d380_1875.xml.

Crump v. Beckley Newspapers, Inc., 173 W.Va. 699 (1983). http://wv.findacase.com/research/wfrmDocViewer.aspx/xq/fac.19831110_9999.WV.htm/qx.

Eastwood v. Superior Court of Los Angeles County, 198 Cal.Rptr. 342 (1983). http://www.markroesler.com/pdf/caselaw/Eastwood%20v.%20Superior%20Court.pdf.

Hoffman v. Capital Cities/ABC, Incorporated and L.A. Magazine, Inc. 255 F.3d 1180 (9th Cir. 2001). http://caselaw.findlaw.com/us-9th-circuit/1004607.html.

Hustler Magazine and Larry C. Flynt v. Jerry Falwell, 485 U.S. 46 (1988). http://www.law.cornell.edu/supct/html/historics/USSC_CR_0485_0046_ZO.html.

Jennings v. Telegram-Tribune Company, 164 Cal. App.3d 119 (1985). http://law.justia.com/cases/california/calapp3d/164/119.html.

KOVR-TV, Inc. v. Superior Court of Sacramento County (31 Cal. App.4th 1023, 1995). http://law2.umkc.edu/faculty/projects/ftrials/communications/kovr-tv.html.

Miller, Brownie v. National Broadcasting Company 187 Cal. App.3d 1463 (1986). http://www.firstamendmentcoalition.org/handbook/cases/Miller_v_NBC.pdf.

Montana v. San Jose Mercury News, Inc., 34 Cal. App.4th 790 (1995). http://caselaw. findlaw.com/us-9th-circuit/1004607.html.

Peoples Bank and Trust Company of Mountain Home, as Conservator of the Estate of Nellie Mitchell, an Aged Person v. Globe International Publishing, Inc., doing business as "Sun," 978 F.2d 1065 (8th Cir. 1992). http://law2.umkc.edu/faculty/ projects/ftrials/communications/peoplesbank.html.

Restatement of the Law, Second, Torts (Philadelphia: American Law Institute, 1977).

Seattle Post-Intelligencer, November 17, 2006, p. 1.

Spahn v. Messner, 21 N.Y.2d 124 (1967). http://ny.findacase.com/research/wfrm-DocViewer.aspx/xq/fac.19661027_0043700.NY.htm/qx.

Stewart v. NYT Broadcast Holdings, L.L.C., and Griffin Communications, L.L.C., Okla.Civ.App. 89, 240 P.3d 722 (2010). http://law.justia.com/cases/oklahoma/ court-of-appeals-civil/2010/461253.html.

Time, Inc. v. Hill, 385 U.S. 374 (1967). http://www.bc.edu/bc_org/avp/cas/comm/ free_speech/time.html.

Tiwari v. NBC Universal, Inc., No. C-08–3988 EMC (N.D. Cal. 2011). http:// www.leagle.com/xmlResult.aspx?xmldoc=In%20FDCO%2020111025D32. xml&docbase=CSLWAR3–2007-CURR.

Yeakey v. Hearst Communications, Inc., 156 Wn.App. 787 (2010). http://caselaw. findlaw.com/wa-court-of-appeals/1530905.html.

Zacchini v. Scripps-Howard Broadcasting Co., 433 U.S. 562 (1977). http://www. bc.edu/bc_org/avp/cas/comm/free_speech/zacchini.html.

7

Fair Trial v. Free Press

"Whatever disagreement there may be as to the scope of the phrase 'due process of law' there can be no doubt that it embraces the fundamental conception of a fair trial, with opportunity to be heard."
—Justice Oliver Wendell Holmes, Jr., *Frank v. Magnum,* 1915

In spite of the exhortations of Justice Hugo Black and Justice William O. Douglas, the First Amendment is not absolute. It does not trump all other rights. Over the years the courts have resolved conflicts between rights, especially constitutional rights, by balancing and weighing one fundamental right against another. Nowhere is this balancing act more evident than in the recurring tensions between free press and a defendant's right to a fair trial, guaranteed by the Sixth Amendment of the U.S. Constitution. The Sixth Amendment states:

> "In all criminal prosecutions, the accused shall enjoy the right to a speedy and public trial, by an impartial jury . . . and to be informed of the nature and cause of the accusation; to be confronted with the witnesses against him; to have compulsory process for obtaining Witnesses in his favor, and to have the Assistance of Counsel for his defense."

The amendment, like the entire Bill of Rights (the first ten amendments), is made applicable to the states by the Fourteenth Amendment's "due process" clause: "[N]or shall any State deprive any person of life, liberty, or property, without due process of law." (The state constitutions also guarantee fair trial.) Unfortunately, crime and criminals make the news, virtually every day, and it's inevitable that every general-assignment journalist will cover crime stories at one time or another. So understanding how the courts balance the rights to a fair trial and the freedom of the press is essential.

Like the First Amendment, the Sixth Amendment—a concise enumeration of six separate rights—wasn't strictly enforced by the U.S. Supreme Court until the twentieth century, beginning with the advent of Chief Justice Earl Warren (1953–1969). Since the resurrection of both amendments, there have been many points of conflict between freedom of the press and the right to a fair trial, from concerns about polluting the minds of prospective jurors with prejudicial pretrial publicity to closing courtrooms, from access to court documents to cameras in court. And here, as with defamation and invasion of privacy, there may be times when the law permits a journalist to act in ways that ethical considerations might reject.

Prejudicial Pretrial Publicity

Can extensive media coverage of a crime engender a widespread public belief that the accused is guilty even before he's tried? If so, that threatens his right to a fair trial, because it may be difficult to select a jury of local residents (drawn from the list of registered voters) who have not already formed an opinion about the defendant's guilt.

Most criminal trials take place in state courts, but several of our cases will focus on U.S. Supreme Court reviews of state trials. How does a state prosecution get into the federal system? This may occur when a convicted defendant, his appeal having been rejected by the state's highest court, seeks a writ of habeas corpus, in effect a nullification of his state conviction, from a federal court on the grounds that his trial did not comport with the Sixth Amendment's guarantee of a fair trial. Enacted by Congress, the habeas corpus jurisdiction of the federal courts empowers them to set aside state court convictions in "all cases where any person may be restrained of his . . . liberty in violation of the constitution, or of any treaty or law of the United States. . . ."

The "exhaustion of state remedies" requirement is a significant prerequisite to federal intervention. In one of the early cases testing this requirement, an Indiana man named Leslie Irvin was convicted of murder and sentenced to death, even though the prosecutor had made it difficult to find impartial jurors by announcing publicly that Irvin had confessed to killing six people. Because of the widespread publicity about the murders and the confession, 355 prospective jurors had to be questioned before 12/4 of whom admitted they believed Irvin was guilty—were seated as his jury. The Indiana Supreme Court affirmed the verdict, but without carefully exploring the defendant's claim that the pretrial publicity had violated his Sixth Amendment right to a fair trial.

So Irvin turned to the federal courts for a writ of habeas corpus. His claim rose through district and appellate courts to the U.S. Supreme Court, where the justices divided. They all noted that the Indiana Supreme Court, which pointed out that Irvin had escaped from prison and was still at large, rested its denial primarily on a state law that disallowed claims of an escapee and had given short shrift to the pretrial publicity argument. So there was a question about whether Irvin had exhausted his state remedies. Rather than ask Indiana for clarification, a majority of five U.S. Supreme Court justices decided lamely in *Irvin v. Dowd*, 359 U.S. 394 (1959) that the federal appellate court that had most recently ruled on the case, also rejecting Irvin's claim, should assess the sufficiency of the Indiana Supreme Court's handling of the publicity issue. But four dissenters remonstrated that the U.S Supreme Court itself should be ruling on that constitutional question, and then, if a violation was found, send the case back to the Indiana Supreme Court to determine whether its denial of Irvin's appeal was adequately grounded in the state law disallowing claims of escaped prisoners.

The U.S. Seventh Circuit Court of Appeals again ruled against Irvin, but this time the Supreme Court, in *Irvin v. Dowd*, 366 U.S. 717 (1961), finally concluded that Irvin's trial indeed had been prejudiced by pretrial publicity and granted the writ of habeas corpus, opening the door to a new trial in Indiana. Irvin was recaptured, tried again by a new jury, and was convicted and sentenced to life in prison, where he later died.

We have examined the sequence of events in the Irvin case to see how carefully the federal courts will evaluate and decide the threshold question: did the defendant exhaust his state remedies?

Another early habeas corpus case, with even greater ramifications still today, grew out of the murder of the thirty-year-old pregnant wife of a socially prominent, Cleveland-area osteopathic surgeon, Samuel Sheppard. Partly because Sheppard had had an extramarital affair, and because the police could identify no other suspects, suspicion immediately focused on him. He said he was asleep on a couch downstairs but glimpsed a shadowy figure who knocked him unconscious as he fled.

Though he repeatedly denied killing his wife, three Cleveland daily newspapers and other media, local and national, headlined every hint of Sheppard's guilt that they could dig up or manufacture. "Testify Now In Death, Bay Doctor Is Ordered," "Doctor Balks at Lie Test; Retells Story," the headlines blared. A hostile front-page editorial shrieked that somebody is "getting away with murder," and another editorial asked, "Why Isn't Sam Sheppard in Jail?" All along Sheppard cooperated with investigators, answering hours of questions on several occasions without his lawyer present. At the end of one session a police officer told him bluntly, "I think you killed your wife."

The authorities helped inflame the public. For instance, the coroner, prodded by the press, conducted a public inquest in a school gymnasium, with a long table up front for reporters and broadcasters, who aired the three-day session live. Sheppard's counsel was allowed to attend but not to participate, barred from even submitting documents for the record.

Sheppard's trial was conducted in a small Cuyahoga County courtroom where a long press table was placed directly behind the lawyers' table, in front of the bar rail separating the public section, most of whose seats were also allotted to the press. A room next to the jury room was given over to a local radio station, which broadcast frequent reports, even as the jurors took breaks and later deliberated on their verdict. Photographers and reporters wandered about the courtroom and the hallway outside. Though photos of the trial proceedings were not permitted, the trial judge made sure the photographers had time to get pictures of Sheppard and the jurors in the courtroom for a few minutes before each session started. Jurors' names and addresses were released and printed in the papers, stimulating calls and letters to them from the public. The jurors weren't sequestered or forbidden to watch or read daily stories about the trial. Defense motions to move the trial to another district were denied. The circus lasted for five weeks, and, not surprisingly, Sheppard was convicted. He was sentenced to life in prison. The Ohio Supreme Court affirmed the verdict.

From jail, Sheppard sought a writ of habeas corpus in federal district court, alleging a denial of his right to a fair trial. The district court granted the writ, but the Sixth Circuit Court of Appeals reversed. The case moved on to the Supreme Court.

In *Sheppard v. Maxwell*, 384 U.S. 333 (1966), the appalled Supreme Court reversed the appellate court and granted the writ of habeas corpus. Justice Tom Clark, a former U.S. attorney general, wrote the opinion, pointing out that the trial began just two weeks before an election in which the prosecutor was running for judge, and the trial judge was a candidate for reelection. Clark characterized the trial as being conducted in a "carnival atmosphere" and castigated the press, local officials, and especially the trial judge for failing to ensure a fair trial. "The fact is," Clark declared, "that bedlam reigned at the courthouse during the trial and newsmen took over practically the entire courtroom, hounding most of the participants in the trial, especially Sheppard. Participants in the trial, including the jury, were forced to run a gauntlet of reporters and photographers each time they entered or left the courtroom." Justice Clark was particularly critical of leaks, rumors, and innuendos published by the media:

> Much of the material printed or broadcast during the trial was never heard from the witness stand, such as the charges that Sheppard had purposely impeded the murder investigation and must be guilty since he had hired a prominent criminal lawyer; that Sheppard was a perjurer; that he had sexual relations with numerous women; that his slain wife had characterized him as a "Jekyll-Hyde"; that he was "a bare-faced liar" because of his testimony

as to police treatment; and, finally, that a woman convict claimed Sheppard to be the father of her illegitimate child. . . . At one point, a front-page picture of Mrs. Sheppard's blood-stained pillow was published after being "doctored" to show more clearly an alleged imprint of a surgical instrument. (*Sheppard v. Maxwell,* 356–57)

Clark went on to enumerate strong, specific criticisms of the trial judge and prescribe several recommendations to help future judges in such highly publicized cases to ensure a fair trial:

1. The judge should have adopted stricter rules governing the use of the courtroom by newsmen. . . . The number of reporters in the courtroom itself could have been limited. . . . They certainly should not have been placed inside the bar.
2. The court should have insulated the witnesses. All of the newspapers and radio stations apparently interviewed prospective witnesses at will, and in many instances disclosed their testimony.
3. The trial court might well have proscribed extrajudicial statements by any lawyer, party, witness, or court official which divulged prejudicial matters, such as the refusal of Sheppard to submit to interrogation or take any lie detector tests; any statement made by Sheppard to officials; the identity of prospective witnesses or their probable testimony; any belief in guilt or innocence; or like statements concerning the merits of the case.
4. Reporters who wrote or broadcast prejudicial stories could have been warned as to the impropriety of publishing material not introduced in the proceedings.
5. Where there is a reasonable likelihood that prejudicial news prior to trial will prevent a fair trial, the judge should continue [postpone] the case until the threat abates, or transfer it to another county not so permeated with publicity.
6. Sequestration of the jury was something the judge should have raised *sua sponte* [on his own] with counsel.
7. If publicity during the proceedings threatens the fairness of the trial, a new trial should be ordered. (*Sheppard v. Maxwell,* 358–63)

These recommendations have stood the test of time and remain applicable to trials today.

Gag Orders

To safeguard a defendant's right to a fair trial, on occasion judges have issued orders restricting coverage by journalists, on pain of being held in contempt of court, which can mean jail. Any such "gag order," however, runs afoul of the First Amendment and should be challenged. (An order to gag the press should not be confused with an order to gag law enforcement and court personnel and lawyers, as suggested in *Sheppard,* for they are under the jurisdiction of the court and may be disciplined by the trial judge.)

The most notable Supreme Court decision on gag orders in a criminal case related to the grisly murders of all six members of the Henry Kellie family, allegedly in connection with a sexual assault, in tiny Sutherland, Nebraska, population 850. A suspect named Erwin Charles Simants was promptly arrested and charged with the crimes. The publicity, both local and national, was immense. A preliminary hearing was scheduled, but the prosecutor requested, and the county judge issued, an order to all attending the hearing not to disclose anything said there that might undermine Simants' right to a fair trial, in particular any mention of a confession he might have made to law enforcement authorities. That restriction was approved by the Nebraska Supreme Court.

Even though the case was over, for future guidance Nebraska news media contested the gag order at the U.S. Supreme Court, in *Nebraska Press Association v. Stuart,* 427 U.S. 539 (1976). For a unanimous Court, Chief Justice Warren Burger acknowledged,

> as the Nebraska courts held, that there was indeed a risk that pretrial news accounts, true or false, would have some adverse impact on the attitudes of those who might be called as jurors. But on the record now before us it is not clear that further publicity, unchecked, would so distort the views of potential jurors that 12 could not be found who would, under proper instructions, fulfill their sworn duty to render a just verdict on the evidence presented in open court. (*Nebraska Press Association v. Stuart,* 568–69)

In fact, the Court found fault with several aspects of the Nebraska proceedings. The judges had not made a specific determination of the harm that would be done by pretrial publicity. There was no Court finding that that "the restraining order actually entered would serve its intended purpose," because news of the crime and the hearing would naturally spread rapidly in such a small, rural community. Perhaps, the justices suggested, a more precisely tailored restriction might have sufficed. So the Court deemed the Nebraska restriction a prior restraint of publication: "We hold that, with respect to the order entered in this case prohibiting reporting or commentary on judicial proceedings held in public, the barriers have not been overcome; to the extent that this order restrained publication of such material, it is clearly invalid."

Justice William Brennan, concurring in the judgment but preferring an even broader interpretation of the First Amendment's protection, wrote tartly, "the press may be arrogant, tyrannical, abusive, and sensationalist, just as it may be incisive, probing, and informative. But at least in the context of prior restraints on publication, the decision of what, when, and how to publish is for editors, not judges. Every restrictive order imposed on the press in this case was accordingly an unconstitutional prior restraint on the freedom of the press. . . ."

But the Supreme Court's opposition to press gag orders hasn't always been honored, even in federal courts. In 1990 a U.S. District Court ordered CNN not to air portions of a Miami jailhouse conversation between a former military governor of Panama accused of international drug trafficking and his lawyer. It was a bizarre case in every respect. In 1989, while still in his Panama post, General Manuel Noriega was indicted in the U.S. for facilitating the transport of cocaine from the notorious Medellin drug cartel in Colombia through Panama and on to the United States. He responded by declaring that a state of war existed between Panama and the United States, prompting President George H. W. Bush to dispatch U.S. forces to Panama to find and arrest Noriega, which they did.

As Noriega awaited trial in Miami, the government recorded his phone conversations with his lawyer (with his knowledge), and somehow CNN obtained a copy of those recordings. Noriega protested in U.S. District Court that broadcasting the recordings would jeopardize his right to a fair trial. Judge William M. Hoeveler issued a temporary restraining order directing CNN not to air the recordings but to turn them over to him so he could determine whether publicizing them would have a prejudicial effect. While appealing the order, CNN defied it by broadcasting two segments of the conversations. In *United States of America v. Noriega and Cable News Network*, 917 F.2d 1543 (11th Cir. 1990), the appellate court affirmed Judge Hoeveler's order, and CNN then delivered copies of its tapes to him. After reading transcripts of them, he concluded that publicizing them would not adversely impact Noriega's trial, at which point the *Miami Herald,* Post-Newsweek, the Associated Press, and Gannett all sought access to the transcripts. Over CNN's objection, Hoeveler complied, holding that "the transcripts are properly considered to be judicial or court records" and thus open to the public. (Noriega, who was found to have stashed away at least twenty-three million dollars from his drug dealings, was convicted by a jury and sentenced to forty years in prison.)

Other judges on occasion have issued very limited gag orders. In 2010 and 2011, U.S. District Court Judge James Zagel presided over two trials in Chicago of former Illinois Governor Rod Blagojevich. Blagojevich was charged with conspiring to commit mail and wire fraud and of solicitation of bribery in connection with his appointment of a replacement for former U.S.

Senator Barack Obama. At the commencement of each trial Zagel ordered the media not to publish the names of the jurors until after the trial. In the first instance, Chicago media lawyers challenged Zagel's order as a violation of freedom of the press, but he held firm and the press complied. (The trial ended in a hung jury.) In the second trial, Zagel's order again was observed. (Blagojevich was convicted and sentenced to fourteen years in prison.) In another Chicago case, the trial of William Balfour, accused of killing three family members of prominent actress Jennifer Hudson, the judge also ordered the media not to publish the jurors' names during the trial, and that restriction was honored. (Balfour, too, was convicted.)

Closed Courtrooms

Trials

The Sixth Amendment, like the common law of England and its progeny in the American colonies, provides that a trial should be public, to ensure that justice is done. Thus the prosecutor and the trial judge may be scrutinized by the press and the public to ensure that the trial is fair, measuring up to all legal standards and requirements.

But it took a Supreme Court decision in a relatively recent Virginia case to nail down the requirement of an open trial. "One Stevenson," as the Supreme Court later identified him, was tried four times in Hanover County for the same murder: one conviction was overturned by the Virginia Supreme Court, there were two mistrials, and finally a judge, after excluding the press and public from the courtroom, acquitted Stevenson. The reason for closing the fourth trial was a request by the defendant's lawyer, who said, according to the transcript: "[There] was this woman that was with the family of the deceased when we were here before. She had sat in the Courtroom. I would like to ask that everybody be excluded from the Courtroom because I don't want any information being shuffled back and forth when we have a recess as to what—who testified to what."

The prosecuting attorney didn't object, so the judge obliged. Among those ushered out were two reporters for the *Richmond Times-Dispatch*. (Oddly, they did not protest.) After the prosecution presented its case, the judge granted a defense motion to strike the prosecution's evidence and find the defendant not guilty. Though the trial was over, the newspaper's parent company was permitted to intervene in order to challenge the closure, and the Virginia Supreme Court upheld it.

In *Richmond Newspapers, Inc. v. Virginia*, 448 U.S. 555 (1980), the U.S. Supreme Court reversed the Virginia courts by a vote of 7–1 (one justice not participating), and proclaimed firmly that criminal trials, in accordance with long-established practice in England as well as in the United States, must be conducted in public. As in *Sheppard v. Maxwell,* the justices prescribed other ways the trial might have been conducted. Chief Justice Warren Burger wrote for the majority:

> There was no suggestion that any problems with witnesses could not have been dealt with by their exclusion from the courtroom or their sequestration during the trial. Nor is there anything to indicate that sequestration of the jurors would not have guarded against their being subjected to any improper information. All of the alternatives admittedly present difficulties for trial courts, but none of the factors relied on here were beyond the realm of the manageable. (*Richmond Newspapers, Inc. v. Virginia,* 606)

Notably, there was a strong dissent from Justice (later Chief Justice) William Rehnquist, who contended that the Court was over-reaching in its objection to a state legal proceeding:

> [I]t is basically unhealthy to have so much authority concentrated in a small group of lawyers who have been appointed to the Supreme Court and enjoy virtual life tenure. . . . The issue here is not whether the "right" to freedom of the press conferred by the First Amendment to the Constitution over-rides the defendant's "right" to a fair trial conferred by other Amendments to the Constitution; it is instead whether any provision in the Constitution may fairly be read to prohibit what the trial judge in the Virginia state-court system did in this case. Being unable to find any such prohibition in the First, Sixth, Ninth, or any other Amendment to the United States Constitution, or in the Constitution itself, I dissent. (*Richmond Newspapers, Inc. v. Virginia,* 606)

Rehnquist made no effort to explain away the Sixth Amendment's guarantee of a "speedy and public trial."

Later, as chief justice, Rehnquist became known for championing "federalism," by which he meant greater recognition of state authority when it overlaps or bumps up against federal law. Therefore, his *Richmond Newspapers* dissent was consistent with that view.

Pretrial Hearings

At about the same time, other cases questioned whether an open courtroom rule also applied to pretrial (or preliminary) hearings, which sometimes reveal important aspects of a pending case. Simply put, may a trial judge conduct a pretrial hearing in private as a way of ensuring a fair trial later? Or is a pretrial hearing just as much the public's business as the trial itself?

A pretrial, or preliminary, hearing takes place in court, before the trial judge, with lawyers for both sides participating, but with no jury. Such hearings often deal with matters that will be important in determining guilt or innocence, and can be highly newsworthy. For instance, was the weapon seized without a search warrant? If so, the judge is likely to order it suppressed, or excluded from the trial, a considerable disadvantage to the prosecution. At the same time, disclosing persuasive evidence in advance may make it difficult to select jurors who haven't already made up their minds about the case, thus jeopardizing the accused's right to a fair trial before an impartial jury. A pretrial hearing about suppressing evidence is commonly called a suppression hearing.

Several important decisions by the Supreme Court have tended to support the media's right of access to pretrial hearings but have established criteria for imposing selective limitations on that right. The decisions require trial judges to consider carefully how far they can go to protect the right to a fair trial while still respecting freedom of the press. These nuances are important for reporters and editors to understand, for if a trial judge goes beyond these strictures and bars reporters from a pretrial hearing, reporters should object on the spot, and media companies should promptly file formal legal objections that may induce the judge to articulate his reasoning, and perhaps reconsider the correctness of his ruling.

Wayne Clapp, a forty-two-year-old former local policeman in Henrietta, New York, went fishing one day on Seneca Lake with sixteen-year-old Kyle Greathouse, from Texas, and twenty-one-year-old David Jones, from South Carolina. Only the two companions returned to shore. They drove away in Clapp's truck. His boat was found riddled with bullet holes. His family reported him missing. Assuming the worst, the police began dragging the lake for Clapp's body. It was never found. The two companions were arrested in Michigan, along with Greathouse's wife, also sixteen.

The apparent murder commanded extensive media coverage and was followed especially closely by the two nearby Rochester daily newspapers, the *Democrat & Chronicle* and the *Times-Union,* both owned by Gannett Co., Inc. They reported that the Seneca County police theorized that Clapp was shot with his own pistol and robbed of cash and a credit card, and his body dumped in the lake. The *Democrat & Chronicle* then reported that Michigan police had seized the trio, and Greathouse had led them to a spot where he had buried Clapp's .357 Magnum revolver.

Back in New York, Greathouse and Jones were indicted by a grand jury on charges of second-degree murder, robbery, and grand larceny. (Greathouse's wife was charged with grand larceny.) They were arraigned and pleaded not guilty. Their attorneys soon filed motions to suppress any statements they had made to the police on the grounds that they were given involuntarily, and to suppress physical evidence that they contended was the fruit of the alleg-edly involuntary statements, primarily the gun. At a pretrial hearing on the defense's motion to suppress, the defendants' attorneys asked that the hearing be closed to avoid publicizing any evidence that would be inadmissible at trial. The prosecutor did not object, and Judge Daniel A. DePasquale closed the hearing. The newspapers contested the closure, but New York's highest court, the Court of Appeals, upheld it.

So did the U.S. Supreme Court, in *Gannett Co., Inc. v. DePasquale*, 443 U.S. 368 (1979), although four justices dissented in part. In the majority opinion, Justice Potter Stewart explained:

> Publicity concerning pretrial suppression hearings such as the one involved in the present case poses special risks of unfairness. The whole purpose of such hearings is to screen out unreliable or illegally obtained evidence and insure that this evidence does not become known to the jury. Publicity concerning the proceedings at a pretrial hearing, however, could influ-ence public opinion against a defendant and inform potential jurors of inculpatory information wholly inadmissible at the actual trial. (*Gannett v. DePasquale*, 378)

Justice Lewis Powell added in a concurring opinion:

> In our criminal justice system as it has developed, suppression hearings often are as important as the trial which may follow. The government's case may turn upon the confession or other evidence that the defendant seeks to suppress, and the trial court's ruling on such evidence may determine the outcome of the case. Indeed, in this case there was no trial as, following the suppression hearing, plea bargaining occurred that resulted in guilty pleas. In view of the special significance of a suppression hearing, the public's interest in this proceeding often is comparable to its interest in the trial itself. (*Gannett Co., Inc. v. DePasquale*, 398)

Despite the firmness of their reasoning in *Gannett Co., Inc. v. DePasquale*, the justices backed away from it in later cases, giving greater weight to the First Amendment while striving to lay down criteria to help trial judges de-termine when a closure of any part of the criminal justice process might be justified.

One vital part of that process is the questioning of prospective jurors to select people who are both willing to serve and who can render an impartial verdict based solely on the evidence and testimony in court. This selection process is called the *voir dire,* from the French for "to see, to say." When a heinous crime is widely reported by the news media, the process of finding an impartial jury may be long and difficult. In 1807 Chief Justice John Marshall needed several weeks to find twelve residents of Virginia who had not formed an opinion about whether Aaron Burr, the former vice president of the United States, committed treason when he formulated rather imprecise plans to take control of a vast area of western U.S. real estate. (He was acquitted.)

Like trials, historically the questioning of prospective jurors was open to the public in both England and the early United States, in order to ensure fairness and protection of the accused's rights. So when a California judge conducted an extraordinary six-week *voir dire* behind closed doors, it was unsuccessfully challenged by the Riverside *Press-Enterprise*. The trial judge defended the closure on the grounds of protecting the prospective jurors' privacy.

But the U.S. Supreme Court took the case, and reversed it. Calling the lengthy closure "incredible," a unanimous Court ordered that a transcript of the proceedings be made public, in *Press-Enterprise Co. v. Superior Court*, 464 U.S. 501 (1984)—now referred to as *"Press Enterprise I"* to distinguish it from a later case. Chief Justice Warren Burger wrote that the trial judge "failed to consider whether alternatives were available to protect the interests of the prospective jurors." For instance, he said, noting that the case involved the alleged rape of a teenage girl, "a prospective juror might privately inform the judge that she, or a member of her family, had been raped but had declined to seek prosecution because of the embarrassment and emotional trauma from the very disclosure of the episode. . . . [T]hose individuals . . . may properly request an opportunity to present the problem to the judge *in camera* [in private] but with counsel present and on the record."

In fact, Burger criticized the trial court in considerable detail:

> [T]he trial judge provided no explanation as to why his broad order denying access to information at the *voir dire* was not limited to information that was actually sensitive and deserving of privacy protection. Nor did he consider whether he could disclose the substance of the sensitive answers while preserving the anonymity of the jurors involved. . . . [T]here was also a failure to consider alternatives to closure and to total suppression of the transcript. The trial judge should seal only such parts of the transcript as necessary to preserve the anonymity of the individuals sought to be protected. (*Press-Enterprise I v. Superior Court*, 513)

Following up on *Press-Enterprise I*, the Supreme Court prescribed a helpful lesson about suppression hearings in a Georgia case involving several men indicted for violating state criminal statutes by operating a large lottery tied to the volume of stocks and bonds traded on the New York Stock Exchange. Their operation was seen by the prosecutor as gambling. The defendants filed a motion to suppress wiretap evidence, arguing that, although the police had obtained court warrants authorizing them to listen in, the warrants allegedly were unsupported by probable cause (always a necessary justification for a warrant) and based on overly general information. The defense also contended that the taps were conducted without adequate supervision, and the resulting searches were indiscriminate and exploratory.

This time it was the prosecution that moved to close the hearing, on the grounds that in order to validate the seizure of evidence derived from the wiretaps, prosecutors would have to play recordings that would identify other persons who might themselves be indicted later. Premature disclosure of evidence concerning them, the prosecutors contended, would taint the use of that evidence so it could not be used against them if they were brought to trial. The trial judge agreed and closed the hearing. It went on for seven days, but only two and half hours were devoted to listening to recordings of intercepted telephone conversations, and only one person, not already indicted, was heard.

In the criminal trial that followed, the defendants were acquitted of one charge but convicted of the gambling offenses. The Georgia Supreme Court upheld the convictions, affirming the closure of the suppression hearing. But the U.S. Supreme Court reversed, in *Waller v. Georgia*, 467 U.S. 39 (1984), ruling that the closure did not meet the *Press-Enterprise* tests, to wit: "the party seeking to close the hearing must advance an overriding interest that is likely to be prejudiced, the closure must be no broader than necessary to protect that interest, the trial court must consider reasonable alternatives to closing the proceeding, and it must make findings adequate to support the closure." In this case, Justice Lewis Powell's unanimous opinion went on:

> [T]he only evidence about which the prosecutor expressed concern was the information derived from the wiretaps. . . . [T]he State's proffer was not specific as to whose privacy interests might be infringed, how they would be infringed, what portions of the tapes might infringe them, and what portion of the evidence consisted of the tapes. As a result, the trial court's findings were broad and general, and did not purport to justify closure of the entire hearing. The court did not consider alternatives to immediate closure of the entire hearing: directing the government to provide more detail about its need for closure, *in camera* if necessary, and closing only those parts of the hearing that jeopardized the interests advanced. As it turned out, of course,

the closure was far more extensive than necessary. The tapes lasted only 2 1/2 hours of the 7-day hearing, and few of them mentioned or involved parties not then before the court. (*Waller v. Georgia*, 48)

The Court ordered a new suppression hearing with "significant portions" open to the public, allowing for some restricted closure. But Powell added that, unless the new hearing resulted in suppression of "material evidence" not suppressed originally, or produced "some other material change in the positions of the parties," a new trial was not warranted.

Press-Enterprise Co. v. Superior Court, 478 U.S. 1 (1986), referred to as *"Press-Enterprise II,"* pitted the same newspaper publisher against another closure by the same California trial court. This time the court closed an impossibly long preliminary hearing, convened to determine whether there was probable cause to formally charge the defendant. It dragged on for forty-one days. It was closed at the request of the accused, a nurse named Robert Diaz, suspected of murdering twelve patients by administering massive doses of Lidocaine, a heart drug. He contended that closure was necessary to protect his right to a fair trial after massive national publicity about the case. A magistrate agreed. During the long hearing, Diaz's lawyer vigorously cross-examined most of the witnesses, but presented no evidence. The magistrate declined even to release a transcript of the hearing after it was over, and the California Supreme Court affirmed.

The U.S. Supreme Court, in a 7–2 decision reversing the California courts (*Press-Enterprise Co. v. Superior Court,* 478 U.S. 1, 1986), explained that under California law, a prosecutor may proceed against a suspect either by asking a grand jury to issue an indictment or by conducting a preliminary hearing to determine probable cause. "If the magistrate determines that probable cause exists," Chief Justice Warren Burger wrote for the majority, "the accused is bound over for trial; such a finding leads to a guilty plea in the majority of cases."

Burger carefully limited the Court's ruling to this unusual California process: "Because of its extensive scope, the preliminary hearing is often the final and most important step in the criminal proceeding. . . . The absence of a jury . . . makes the importance of public access to a preliminary hearing even more significant. . . . We therefore conclude that the qualified First Amendment right of access to criminal proceedings applies to preliminary hearings as they are conducted in California."

Justice John Paul Stevens, joined in part by Justice William Rehnquist, argued in dissent that California's preliminary hearing was so similar to the always-secret grand jury, employed by the federal government and most other states as well as California, that the Court's ruling—"if carried to its logical outcome"—threatened to undermine the secrecy of the grand jury as well. (Nevertheless, that secrecy remains sacrosanct today.)

Access to Court Documents

United States common law, the law made by judges rather than legislatures, has long held that court documents are public documents, open to the public and the press. The Supreme Court confirmed this in a case called *Nixon v. Warner Communications, Inc.*, 435 U.S. 589 (1978), in which Warner, ABC, CBS, NBC, PBS, and the Radio-Television News Directors Association sought to copy taped White House conversations between President Richard M. Nixon and other persons, following the Republicans' 1972 burglary of Democratic Party offices at the Watergate building complex in Washington, D.C. This was the scandal that led to Nixon's disgrace and resignation in 1975. Long segments of the tapes were played during the 1974 trial of several Nixon associates for conspiracy to obstruct justice during the investigation of the burglary. (Three of his associates were convicted.) The media companies wanted to sell copies of the tapes to the public.

"It is clear," the Supreme Court held, "that the courts of this country recognize a general right to inspect and copy public records and documents, including judicial records and documents." It cited a number of federal and state court rulings that recognized this "general right," commencing with the District of Columbia courts in 1894. However, after embracing the common law, the Court did not apply it in this prominent case, on the grounds that a special act of Congress required that the former president's papers and tapes be collected and administered by the government's General Services Administration.

Still, the principle of open access to court documents was firmly established, and an appellate court applied it later in the case of Theodore Kaczynski, the reclusive murderer known as the "Unabomber," *United States of America v. Kaczynski*, 154 F.3d 930 (9th Cir. 1998). After Kaczynski was discovered hiding in his cabin in Montana, a U.S. Bureau of Prisons psychiatrist examined him and found him competent to stand trial. He then pleaded guilty in U.S. District Court and was sentenced to life imprisonment without the possibility of parole. CBS, the *Sacramento Bee,* and the *San Francisco Examiner* requested copies of the psychiatrist's report. The trial judge ordered some redactions (deletions) of material he considered private and not relevant to the case, and granted the request. On Kaczynski's appeal, the Ninth Circuit Court of Appeals affirmed, citing common law, and explaining:

> [T]he media made the necessary threshold showing. It established that disclosure of Kaczynski's psychiatric report would serve the ends of justice

by informing the public about the court's competency determination and Kaczynski's motivation for committing the Unabomber crimes. . . . We conclude that the public and the media have a legitimate interest in disclosure of the report. We also conclude that the district court properly balanced the public's legitimate interest in access to the report, that is, its interest in obtaining information bearing on the workings of the criminal justice system, with the countervailing privacy interests asserted by Kaczynski. (*United States of America v. Kaczynski*, 931, 932)

Cameras in Court

Even in the disgraceful trial of Samuel Sheppard in Ohio, taking pictures during the trial was forbidden. That was the common rule, and it still is. Trial judges control their own courtrooms, and the notion of photographers moving around and shooting pictures has always been considered inimical to courtroom dignity and decorum. That's why trial scenes are often depicted on television by skillful, remarkably fast courtroom artists. But television cameras? Surprisingly, although they are still controversial today, the Supreme Court confronted their use decades ago.

A television station in Lake Charles, Louisiana, aired a jail-cell confession of murder, armed robbery, and kidnapping given by Wilbert Rideau to the sheriff of Calcasieu Parish. Rideau subsequently was found guilty by a jury but challenged the conviction on the grounds that the TV interview precluded a fair trial in that community. The U.S. Supreme Court agreed and reversed Rideau's conviction. Writing for a majority of seven in *Rideau v. Louisiana*, 373 U.S. 723 (1963), Justice Potter Stewart declared that "due process of law in this case required a trial before a jury drawn from a community of people who had not seen and heard Rideau's televised 'interview.'"

A few years later another conviction was thrown out because of television. A colorful Texas deal-maker, Billie Sol Estes, was considered a "notorious character," as the Supreme Court put it. He was convicted in the town of Tyler of swindling farmers by selling them liquid fertilizer tanks and equipment that didn't exist, akin to the mythical sale of the Brooklyn Bridge. Texas previously had authorized cameras in court, and the trial judge approved, for a pretrial hearing and the trial itself, four TV cameras, radio reporters with recorders, and still photographers, with few guidelines to restrict their activities during the trial. The deplorable result, according to Justice Tom Clark's majority opinion in *Estes v. Texas*, 381 U.S. 532 (1965), was this:

[T]he courtroom was a mass of wires, television cameras, microphones and photographers. The petitioner [Estes], the panel of prospective jurors, who were sworn the second day, the witnesses and the lawyers were all exposed to this untoward situation. . . . This emphasized the notorious nature of the coming trial, increased the intensity of the publicity on the petitioner and together with the subsequent televising of the trial beginning 30 days later inherently prevented a sober search for the truth. This is underscored by the fact that the selection of the jury took an entire week. As might be expected, a substantial amount of that time was devoted to ascertaining the impact of the pretrial televising on the prospective jurors. . . . [F]our of the jurors selected had seen all or part of those broadcasts. The trial, on the other hand, lasted only three days.

Moreover, the trial judge was himself harassed. After the initial decision to permit telecasting he apparently decided that a booth should be built at the broadcasters' expense to confine its operations; he then decided to limit the parts of the trial that might be televised live; then he decided to film the testimony of the witnesses without sound in an attempt to protect those under the rule; and finally he ordered that defense counsel and their argument not be televised, in the light of their objection. Plagued by his original error—recurring each day of the trial—his day-to-day orders made the trial more confusing to the jury, the participants, and to the viewers. Indeed, it resulted in a public presentation of only the State's side of the case. (*Estes v. Texas,* 550, 551)

Citing *Irvin v. Dowd* and *Rideau v. Louisiana,* among other cases, Justice Clark went on and on to detail numerous distractions, interruptions, and inconveniences caused by the photographers and their activities, criticizing them as well as the judge. Journalists' "right to attend trials," he declared, "does not bring with it the right to inject themselves into the fabric of the trial process to alter the purpose of that process." Clark concluded that Estes "was deprived of his right under the Fourteenth Amendment to due process by the televising and broadcasting of his trial. Both the trial court and the Texas Court of Criminal Appeals found against the petitioner. We hold to the contrary and reverse his conviction."

In a robust concurrence joined by Justices Arthur Goldberg and William O. Douglas, Chief Justice Earl Warren, who had been a longtime California prosecutor, came down hard on the very idea of televising a trial:

I believe that it violates the Sixth Amendment for federal courts and the Fourteenth Amendment for state courts to allow criminal trials to be televised to the public at large. I base this conclusion on three grounds: (1) that the televising of trials diverts the trial from its proper purpose in that it has an inevitable impact on all the trial participants; (2) that it gives the public the wrong impression about the purpose of trials, thereby detracting from the dignity of court proceedings and lessening the reliability of trials; and (3) that it singles out certain defendants and subjects them to trials under prejudicial conditions not experienced by others. (*Estes v. Texas,* 565)

Despite the strong opinions for reversal, there were four dissenters. Justice Potter Stewart, joined by Justices Hugo Black, William Brennan, and Byron White, voiced opposition to permitting TV cameras in trials, but declared: "I am unable to find, on the specific record of this case, that the circumstances attending the limited televising of the petitioner's trial resulted in the denial of any right guaranteed to him by the United States Constitution."

In light of these discordant opinions in *Estes,* perhaps it's not surprising that the Supreme Court later took a Florida case that raised squarely the question of whether televising a trial passed constitutional muster, even in the face of an objection by the defendant. Compared to *Estes,* it was a modest test indeed. A single camera filmed only one afternoon of the trial, and just two minutes and fifty-five seconds were broadcast. But the case had additional cachet: the defendants were two Miami Beach policemen, accused of burglarizing a local restaurant. The prosecution's principal witness was an amateur radio operator who by chance had overheard and decided to record the cops talking to each other on their police walkie-talkies during the burglary. The policemen objected to the presence of the camera, so when they were found guilty, they claimed that it had deprived them of their constitutional right to a fair trial, noting that the segment broadcast was entirely of the prosecution's case and nothing of the defense. But the Florida Supreme Court, which had authorized experimenting with cameras in court, upheld the guilty verdict.

In *Chandler v. Florida,* 449 U.S. 560 (1981), a unanimous Supreme Court affirmed, finding no violation of the Constitution. Chief Justice Warren Burger wrote, "The appellants have offered no evidence that any participant in this case was affected by the presence of cameras. In short, there is no showing that the trial was compromised by television coverage, as was the case in *Estes. . . .* Absent a showing of prejudice of constitutional dimensions to these defendants, there is no reason for this Court either to endorse or to invalidate Florida's experiment."

With no constitutional barrier, over time several state supreme courts have authorized televising trials, generally just a single camera, while barring any pictures of the jury. Some states require the acquiescence of the accused, while others say merely that the parties' views should be heard and considered, and all states leave the final decision up to the trial judge. The first widespread use of TV in trials came in 1991 when a journalist named Steven Brill founded *CourtTV,* a cable program that covered trials in their entirety.

However, the trial that unquestionably reached the entire country was that of actor and former football star O.J. Simpson, accused of murdering his former wife Nicole Brown Simpson and her friend Ronald Goldman. Los Angeles Judge Lance Ito granted the request for a single camera to televise the proceedings, which ultimately swept up one hundred fifty witnesses and lasted more than nine months in 1995. Americans were aghast and agog as the story unfolded. In the end, the jury of ten women and two men acquitted Simpson (though he subsequently was ordered to pay $46.1 million in damages in civil suits brought by the Goldman and Brown families). Simpson's lawyer, Alan M. Dershowitz, was quoted later as stating that the gripping tale was the subject of 2,237 television news segments from 1994 through 1997. Newspapers were similarly committed to the coverage. The *Los Angeles Times* played the story on page one for more than three hundred consecutive days after the murders. The brutal crime and the made-for-TV trial with numerous assertive and sometimes shady personalities were the subject of endless conversations, speculation, and theorizing across the country.

Despite the Simpson case, or perhaps because of it, more and more states have authorized televising of trials, most recently Illinois, Indiana, and Minnesota, all on a carefully controlled trial basis. But cameras are still not allowed in federal trials.

Separately, two-thirds of the states now provide for televising state supreme court oral arguments. This is an easier decision, for the august proceedings of an appellate court involve only the judges and lawyers—no jury, no witnesses, and usually few spectators. Typically there are no camera operators in the courtroom. Instead small cameras are permanently installed in an obscure spot or two, and remotely operated. No fuss, no muss, no bother. Two federal appellate courts have experimented extensively with television. Judges and lawyers report salutary results—no grandstanding, no playing to the cameras, no ill effects at all. Nevertheless, some justices of the U.S. Supreme Court worry that cameras in their courtroom might impair the Court's process and dignity, so the outlook for Supreme Court television is dim.

Crime Coverage

We should also note that the need for fairness in covering crime and those accused of it is not limited to formal proceedings like pretrial hearings and trials. Much of the routine press coverage of accused persons is faulted as "cheap entertainment" by Andrea D. Lyon of DePaul University's College of Law in Chicago, who defended more than one hundred capital cases as a Cook County public defender over thirty years. She also was on the defense team of Casey Anthony, the young Florida mother accused (and acquitted) in 2011 of killing her two-year-old daughter.

Writing in *Reynolds Courts & Media Law Journal* (Lyon 2011), Lyon alleges media unfairness in the Anthony case:

> What is troubling is the public's fascination with this case, the need to make Anthony a villain, and how the media helped feed this mob mentality. In particular, nearly all the TV pundits castigated my former partner and friend Jose Baez [the lead defense attorney], literally raking his personal professional life over the coals. They landed, heavily, on any witness who spoke up in Anthony's favor, making witnesses extraordinarily difficult to find and interview because everyone was afraid of the backlash from the public and the prosecution. There were exculpatory witnesses who were intimidated to the point that they feared coming forward. (Word on the street? Helping Anthony is dangerous.) I was even physically assaulted myself while investigating this case. I have continued to receive hate mail of a type that is hard to imagine. (Lyon 2011:430)

Professor Lyon is especially critical of what law enforcement officers call the "perp [short for perpetrator] walk," in which "the defendant is in handcuffs and paraded in front of the media." It's defended, she says, as a way of showing the public "that law enforcement is doing its job," but Lyon argues, "the perp walk actually further conflates the charging stage with the verdict stage, undermining the importance of a hearing before a fair and neutral tribunal, which is supposedly central to our notion of justice."

Could a journalist resist taking a picture of a "perp walk"? Even a confession should be viewed cautiously, Lyon warns. She recalls one client, a terrified young man, who confessed before a court reporter to a triple homicide because he knew one of the actual killers, saw the incident start, and was so afraid of retribution that "he decided confessing was safer for him and his family." After long police interrogation, he finally divulged the other person's name. The young man still faced trial, but "the jury acquitted him in less than an hour."

As Lyon so rightly declares, "the media must take responsibility when its profit-driven coverage takes a human toll."

Questions for Discussion

1. Do journalists have any responsibility to avoid publishing prejudicial pretrial stories, or is that solely a matter for the court?
2. Could a trial judge order a defense lawyer (who's not an employee of the court) not to talk to the press? If he does make the order, and the lawyer declines to be bound by the gag order, what would happen?

3. Describe how a trial judge can assure a fair trial without impinging on the First Amendment.

4. Would a change of venue (location) mean that reporters who have commenced covering the case are barred from covering the trial in the new location?

5. What should a reporter do if a trial judge closes a pretrial hearing and orders the press out?

6. If television journalists want to cover a trial in a state that permits cameras in court, to whom should they talk?

7. Should a journalist refrain from photographing a "perp walk"? Why or why not?

References

Chandler v. Florida, 449 U.S. 560 (1981). http://openjurist.org/449/us/560/chandler-v-florida.

Estes v. Texas, 381 U.S. 532 (1965). http://caselaw.lp.findlaw.com/scripts/getcase.pl?court=us&vol=381&invol=532.

Gannett Co., Inc. v. DePasquale, 443 U.S. 368 (1979). http://supreme.justia.com/cases/federal/us/443/368/case.html.

Irvin v. Dowd, 359 U.S. 394 (1959). http://openjurist.org/359/us/394/irvin-v-f-dowd.

Irvin v. Dowd, 366 U.S. 717 (1961). http://supreme.justia.com/cases/federal/us/366/717/case.html.

Lyon, Andrea D., "Criminal Coverage: News Media, Legal Commentary, and the Crucible of the Presumption of Innocence," *Reynolds Courts & Media Law Journal* 1, no. 4 (2011): 427–42.

Nebraska Press Association v. Stuart, 427 U.S. 539 (1976). http://law2.umkc.edu/faculty/projects/ftrials/conlaw/nebpress.html.

Nixon v. Warner Communications, Inc., 435 U.S. 589 (1978). http://caselaw.lp.findlaw.com/scripts/getcase.pl?navby=case&court=us&vol=435&invol=589.

Press-Enterprise Co. v. Superior Court, 464 U.S. 501 (1984). http://caselaw.lp.findlaw.com/scripts/getcase.pl?court=us&vol=464&invol=501.

Press-Enterprise Co. v. Superior Court, 478 U.S. 1 (1986). http://www.law.cornell.edu/supct/html/historics/USSC_CR_0478_0001_ZO.html.

Richmond Newspapers, Inc. v. Virginia, 448 U.S. 555 (1980). http://www.law.cornell.edu/supct/html/historics/USSC_CR_0448_0555_ZS.html.

Rideau v. Louisiana, 373 U.S. 723 (1963). http://caselaw.lp.findlaw.com/scripts/getcase.pl?navby=case&court=us&vol=373&invol=723.

Sheppard v. Maxwell, 384 U.S. 333 (1966). http://www.bc.edu/bc_org/avp/cas/comm/free_speech/sheppard.html.

United States of America v. Kaczynski, 154 F.3d 930 (9th Cir. 1998). http://openjurist.org/154/f3d/930/united-states-v-kaczynski.

United States of America v. Noriega and Cable News Network, 917 F.2d 1543 (11th Cir. 1990). https://bulk.resource.org/courts.gov/c/F2/917/917.F2d.1543.90-5932.90-5927.html.

Waller v. Georgia, 467 U.S. 39 (1984). http://www.law.cornell.edu/supct/html/historics/USSC_CR_0467_0039_ZO.html.

8

Anonymous Sources and the
Journalist's Privilege

*"Identify sources whenever feasible. The public is entitled to as
much information as possible on sources' reliability."*
—Society of Professional Journalists Code of Ethics

Every journalist promises confidentiality to sources to induce them to talk freely and frankly. It's a natural resort when you're questioning a source who has the information you need for your story, but who doesn't want to be quoted or even identified. "What did the boss say in private? I won't quote you." "Just tell me who has the document. I won't mention your name at all." "Who else could I talk to about this? I'll keep you out of it." This may sound like a harmless ploy, and sometimes it's productive: You get the name, document, or frank comment for which you're looking. Especially in political, law enforcement, and business stories, the front pages and the evening news are rife with stories and quotations attributed to "a person familiar with the situation who wasn't authorized to talk about it publicly" or some such cloak of anonymity.

For example, the *Wall Street Journal* often capitalizes on its sterling reputation for reliability in this way. "Amazon.com Inc. is ratcheting up pricing pressure in the gadget wars with an advertising-supported tablet that will be priced lower than similar models, according to people involved in the discussions," the *Wall Street Journal* reported in its weekend edition of September 1–2, 2012. None of those "people" was named in the story. However, if the reader believes the *Wall Street Journal* is credible, and most readers do, then the story sounds solid.

You can see how this modest subterfuge of attributing the story to "people involved in the discussions" satisfies the admonition from the Society of Professional Journalists given at the start of this chapter. You get your facts or quotes, you get your story (preferably with confirmation from other, identified sources), and you give your readers and viewers reason to believe that your anonymous sources are authoritative, because they're "involved in the discussions." Is this good journalism? Indeed it is. Many fine stories would never see the light of day if an inquiring reporter hadn't found the right source and promised anonymity. Reporters would be more dependent on press releases and spokespersons touting the official line.

So what's the downside? Unfortunately, it could be jail. Especially if your story depicts apparently illegal activity, you could be called before a federal or local grand jury investigating the crime and the people involved. If you're asked for the confidential source for your story, will you break your promise of anonymity, or will you risk being held in civil contempt of court and possibly being sent to prison? It is important to note that the imprisonment is not for a prescribed period, like a criminal sentence. Rather it's intended to persuade the journalist to reveal the anonymous source. As soon as the source is revealed, the journalist will be released. So the question arises, can a journalist be forced, by the threat of contempt of court and jail, to disclose the name of a confidential source to a grand jury? It's not just hypothetical.

The grand jury is entirely different from the trial (or petit) jury that decides guilt or innocence. In the enforcement of both federal and state criminal statutes the most common way for a prosecutor to formally charge a person with a crime is through the grand jury process. The grand jury, as the name implies, in larger than the trial jury, usually twenty-three persons, selected at random from voter lists, as are trial jurors. And the grand jury doesn't deal with just a single case, as the trial jury does. It sits for a relatively long period of time, commonly eighteen months, and it hears evidence from the prosecutor about any number of alleged crimes during that time. When the prosecutor thinks she has a case ready to bring against a person, she presents her evidence to the grand jury and usually calls witnesses. The accused person, not yet charged, isn't notified or represented at the grand jury hearing. This is called *ex parte,* meaning only one side is heard. The prosecutor answers questions from the grand jurors, then asks them to vote to indict, or formally accuse, a person or persons with a specific violation of criminal law. It's very unusual for a grand jury to refuse the prosecutor's recommendation.

But, in fact, there's no scorecard available for the grand jury hearings, and often even the fact that the grand jury is deliberating is totally secret. Witnesses are admonished not to reveal to anyone that they've testified before the grand jury or to disclose any of their testimony. Only when the grand jury hands up an indictment does its work become public. (Hands *up* because the indictment is delivered to a trial judge, envisioned on the bench, as opposed to the judge's handing *down* a ruling.) The reasons for secrecy are apparent: if a suspect is discussed but never indicted, the humiliation on all sides would be enormous; and if the target is liable to flee to avoid prosecution, the secrecy avoids a tip-off that the prosecutor is on his trail. And of course, a person who is indicted will have his day in court to defend himself, for the grand jury evidence and witness testimony will be presented again, in public, subject to cross-examination, rebuttal, and denial.

Federal Law

Branzburg v. Hayes

Unfortunately for journalism, and contrary to the Supreme Court's generally supportive First Amendment rulings on libel, privacy, and other issues affecting the media, there's a powerful, long-standing Supreme Court precedent casting a shadow over the issue of a journalist protecting a source, called *Branzburg v. Hayes*, 408 U.S. 665 (1972). Three reporters, doing four different stories, received subpoenas (a court order) to appear and answer questions before four different grand juries. All four situations involved a promise of confidentiality to the sources, and the Supreme Court consolidated the cases as one.

Paul Branzburg wrote a front-page story for the *Louisville Courier-Journal* with the headline, "The Hash They Make Isn't to Eat," describing his observations of two young men, no names given, of course, synthesizing hashish from marijuana, which the story stated earned them about five thousand dollars in three weeks. The article was accompanied by a photo of a pair of hands working with a substance identified as hashish. Branzburg was subpoenaed to testify before the Jefferson County grand jury; he appeared but declined to reveal the names of the two young men because he had promised them anonymity. He claimed the "journalist's privilege" under a Kentucky statute called the shield law. Kentucky, like most states but not the federal government, provides that in certain situations a journalist may decline to answer a grand jury's questions, but the Kentucky courts ruled that the shield law didn't permit Branzburg to duck testifying about events he had witnessed personally.

The second case before the Supreme Court also involved Paul Branzburg. Once again his subject was narcotics, this time describing the use of drugs in Frankfort, the capital of Kentucky. He wrote that his story was based on "two weeks of interviewing several dozen drug users in the capital city." No names were mentioned, and again Branzburg refused to give them to a grand jury, this time in Franklin County. Again the Kentucky courts stood by the subpoena.

The third case came from Massachusetts. TV reporter Paul Pappas gained entrance to the New Bedford storefront office of the Black Panther Party, a militant civil rights organization that was anticipating a confrontation with the police, on the condition that he'd reveal nothing of what he observed inside the office. The confrontation never happened. Pappas produced no story, but was called before the Bristol County Grand Jury anyway. True to his promise, he refused to answer questions about what he saw and who was there. Massachusetts had no shield law, but he claimed the First Amendment authorized him to honor his pledge of confidentiality. The Massachusetts courts said no.

The fourth case came from a federal court in California. It, too, involved coverage of the Black Panther Party. Earl Caldwell of the *New York Times* wrote several stories about the organization, including a quotation from one leader saying, "we advocate the very direct overthrow of the Government by way of force and violence." Caldwell was subpoenaed to appear before a federal grand jury and to bring with him notes and tape recordings of interviews given to him for publication by Black Panther leaders. Caldwell refused, citing the First Amendment but without claiming any promises of confidentiality. The U.S. District Court for the Northern District of California adjudged him in contempt of court, but the Ninth Circuit Court of Appeals reversed, holding that the First Amendment entitled him to a "qualified testimonial privilege."

In U.S. law there are certain well-established testimonial privileges, holding, for instance, that spouses cannot be required to testify against each other; that a physician cannot be required to testify against a patient; nor a lawyer against a client; nor a clergyman against a parishioner. State shield laws grant such a testimonial privilege to journalists, and in most states it's "qualified," meaning it doesn't apply in all situations. But, as we noted earlier, there is no federal shield law (and repeated efforts to pass one have failed in Congress).

Addressing these four cases, coming from both federal and state courts, the Supreme Court split, 5–4. Writing for the majority, Justice Byron White acknowledged the importance of freedom of the press, noting significantly, "Nor is it suggested that news gathering does not qualify for First Amendment protection; without some protection for seeking out the news, freedom of the press could be eviscerated." But White drew the line at refusing to testify before a grand jury:

> Fair and effective law enforcement aimed at providing security for the person and property of the individual is a fundamental function of government, and the grand jury plays an important, constitutionally mandated role in this process. On the records now before us, we perceive no basis for holding that the public interest in law enforcement and in ensuring effective grand jury proceedings is insufficient to override the consequential, but uncertain, burden on news gathering that is said to result from insisting that reporters, like other citizens, respond to relevant questions put to them

in the course of a valid grand jury investigation or criminal trial. (*Branzburg v. Hayes*, 690–91)

Unequivocal as this pronouncement seems, the justices produced that day two other *Branzburg* opinions that have had powerful and quite surprising ramifications in subsequent claims of journalists' privilege. Justice Lewis Powell, who voted with the majority, wrote a short concurring opinion suggesting that the federal courts might on occasion recognize a journalist's privilege. Powell declared:

> If a newsman believes that the grand jury investigation is not being conducted in good faith he is not without remedy. Indeed, if the newsman is called upon to give information bearing only a remote and tenuous relationship to the subject of the investigation, or if he has some other reason to believe that his testimony implicates confidential source relationships without a legitimate need of law enforcement, he will have access to the court on a motion to quash [the subpoena]. (*Branzburg v. Hayes*, 710)

Even more significantly, Powell went on to further undermine the firm rule that he had just agreed to in Justice White's majority opinion, by advocating judicial examination of each situation individually:

> The asserted claim to privilege should be judged on its facts by the striking of a proper balance between freedom of the press and the obligation of all citizens to give relevant testimony with respect to criminal conduct. The balance of these vital constitutional and societal interests on a case-by-case basis accords with the tried and traditional way of adjudicating such questions. . . . [In a footnote:] [T]he court—when called upon to protect a newsman from improper or prejudicial questioning—would be free to balance the competing interests on their merits in the particular case. (*Branzburg v. Hayes*, 710)

In one of the Supreme Court's most persuasive and influential dissents ever written, Justice Potter Stewart, joined by Justices William Brennan and Thurgood Marshall, declared that "the longstanding rule making every person's evidence available to the grand jury is not absolute." Stewart proposed a three-point test to determine whether a court should recognize a journalist's privilege in a particular case:

> [W]hen a reporter is asked to appear before a grand jury and reveal confidences, I would hold that the government must:

1. show that there is probable cause to believe that the newsman has information that is clearly relevant to a specific probable violation of law;
2. demonstrate that the information sought cannot be obtained by alternative means less destructive of First Amendment rights; and
3. demonstrate a compelling and overriding interest in the information. (*Branzburg v. Hayes*, 743)

The Supreme Court still holds to its majority ruling in *Branzburg v. Hayes*. For instance, in 2004, *New York Times* reporter Judith Miller refused to tell a federal grand jury the name of the source who had divulged the name of CIA undercover agent Valerie Plame, a disclosure that's forbidden by federal law. (The leaking of the name was a tawdry effort by the George W. Bush administration to retaliate against her husband, a former ambassador who investigated and flatly contradicted Bush's claim that Iraq was trying to buy nuclear-bomb material in Africa, one of Bush's justifications for attacking Iraq.) The U.S. Court of Appeals for the District of Columbia (*In re: Grand Jury Subpoena Judith Miller*, 397 F.3d 964, D.C. Cir. 2005) affirmed a contempt and imprisonment ruling by the U.S. District Court for the District of Columbia, and the Supreme Court declined to review the ruling. Miller remained in jail eighty-five days, until her source released her from her pledge of confidentiality, so she relented. (Her source was Vice President Dick Cheney's chief of staff, I. Lewis "Scooter" Libby, who was subsequently convicted of lying and obstructing the leak investigation.)

Such punishment isn't confined to journalists whose well-heeled employer will pay the legal expenses. A freelance videographer, Joshua Wolf, was jailed in 2006 for refusing to respond to a grand jury investigation of violence during a San Francisco street protest against a meeting of the G8 nations. Wolf shot video that was used on-air and on a website. His video included a scene of a protester being choked by a police officer and other officers threatening passersby with stun guns. The police and FBI wanted Wolf's whole tape and his testimony as well to identify protestors who injured a policeman and burned his car. Wolf resisted, was held in contempt, and the Ninth Circuit Court of Appeals affirmed the judgment in *Wolf v. United States*, 201 Fed. Appx. 430 (9th Cir. 2006). He spent 226 days, more than seven months, in prison, until he made a deal to turn over the tape but not to testify.

Wolf's jailhouse tenure established a new American record, surpassing freelance writer Vanessa Leggett's 168 days for refusing to hand over notes of her interview of a wealthy man accused of conspiring to murder his wife. The suspect, a Houston bookmaker and police informant named Robert Angleton, subsequently committed suicide in jail. In *Vanessa Leggett v. United States*,

535 U.S. 1011 (2002) the U.S. Supreme Court declined to review the ruling of the Fifth Circuit Court of Appeals. Leggett was released from jail when the term of the grand jury expired.

In another notable case, Jim Taricani, an investigative reporter for the NBC affiliate in Providence, Rhode Island, was found in contempt in federal court for refusing to reveal the source of an FBI surveillance videotape that showed a city official taking a bribe. In ill health, Taricani was sentenced to six months of probation in home confinement, even though a defense lawyer who originally denied culpability eventually admitted he had given Taricani the tape. The judgment was upheld by the First Circuit Court of Appeals in *In re: Special Proceedings (Jim Taricani)*, 373 F.3d 37 (lst Cir. 2004).

The First Amendment Center in Washington, D.C., and Nashville, which keeps tab on such matters, reports that in most years between 1989 and 2007 at least one reporter was held in contempt of court for refusing to divulge a source, and almost all of them served jail time.

Civil Cases Are Different

Despite *Branzburg,* commencing soon after that decision most federal appellate courts have taken Justice Powell's "case-by-case" concurrence to heart, recognizing a qualified or limited journalist's privilege in certain situations, notably in civil litigation, where there's no grand jury involved. The critical factor in a number of these appellate decisions was the unexplored possibility of obtaining the information from other sources.

For instance, just months after *Branzburg,* the Second Circuit Court of Appeals in New York upheld a trial court's refusal to compel a journalist to reveal confidential sources in *Baker v. F & F Investment,* 470 F.2d 778 (2d Cir. 1972). A decade before the court case a Chicago writer, Alfred Balk, had written a potent magazine story that relied heavily on a pseudonymous real estate agent. The agent told how he, other agents, and real estate speculators had misled and overcharged black buyers of homes in previously white neighborhoods of Chicago (Balk 1962). When a group of those buyers filed a class-action suit "in behalf of all Negroes in the City of Chicago who purchased homes from approximately 60 named defendants between 1952 and 1969," the defendants wanted Balk, by then living in New York, where he was the editor of the *Columbia Journalism Review* and a lecturer at Columbia's Graduate School of Journalism, to disclose the name of his confidential source. Relying on the First Amendment, he refused. The U.S. District Court in Manhattan sustained his refusal, and so did the Court of Appeals.

The appellate court, citing the ringing affirmation of freedom of the press in *New York Times v. Sullivan,* declared:

> Compelled disclosure of confidential sources unquestionably threatens a journalist's ability to secure information that is made available to him only on a confidential basis—and the district court so found. The deterrent effect such disclosure is likely to have upon future "undercover" investigative reporting, the dividends of which are revealed in articles such as Balk's, threatens freedom of the press and the public's need to be informed. It thereby undermines values which traditionally have been protected by federal courts applying federal public policy. . . . It is axiomatic, and a principle fundamental to our constitutional way of life, that where the press remains free so too will a people remain free. (*Baker v. F & F Investment,* 782, 785)

The appellate court went on to explain that *Branzburg,* a criminal case, was not controlling in this instance, but nevertheless quoted Justice Powell's recommendation of a case-by-case analysis. This approach, the court declared, led to an affirmation of the District Court's conclusion that the real estate agents had not exhausted other means of learning the identity of the tipster and therefore "disclosure by Balk of his source was not essential to protect the public interest in the orderly administration of justice in the courts."

Similarly, the Circuit Court of Appeals for the District of Columbia ruled in *Carey v. Hume,* 492 F.2d 631 (D.C. Cir. 1974) that *Branzburg* was not a binding precedent in civil cases. Edward L. Carey, a labor union lawyer, sought the names of sources in his union, the United Mine Workers, for a column by Britt Hume, co-author of the widely syndicated Washington Merry-Go-Round (and later a fixture on cable television news). The column stated that the lawyer and union President Tony Boyle, facing a Justice Department investigation of the union's finances, "were seen removing box-fuls [sic] of documents from Boyle's office." In a libel suit against him, the U.S. District Court for the District of Columbia ordered Hume to reveal his sources. The Circuit Court of Appeals, also citing Justice Powell in *Branzburg,* acknowledged that "the identity of appellant's [Hume's] sources is critical to appellee's [Carey's] claim, but nevertheless came down on Hume's side. It noted that the record in the case "discloses no wide-ranging and thorough investigatory effort by appellant" and declared, "The courts must always be alert to the possibilities of limiting impingements upon press freedom to the minimum; and one way of doing so is to make compelled disclosure by a journalist a last resort after pursuit of other opportunities has failed."

In 1981, journalists won again in the Court of Appeals for the D.C. Circuit. Seth Kantor and other reporters for the *Detroit News* had written investigative articles on the Detroit crime syndicate. Said to be based on FBI logs, the articles identified Anthony Zerilli as the Detroit mob leader and Michael Polizzi as a mob cohort. However, as a federal prosecution of the two unfolded, the government admitted that it had tapped the phone of the Home Juice Company without a warrant, so the trial judge ordered the transcripts of overheard conversations sealed and not revealed to the public. Zerilli and Polizzi contended that the *Detroit News* articles contained material from those transcripts and so demanded that Kantor reveal who provided that information.

Kantor balked, claiming First Amendment protection, and the trial judge upheld his refusal, stating that the two men had not exhausted alternative sources of information. The Circuit Court of Appeals affirmed, in *Zerilli v. Smith*, 656 F.2d 705 (D.C. Cir. 1981), while giving still another nod to Justice Powell's *Branzburg* concurrence. It also cited its own decision in *Carey v. Hume* as well as similar decisions by other Circuit Courts of Appeals. The court noted that Kantor was not a defendant, as in a libel action, declaring: "When the journalist is a party, and successful assertion of the privilege will effectively shield him from liability, the equities weigh somewhat more heavily in favor of disclosure." Making the same point as other appellate courts, the D.C. Circuit said of Zerilli and Polizzi:

> [They] clearly have not fulfilled their obligation to exhaust possible alternative sources of information. In response to appellants' interrogatories the Department of Justice provided a list of the names of four employees who knew most about the wiretap logs. During the 1971 criminal trial the Government also provided a list of employees who had been given access to the transcripts. Yet appellants made no attempt to depose any of these individuals. . . . It is quite possible that interviewing these four individuals could have shed further light on the question whether the Justice Department was responsible for the leaks. (*Zerilli v. Smith*, 714–15)

An author of books on public affairs, Ronald J. Watkins, interviewed the founder of U-Haul Company, Leonard Shoen, while gathering information to write about a sordid family dispute over control of the highly successful company, whose revenues were then approaching one billion dollars. As Shoen was confronted by two of his sons, the wife of a third son was brutally murdered in her family's log cabin in Telluride, Colorado. The Associated Press reported, "In a telephone interview from his home in Las Vegas, the eldest Shoen said he believes his two sons are mentally ill and that he suspects they are indirectly connected to the killing. . . ." He also made other accusatory statements to the media, at which point the two sons sued him for libel in the U.S. District Court for Arizona. They served Ronald Watkins with a subpoena (also used in civil cases) to appear at a deposition and bring with him any notes or recordings he had that related to the murder. A deposition, at which a witness gives sworn testimony in the presence of lawyers for both sides, is standard procedure in the pretrial "discovery" process of U.S. civil litigation. Watkins appeared but without his notes and recordings. He filed a motion to quash the subpoena on First Amendment grounds, but it was denied by the trial judge and eventually he was held in contempt of court.

In *Shoen v. Shoen*, 5 F.3d 1289 (9th Cir. 1993), the Ninth Circuit Court of Appeals reversed. It ruled that the sons had not exhausted other sources, namely their own father: "we do not say that plaintiffs will never be able to overcome the presumption in favor of the [journalist's] privilege, we say only that they have failed to provide a sufficiently compelling reason to do so at this stage of the litigation."

In a case that went the other way, *Gonzales v. National Broadcasting Company, Inc.*, 194 F.3d 29 (2d Cir. 1998), the Second Circuit Court of Appeals nevertheless affirmed the existence of a journalist's privilege based on the First Amendment, even for materials obtained without any promise of confidentiality. NBC's *Dateline* aired a segment on what it described as pervasive abuses of motorists by Louisiana police, alleging that traffic stops often led to harassment and seizure of property. The program included a secretly videotaped, allegedly unprovoked stop of two of NBC's own employees, a *Dateline* producer named Pat Weiland and a cameraman.

Albert and Mary Gonzales, complaining of a previous stop they deemed without any reasonable suspicion, already had commenced a federal civil rights action against a Louisiana deputy sheriff, alleging that Hispanics and other minorities were targeted in order to extort money from them. When the *Dateline* segment aired, the Gonzaleses served subpoenas on NBC to obtain its entire videotape, and NBC claimed the journalist's privilege. While recognizing that the privilege, as applied in the Second Circuit, covered non-confidential information, the trial court nevertheless ruled against NBC. The appellate court applied a three-point test that sounded very much like that of Justice Potter Stewart in his *Branzburg* dissent, concluding that the tapes were "highly material and relevant" to the Gonzaleses' lawsuit, that the tapes were "necessary or critical to the maintenance of their claim," and that the materials sought "are not reasonably obtainable through other available sources."

But *Gonzales v. National Broadcasting Company, Inc.* was not entirely a lost cause for journalism. It was cited by the U.S. District Court in Manhattan in rejecting an effort by a bicyclist arrested during the Republican National Convention in 2004 who was trying to obtain Associated Press photographs showing his arrest. In *In re Subpeona Directed to the Associated Press; Nikolas Sikelianos v. City of New York*, 36 Media L. Rep. 2087 (S.D. N.Y. 2008), the District Court said that access to non-confidential materials doesn't permit "unfettered access" to sift through journalists' files, because that would foster the notion that the press is an "investigative arm" of the government or private litigants. Sikelianos contended that AP photos might be used to "refresh the recollection of witnesses who were on the scene," but the court countered that "this reasoning could apply to any photograph of the plaintiff's arrest; it is not sufficient to show a particularized need for the photos in AP's possession." To Sikelianos's argument that the photos might be relevant to the question of whether the police had probable cause to stop him and remove him from his bicycle, the court responded, "there is no indication that any of the photos in AP's possession show whether Mr. Sikelianos was obstructing the roadway or violating traffic rules." AP's motion to quash the subpoena was granted.

Wen Ho Lee v. Department of Justice

New York Times stellar reporter James Risen has tussled more than once with authorities demanding to know the names of his anonymous sources. In a case that reverberated through the federal government, longtime government nuclear scientist Wen Ho Lee was suspected of spying for China. He lost his job. Newspapers carried a number of stories detailing the suspicions against him. The government indicted Lee on fifty-nine counts of mishandling classified computer files and held him in solitary confinement for nine months pending his trial, but in the end the government settled for a guilty plea on just a single count.

Wen Ho Lee filed a suit under the Privacy Act, which prohibits disclosure of private information about government employees, alleging that the Department of Energy, where he had worked, the Department of Justice, and the FBI (which is in fact a part of the Department of Justice) had improperly disclosed to the news media personal information about him and the investigation. Risen and four other journalists who had written about Lee were subpoenaed to provide testimony and documents relating to the leaks, in particular their sources. The U.S. District Court for the District of Columbia denied their motions to quash the subpoenas. The court held that the information the scientist sought went to the heart of his case and that he had exhausted other possible sources of the information. The journalists refused to appear, were held in contempt of court, and fined five hundred dollars a day until they complied with the subpoenas, suspended pending appeal.

In *Wen Ho Lee v. Department of Justice*, 413 F.3d 53 (D.C. Cir. 2005), the Circuit Court of Appeals for the District of Columbia affirmed the contempt judgment against four of the five journalists—Risen, Josef Hebert of the Associated Press, Bob Drogin of the *Los Angeles Times,* and Pierre Thomas of CNN. (The contempt of Jeff Gerth of the *New York Times* was reversed.) Not a happy result for journalism, but the court's reasoning is worth understanding.

Dr. Lee alleged in his Privacy Act suit that leaks about him were designed to smear his image and distract from the government's own security lapses. According to the court, "He claimed that the leaked information included his and his wife's employment history, their financial transactions, details of their trips to Hong Kong and China, details of the investigation and interrogation of Lee, and purported results of polygraph tests. . . ." In his quest to learn the sources of the news stories, Lee submitted "at least 420 written discovery requests" to the government, "but was largely rebuffed by assertions of law enforcement privilege. . . ." He deposed six top Department of Energy officials including Secretary Bill Richardson, but they "were unable (or unwilling) to identify the leaker(s)." He also deposed, equally fruitlessly, six Department of Justice and eight FBI officials. The appellate court agreed with the trial court that the information Lee sought went to the heart of his case and that he had exhausted the alternative sources. It derided an assertion by Risen and Gerth that Lee should be required to depose sixty to sixty-five persons, declaring that their description of a prior decision was "inaccurate to a point approaching deceptiveness."

The Court of Appeals lowered the boom on Risen, affirming his contempt order and stating that he had invoked the journalist's privilege "at least 115 times" to avoid answering numerous questions:

(1) whether he had spoken to certain individuals at all;

(2) the source of unattributed quotes in his articles, including whether they came from specific individuals;

(3) further information clarifying the employers of unattributed sources, even when the articles listed them as officials in certain departments;

(4) whether various individuals were close to the Lee investigation or would have had relevant information;

(5) confirmation of information given by others in congressional testimony;

(6) his general practice with respect to unattributed sourcing;

(7) the identity of unattributed sources cited by his colleague, Jeff Gerth;

(8) confirmation of calls placed to government officials by him from an FBI log; and

(9) whether or not his testimony was intended to be inconclusive as to whether certain individuals were his sources.

(*Wen Ho Lee v. Department of Justice*, 62)

Hebert, Drogin, and Thomas got similar tongue-lashings, but the court accepted Gerth's protestation that he didn't know the identity of anonymous sources quoted in articles he cowrote with Risen, so his contempt was overturned.

Confronted with this harsh reality and the puny result of Lee's criminal prosecution, the government and the five news organizations paid one million, six hundred thousand dollars to settle Lee's Privacy Act lawsuit, half of it from the companies. According to the Associated Press (June 2, 2006), the settlement was "the only one of its kind in recent memory, and perhaps ever, legal and media experts said."

Risen Revisited

In his Pulitzer Prize–winning book, *State of War: The Secret History of the CIA and the Bush Administration*, on the Central Intelligence Agency, Risen described efforts by a covert CIA operative, a former Russian scientist recruited for this purpose, to provide Iran with flawed nuclear weapons plans. According to the book, the plans were so clearly defective that the operation failed. Risen told the story from the perspective of the scientist's "personal handler" at the CIA. A federal grand jury in Virginia investigating the leak subpoenaed him to find out who that was. Claiming a journalist's privilege under the First Amendment and the common law as well, Risen moved to quash the subpoena.

When Risen had first learned about the plot, according to telephone records, he had numerous conversations with a CIA agent named Jeffrey Sterling, intending to write a story for the *New York Times*. But after he called the National Security Council's public affairs office seeking comment, National Security Advisor Condoleezza Rice and CIA Director George Tenet responded by calling on Risen and *New York Times* Washington bureau chief Jill Abramson to urge them not to publish the story. A few days later Abramson told the government that the story would not be published.

Testimony by other witnesses before the grand jury in Virginia indicated that Sterling was in contact with "Jim" who was working on a book about the CIA, and a letter to "Jim" was found on Sterling's personal computer. Another witness testified that Risen had told him that Sterling was his source.

In ruling on Risen's motion to quash his subpoena (*In re: Grand Jury Subpoena to James Risen*, 39 Media L. Rep. 1945, E.D. Va. 2011), the U.S. District Court for the Eastern District of Virginia, in Alexandria, noted that the Circuit Court of Appeals for that circuit, the Fourth Circuit, in a previous case (*LaRouche v. National Broadcasting Co.*, 780 F.2d 1134, 4th Cir. 1986) had adopted a three-part test to decide claims of journalist's privilege: "(1) whether the information is relevant, (2) whether the information can be obtained by alternative means, and (3) whether there is a compelling interest in the information."

Although the court didn't attribute it to Justice Potter Stewart's *Branzburg* dissent, the test sounded very much like that opinion. In this ruling and others, the District Court stated, the Fourth Circuit articulated "a clear legal rule. If a reporter presents some evidence that he obtained information under a confidentiality agreement or that a goal of the subpoena is to harass or intimidate the reporter, he may invoke a qualified privilege against having to testify in a criminal proceeding." This wording was drawn from Justice Powell's *Branzburg* concurrence, which the court cited. Apparently focusing on the "alternative means" and "compelling interest" prongs of the three-part test, the court concluded that the grand jury already had "more than enough evidence to establish probable cause to indict Sterling," so to "require a reporter to violate his confidentiality agreement with his source under these facts would essentially destroy the reporter's privilege." The court quashed the subpoena. In sum, despite *Branzburg,* a journalist has a fighting chance of quashing a federal subpoena in civil cases, on the grounds that alternative means of finding the information are still available or that the journalist's information isn't necessary to the case.

State Law

Nearly all states have some sort of journalist's privilege, a few by dint of state supreme court rulings, but most have enacted a shield law creating a testimonial privilege for journalists, though in varying degrees. A few—Alabama, Montana, Nebraska, Nevada, and Washington—grant an "absolute" privilege, meaning that in any legal proceeding in the state, criminal or civil, a journalist may not be required to testify at all. However, most states grant only a qualified or limited privilege, and most pose a three-part test that clearly reflects Justice Stewart's dissent.

New York's Civil Rights Law §79-h (c), for instance, authorizes a court to recognize a journalist's privilege in both civil and criminal cases (but only for information obtained with a promise of confidentiality) unless the information sought

    i.   is highly material and relevant;
    ii.   is critical or necessary to the maintenance of a party's claim, defense or proof of an issue material thereto; and
   iii.   is not obtainable from any alternative source.

Interpretation and application of state shield laws vary widely, and they do not guarantee that a reporter won't be sent to jail. In 2009, Rick Rogers, a *San Diego Union* reporter who claimed a journalist's privilege under both the First Amendment and California's shield law, was nevertheless ordered by a military judge to testify in a court-martial because his testimony was

considered crucial to the defendant, a Marine accused of willfully disobey-
ing an order. The Marine recently had pleaded guilty to passing classified
intelligence to a sheriff's detective and was ordered not to talk to the press
about it, but he granted an interview to Rogers (*San Diego Union,* June 16,
2009). And in the states without a shield law, reporters can appeal only to the
discretion of the trial judge. That didn't work for Claire O'Brien of Kansas's
Dodge City Daily Globe, who in 2010 defied a court order to testify in a grand
jury–like closed hearing about her jailhouse interview with a murder suspect,
and to name a confidential source. She was adjudged in contempt and fined
one thousand dollars a day, whereupon she complied. The judge rescinded the
contempt citation, so she avoided the fine and jail. However, several weeks
later the Associated Press reported that she had been fired. The AP quoted her
as saying it was because she had openly criticized the newspaper's management for the way in which it had handled her legal representation in the case
(*Topeka Capital Journal,* cjonline.com, March 8, 2010).

Price v. Time, Inc.

Another uncertainty, even with a shield law, is exactly what and who is
protected. In a case that embarrassed the newly appointed Alabama football
coach, Michael Price, and cost him his job, *Price v. Time, Inc.,* 416 F.3d 1327
(11th Cir. 2005), a federal court held that under Alabama's shield law, which
specifically protected only newspaper and broadcast reporters, an article in
Sports Illustrated magazine was not covered. The article alleged that the
coach made sexual advances toward female students in a bar and apartment in
Tuscaloosa, and engaged in sexual acts with two women from a strip club in
Pensacola, Florida. One of the alleged participants in the Pensacola incident
was quoted anonymously as saying that the threesome engaged "in some
pretty aggressive sex."

Price sued the magazine's publisher, Time, Inc., and Don Yaeger, the writer,
for libel, demanding to know the name of the source of the Pensacola account.
Although the court ruled that the Alabama shield law did not protect Yaeger
or the magazine, it invoked the First Amendment journalist's privilege, noting that the court had previously recognized such a privilege but ruled that it
could be pierced with this "substantial evidence":

1. that the challenged statement was published and is both factually
   untrue and defamatory;
2. that reasonable efforts to discover the information from alternative sources
   have been made and that no other reasonable source is available
3. that knowledge of the identity of the informant is necessary to proper
   preparation and presentation of the case.

The court held that "Price has taken some depositions, but not enough for us to conclude that he has no other reasonable means of discovering the identity of the confidential sources." Pointing out that Yaeger had named four women in his deposition, the court stated that "Price has not asked any of these women under oath whether she was Yaeger's confidential source, whether she knows who the confidential source is, or whether the allegations attributed to the confidential source are true. . . . Price should be required to depose the four women." It vacated the trial court's order requiring Yaeger to disclose his confidential source. (Ousted at Alabama, Price went on to coach at the University of Texas at El Paso.)

Who's a Journalist?

Questions abound about whether Internet postings by online-only news media, bloggers, and other website operators are covered by a journalist's privilege formulated before the Internet existed. The U.S. District Court for the District of Columbia, in a libel suit against the gossipy online "Drudge Report," *Blumenthal v. Drudge*, 186 F.R.D. 236 (D. D.C. 1999), treated writer Matt Drudge as a reporter covered by the First Amendment reporter's privilege defined earlier in *Zerilli v. Smith.* Similarly, in *O'Grady v. Superior Court*, 139 Cal.App.4th 1423 (2006), a California appellate court granted the journalist's privilege to two online magazines, "O'Grady's PowerPage" and "Apple Insider," covering Apple Macintosh products and technology, in the face of an Apple Computer, Inc. lawsuit alleging that the sites illicitly obtained and published information about the company's secret plans to produce a device that would facilitate the creation of digital live sound recordings on Apple computers.

On the other hand, in Oregon, a U.S. District Court ruled that Crystal Cox, author of a blog that repeatedly called an Oregon lawyer corrupt and a tax fraud, was "not media" under the state's shield law. It provides that "[n]o person connected with, employed by or engaged in any medium of communication to the public shall be required by . . . a judicial officer . . . to disclose, by subpoena or otherwise . . . [t]he source of any published or unpublished information obtained by the person in the course of gathering, receiving or processing information for any medium of communication to the public. . . ." "Medium of communication" is defined broadly by the statute as including, but not limited to, "any newspaper, magazine or other periodical, book, pamphlet, news service, wire service, news or feature syndicate, broadcast station or network, or cable television system."

Despite the wide scope of that definition, in *Obsidian Finance Group, LLC v. Cox*, No. CV-11–57-HZ (D. Ore. 2011), the judge ruled that "although defendant is a self-proclaimed 'investigative blogger' and defines herself as 'media,' the record fails to show that she is affiliated with any newspaper, magazine, periodical, book, pamphlet, news service, wire service, news or feature syndicate, broadcast station or network, or cable television system. Thus, she is not entitled to the protections of the law. . . ."

A similar ruling was handed down by the Supreme Court of New Jersey in *TooMuchMedia v. Hale*, 206 N.J. 209 (2011). Shellee Hale, a former Microsoft employee still residing in Washington State, repeatedly availed herself of Internet message boards to criticize the adult entertainment industry and what she deemed its abuse of women. At one point Hale suggested that a software manufacturer called TooMuchMedia violated New Jersey law in connection with an alleged security breach of its database that allowed confidential personal information of porn subscribers to be disclosed.

TooMuchMedia sued for defamation and false light invasion of privacy. Hale claimed she was an investigative journalist, but the New Jersey court turned her down. It acknowledged that the New Jersey shield law was not limited to traditional news media, but declared that "the Legislature requires that other means of disseminating news be 'similar' to traditional news sources to qualify for the law's coverage. We do not find that online message boards are similar to the types of news entities listed in the statute, and do not believe that the Legislature intended to provide an absolute privilege in defamation cases to people who post comments on message boards."

On the other hand, in *Mortgage Specialists, Inc. v. Implode-Explode Heavy Industries, Inc.*, 160 N.H. 277 (2010), the Supreme Court of New Hampshire took a broad view when confronted by a claim that a commercial website publishing information about mortgage lenders was entitled to the journalist's privilege. The case arose when, according to the court's opinion, the website

> published an article that detailed administrative actions taken by the New Hampshire Banking Department against Mortgage Specialists, Inc. In this article, Implode posted a link to a document that purported to represent Mortgage Specialists' 2007 loan figures. . . . In response to the article, an anonymous website visitor with the username 'Brianbattersby' posted two comments regarding Mortgage Specialists and its president. (*Mortgage Specialists, Inc. v. Implode-Explode Heavy Industries, Inc.*, 231)

The New Hampshire court noted that years earlier it had recognized a journalist's privilege based on the state constitution's commitment to a free press. Also, it quoted *Branzburg v. Hayes* that "Freedom of the press is a fundamental personal right which is not confined to newspapers and periodicals. . . ."

Accordingly, the court ruled that the website "serves an informative function and contributes to the flow of information to the public" and therefore the website "is a reporter for purposes of the newsgathering privilege."

In the same liberal vein, a Chicago trial court granted the journalist's privilege to a firm whose business included soliciting inside information about consumer devices and publishing it on its website. Johns-Byrne Company, based in Illinois, was preparing a manual for the Motorola Droid Bionic smartphone prior to its public release. Images of the phone in the manual were obtained from "an anonymous tipster" and published by TechnoBuffalo LLC in an article several weeks before the phone's release.

In *Johns-Byrne Company v. TechnoBuffalo LLC*, No. 2011 L 009161 (Ill. Circ.Ct. July 13, 2012), the Illinois court rejected an assertion by Johns-Byrne that the state's shield law required active reporting. The law states that the reporter "must be engaged in the business of collecting, writing, or editing news for publication," and the court interpreted "collect" to mean "'gathering' or 'receiving' information in some way." The court concluded that TechnoBuffalo's website, which included a variety of other technology information, was publishing "news" and therefore was covered by the journalist's privilege.

So, what is a journalist to make of this mixed picture? Since every journalist inevitably resorts to granting confidentiality to a source at one time or another, there's a simple answer: know the law of journalist's privilege that covers you. This means, first, whether a state statute or state supreme court ruling creates a journalist's privilege, and its extent. Does it cover non-confidential information as well as confidential? Does it cover criminal cases as well as civil? How does it define "journalist" or "reporter"? Have the state courts interpreted the statute in light of Internet usage? Second, find out what the U.S. Circuit Court of Appeals for your circuit (it may be your whole state or perhaps just a part of it) has ruled about a First Amendment reporter's privilege. As with the state law, what does it cover, and who? Your editor may know the answers to all these questions; every editor should. But if not, don't hesitate to ask for advice from your company lawyer. If you don't have a company or your company doesn't have a lawyer who can answer, at the very least conduct a search for "shield law" and "journalist's privilege" and look for answers to all these questions. If all else fails, track down an expert media lawyer.

Questions for Discussion

1. Does the majority opinion in *Branzburg v. Hayes* enunciate any helpful support for the work of journalists?
2. When is it safe (or unsafe) to promise confidentiality and anonymity to a source? How do you cite or quote an anonymous source? Should you fictionalize a source's name?

3. How would you minimize the possibility of being subpoenaed for the name of an anonymous source?

4. In what you're posting currently, are you covered by a state shield law or a First Amendment journalist's privilege? How do you figure it out?

5. How might you improve your prospects for coverage by a state shield law?

References

Associated Press, "San Diego reporter told to testify in Marine trial," June 16, 2009. http://www.utsandiego.com/news/2009/jun/16/us-marines-stolen-files-061609/.

———, "Writer says 'criticism' led to her firing," Dodge City Daily Globe, March 9, 2010. http://www.dodgeglobe.com/article/20100309/NEWS/303099993/0/SEARCH.

Balk, Alfred, "Confessions of a Block-Buster," *Saturday Evening Post* (July 14, 1962).

Baker v. F & F Investment, 470 F.2d 778 (2d Cir. 1972). https://bulk.resource.org/courts.gov/c/F2/470/470.F2d.778.72-1413.173.html.

Blumenthal v. Drudge,186 F.R.D. 236 (D.D.C. 1999). http://www.internetlibrary.com/pdf/Blumenthal-Drudge.pdf.

Branzburg v. Hayes, 408 U.S. 665 (1972). https://supreme.justia.com/cases/federal/us/408/665/case.html.

Carey v. Hume, 492 F.2d 631 (D.C.Cir. 1974). http://openjurist.org/492/f2d/631/carey-v-hume.

Gonzales v. National Broadcasting Company, Inc., 194 F.3d 29 (2d Cir. 1998). http://caselaw.findlaw.com/us-2nd-circuit/1106890.html.

Johns-Byrne Company v. TechnoBuffalo LLC, No. 2011 L 009161 (Ill. Circ. Ct. July 13, 2012). http://www.citmedialaw.org/sites/citmedialaw.org/files/2012-07-13-Order%20on%20motion%20for%20reconsideration.pdf.

LaRouche v. National Broadcasting Co., 780 F.2d 1134 (4th Cir. 1986). https://bulk.resource.org/courts.gov/c/F2/780/780.F2d.1134.html.

Leggett, Vanessa v. United States, 535 U.S. 1011 (2002). http://www.rcfp.org/browse-media-law-resources/news/high-court-declines-hear-vanessa-leggett%E2%80%99s-appeal.

Miller, Judith, in re: Grand Jury Subpoena, 397 F.3d 964 (D.C. Cir. 2005). http://law.justia.com/cases/federal/appellate-courts/F3/397/964/474679/.

Mortgage Specialists, Inc. v. Implode-Explode Heavy Industries, Inc., 160 N.H. 277 (2010). http://www.courts.state.nh.us/supreme/opinions/2010/2010041mortg.pdf.

New York Civil Rights Law, § 79-h (c). http://codes.lp.findlaw.com/nycode/CVR/7/79-h.

Obsidian Finance Group, LLC v. Cox, No. CV-11–57-HZ (D. Ore. 2011). http://www.dmlp.org/sites/citmedialaw.org/files/2011-11-30-Order.pdf.

O'Grady v. Superior Court, 139 Cal.App.4th 1423 (2006). http://www.firstamendmentcoalition.org/handbook/cases/OGrady.pdf.

Price v. Time, Inc., 416 F.3d 1327 (11th Cir. 2005). http://www.ca11.uscourts.gov/opinions/ops/200413027.pdf.

Risen, James, In re: Grand Jury Subpoena, 39 Media L. Rep. 1945 (E.D.Va. 2011). http://www.fas.org/sgp/jud/sterling/062811-opinion118.pdf.

Risen, James, State of War: The Secret History of the CIA and the Bush Administration (New York: Free Press, 2006).

Shoen v. Shoen, 5 F.3d 1289 (9th Cir. 1993). http://caselaw.findlaw.com/us-9th-circuit/1038870.html.

Sikelianos, Nikolas, In re Subpeona Directed to the Associated Press, v. City of New York, 36 Media L. Rep. 2087 (S.D. N.Y. 2008). http://ny.findacase.com/research/wfrmDocViewer.aspx/xq/fac.20080618_0000476.SNY.htm/qx.

Taricani, Jim, In re: Special Proceedings, 373 F.3d 37 (1st Cir. 2004). http://caselaw.findlaw.com/us-1st-circuit/1378300.html.

TooMuchMedia v. Hale, 206 N.J. 209 (2011). http://www.rcfp.org/newsitems/docs/20110607_153605_toomuchmedia_v_hale.pdf.

Wen Ho Lee v. Department of Justice. 413 F.3d 53 (D.C. Cir. 2005). http://www.firstamendmentcoalition.org/handbook/cases/Lee_v_DepartmentofJustice.pdf.

Wolf v. United States, 201 Fed.Appx. 430 (9th Cir. 2006). http://www.firstamendmentcoalition.org/handbook/cases/joshwolf.pdf.

Zerilli v. Smith, 656 F.2d 705 (D.C. Cir. 1981). http://openjurist.org/656/f2d/705/zerilli-v-smith-j-zerilli.

9

Copyright

> *"The Congress shall have power . . . To promote the*
> *Progress of Science and useful Arts, by securing for*
> *limited Times to Authors and Inventors the exclusive*
> *Right to their respective Writings and Discoveries."*
> —United States Constitution, Article 1, Section 8
> (the "Copyright Clause")

The Internet era provokes endless new questions and controversies about the reach of copyright protection, for it covers the web as well as printed texts and other creative works. For one thing, the law means that even a blogger who invites comments that post automatically without screening may be liable for copyright violation (as well as other possible violations of law, such as defamation and invasion of privacy). Along with sculpture, film, music, and other traditional creations, the law now covers computer software and operating systems. However, ideas and facts may not be copyrighted.

The Copyright Act

To understand the implications of copyright in the future, let's start in the past. The constitutional mandate set forth above means that only the federal government can enact copyright (and patent) law. Congress acted promptly, passing the Copyright Act of 1790. It provided that only the author of a work could sell it or authorize its use by others for fourteen years from the date of publication, with the option to renew for another fourteen years. After these terms, creative works would enter the public domain, freely available for anyone to republish or copy. Congress extended the term of copyright protection four times, in 1831, 1909, 1975, and 1998. The relatively short span between the last two amendments arose from the fact that the copyrights of cartoonist Walt Disney's characters like Mickey Mouse and Donald Duck were approaching expiration, prompting the Walt Disney Company along with other publishing interests—including the estate of composer George Gershwin and the Motion Picture Association of America—to appeal to Congress for extended protection.

Their plea aroused spirited opposition from intellectual-property professors and others who called it "corporate welfare" and predicted it would impose unwarranted costs on the public and discourage new creativity. Nevertheless, the 1998 amendment, called the Copyright Term Extension Act, or CTEA (and facetiously the Mickey Mouse Protection Act), extended copyright terms by twenty years. The term of all existing and future copyrights, commencing with the work's creation (rather than date of publication), jumped from fifty years after the author's death to seventy, harmonizing U.S. law with that of the European Union. Copyrights granted prior to 1978 were extended from seventy-five years from publication to ninety-five years. As to "works made for hire," such as corporate creations, the term was extended from seventy-five years from publication or one hundred years from creation, whichever expired first, to ninety-five years from publication or one hundred twenty years from creation, whichever expires first.

When the CTEA was enacted in 1998 it frustrated Internet publication plans of one Eric Eldred, a New Hampshire resident, former computer programmer and online publisher of the works of Nathaniel Hawthorne and other authors' writings whose copyrights had expired. He intended to scan and publish on the Internet certain additional American literary works copyrighted before 1923 and thus about to enter the public domain under the seventy-five-year term provided by the 1976 Copyright Act. Joined by other small publishers, Eldred sued to set aside the 1998 act, alleging that it exceeded Congress's authority under the Copyright Clause and violated the First Amendment. He lost in both the District Court and the Circuit Court of Appeals in the District of Columbia, but enlisted one of the nation's foremost advocates of copyright relaxation, Stanford law professor Lawrence Lessig, to carry the case on to the Supreme Court.

Eldred's persistence, however, was not rewarded. In *Eldred v. Ashcroft*, 537 U.S. 186 (2003), the Supreme Court affirmed the lower courts' rulings by a vote of 7–2. Writing for the majority, Justice Ruth Bader Ginsburg declared, "we are not at liberty to second-guess congressional determinations and policy judgments of this order, however debatable or arguably unwise they may be." As to Eldred's First Amendment argument, she wrote, "The Copyright Clause and First Amendment were adopted close in time. This proximity indicates that, in the Framers' view, copyright's limited monopolies are compatible with free speech principles. Indeed, copyright's purpose is to *promote* the creation and publication of free expression." She pointed out, significantly, that the "fair use" provision of the Copyright Act "allows the public to use not only facts and ideas contained in a copyrighted work, but also expression itself in certain circumstances."

Reaffirming its judgment that Congress has great discretion in exercising its Copyright Clause mandate, the Supreme Court also upheld a statute that granted copyright protection to foreign works already in the public domain. Congress legislated copyright protection to those works in accordance with an old international agreement, the Berne Convention for the Protection of Literary and Artistic Works, which took effect in 1886, in order to preserve Americans' foreign copyrights. Nevertheless, this belated grant of copyright to old, public works caught the artistic world by surprise. Publishers, orchestra conductors, musicians, and others who had enjoyed free access to foreign works sued, as Eric Eldred had, on the grounds that the congressional action exceeded the authority granted by the Copyright Clause and violated the First Amendment.

The Supreme Court disagreed and ruled 6–2, in *Golan v. Holder*, 132 S.Ct. 873 (2012), with Justice Ginsburg again writing the majority opinion. The statute "falls comfortably within Congress' authority under the Copyright Clause," she affirmed. "Congress determined that exemplary adherence to Berne would serve the objectives of the Copyright Clause. We have no warrant to reject the rational judgment Congress made." Regarding the First Amendment challenge, she declared:

> [N]othing in the historical record, congressional practice, or our own juris-prudence warrants exceptional First Amendment solicitude for copyrighted works that were once in the public domain. Neither this challenge nor that raised in *Eldred,* we stress, allege Congress transgressed a generally applicable First Amendment prohibition; we are not faced, for example, with copyright protection that hinges on the author's viewpoint. (*Eldred v. Ashcroft,* 891–92)

Once more Justice Ginsburg noted that "fair use" provides a legal way to use copyrighted material.

Fair Use

The real question confronting journalists today is not whether works created by others—text, photos, videos, music—are copyrighted. They are, by their authors, from the moment they are "fixed in a tangible form" (although registering them with the U.S. Copyright Office at the Library of Congress enhances enforcement prospects in court). Moreover, websites generally claim a copyright on everything they post. Someone's photo on Facebook, for instance, no matter how newsworthy, is not freely available for your use. So the recurring question is, or at least should be, does "fair use" permit me to use this material without risking a lawsuit for copyright violation? A fair use of copyrighted material is one that requires neither the author's permission nor payment. It can be very narrow, applying to a single classroom, for instance, or as broad as the Internet. The criteria for determining fair use are set forth in the Copyright Act. It states:

> [F]air use of a copyrighted work . . . for purposes such as criticism, comment, news reporting, teaching (including multiple copies for classroom use), scholarship, or research, is not an infringement of copyright. In determining whether the use made of a work in any particular case is a fair use the factors to be considered shall include
>
> 1. the purpose and character of the use, including whether such use is of a commercial nature or is for nonprofit educational purposes;
> 2. the nature of the copyrighted work;
> 3. the amount and substantiality of the portion used in relation to the copyrighted work as a whole; and
> 4. the effect of the use upon the potential market for or value of the copyrighted work.
>
> (Copyright Act, section 107)

Gerald Ford's Autobiography

To get an idea of how courts analyze and weigh these four factors, consider the controversy over the publication of former President Gerald R. Ford's autobiography, *A Time to Heal.* Upon leaving the White House in January 1977, Ford signed a contract with Harper & Row, Publishers, Inc. to write a book that would include his inside view of the explosive Watergate scandal and his pardon of his predecessor, Richard Nixon, who had resigned in disgrace over the Watergate scandal. As the memoir neared completion two years later, Harper & Row granted *Time* magazine the exclusive right to publish a long, 7,500-word excerpt from the book shortly before it reached bookstores. *Time* paid Harper $12,500, and agreed to pay another $12,500 at the time of publication. However, shortly before the book was released, an anonymous person surreptitiously delivered a copy of the Ford manuscript to the *Nation,* a magazine of political commentary, which promptly published a 2,250-word article consisting entirely of quotations, paraphrases, and other information from the book. *Time* abandoned its planned article and refused to pay the second $12,500.

Not surprisingly, Harper & Row sued the *Nation's* publisher for copyright violation. The U.S. District Court declared an infringement, but the Second Circuit Court of Appeals disagreed, ruling that the *Nation's* article fell within the free space called fair use. However, a divided Supreme Court carefully applied the four criteria of the Copyright Act and reversed the appellate court, 6–3. The case was *Harper & Row, Publishers, Inc. v. Nation Enterprises*, 471 U.S. 539 (1985).

Concerning the first criterion of fair use, the "purpose and character of the use," Justice Sandra Day O'Connor wrote for the majority, "we cannot ignore The Nation's stated purpose of scooping the forthcoming hardcover and Time abstracts. . . . The Nation's use had not merely the incidental effect but the *intended purpose* of supplanting the copyright holder's commercially valuable right of first publication." Score one for Harper & Row.

Regarding the "nature of the copyrighted work," Justice O'Connor stated that "'A Time to Heal' may be characterized as an unpublished historical narrative or autobiography. The law generally recognizes a greater need to disseminate factual works than works of fiction or fantasy." However, she went on:

> The Nation did not stop at isolated phrases and instead excerpted subjective descriptions and portraits of public figures whose power lies in the author's individualized expression. Such use, focusing on the most expressive elements of the work, exceeds that necessary to disseminate the facts. In the case of Mr. Ford's manuscript, the copyright holders' interest in confidentiality is irrefutable. . . . A use that so clearly infringes the copyright holder's interests in confidentiality and creative control is difficult to characterize as "fair." (*Harper & Row, Publishers, Inc. v. Nation Enterprises*, 563–64)

On the third criterion, "amount and substantiality of the portion used," Justice O'Connor stated that although the 300 to 400 words quoted verbatim by the *Nation* "were an insubstantial portion" of the book, "the article is structured around the quoted excerpts which serve as its dramatic focal points. . . . In view of the expressive value of the excerpts and their key role in the infringing work, we cannot agree with the Second Circuit that the 'magazine took a meager, indeed an infinitesimal amount of Ford's original language.'" Importantly, this statement stands as the Supreme Court's only ruling on the permissible length of a verbatim quotation from a copyrighted work.

Regarding the fourth criterion, "effect on the market," Justice O'Connor called it "undoubtedly the single most important element of fair use." She noted that the trial court had found "not merely a potential but an actual effect on the market. Time's cancellation of its projected serialization and its refusal to pay the $12,500 were the direct effect of the infringement. . . .

Rarely will a case of copyright infringement present such clear-cut evidence of actual damage." More broadly, she added, "a fair use doctrine that permits extensive prepublication quotations from an unreleased manuscript without the copyright owner's consent poses substantial potential for damage to the marketability of first serialization rights in general."

Thus the Supreme Court awarded all four rounds to the challenger, Harper & Row, concluding that "The Nation's use of these verbatim excerpts from the unpublished manuscript was not a fair use." However, it will come as no surprise to observe that these assessments are all highly subjective, with the exception of the $12,500 withheld by *Time*.

Justice William Brennan, in a dissent joined by Justices Thurgood Marshall and Byron White, disagreed on all four points. He argued that the *Nation's* article consisted mostly of facts and ideas, which cannot be copyrighted, saying they represented an appropriate contribution to a healthy democratic discussion of public affairs. He wrote, "this zealous defense of the copyright owner's prerogative will, I fear, stifle the broad dissemination of ideas and information copyright is intended to nurture." Accusing the majority of relying on "sheer speculation" in its analysis of fair use, Brennan contended that if the six Ford quotations in the article had been included in a book review, "there is little question that such a use would be fair use. . . . It is difficult to see how the use of these quoted words in a news report is less appropriate." He declared unequivocally, "the statutorily prescribed process of weighing the four statutory fair use factors discussed above leads naturally to a conclusion that The Nation's limited use of literary form was not an infringement."

Despite the spirited dissent, Justice O'Connor's majority opinion in *Harper & Row* remains one of the most quoted opinions in the realm of copyright law, particularly its conclusion that 300 to 400 words were too many to qualify as fair use. Nevertheless, as Justice Brennan's disagreement demonstrates, there's wide room for differing analysis of the four fair-use criteria, so it is difficult to know in advance whether a proposed quotation of copyrighted material will or will not constitute an infringement, even when clear attribution is provided. Caution is advised.

Is the Use Transformative?

Another case, arduously fought over a number of years, further illustrates the uncertainty of fair use. Perfect 10, Inc., a California company that distributed photos of nude women via the Internet to paying subscribers only, sued Google Inc. for copyright infringement because Google Image Search enabled a non-customer to access small "thumbnail" versions of the photos and a link to Perfect 10's full-size images. On the face of it, the equities seem clear. Google clearly was facilitating access to Perfect 10's copyrighted photos. And to make matters worse for Google, Perfect 10's business was suffering. Infringement? Surprisingly, the courts said no.

There were half a dozen complex rulings by the U.S. District Court for the Central District of California and the Ninth Circuit Court of Appeals at various stages of this lengthy litigation, but the critical opinion for our purposes was rendered by the Court of Appeals in *Perfect 10, Inc. v. Google, Inc.*, 508 F.3d 1146 (2007). The court analyzed the four fair-use factors this way:

1. *Purpose and Character of the Use:* "The central purpose of this inquiry," the court stated, "is to determine whether and to what extent the new work is 'transformative.'" Did it convey a different expression or message? Yes. "Google's use of thumbnails is highly transformative," the court ruled. "Although an image may have been created originally to serve an entertainment, aesthetic, or informative function, a search engine transforms the image into a pointer directing a user to a source of information. We conclude that the significantly transformative nature of Google's search engine, particularly in light of its public benefit, outweighs Google's superseding and commercial uses of the thumbnails in this case."

2. *The Nature of the Copyrighted Work:* "Once Perfect 10 has exploited this commercially valuable right of first publication by putting its images on the Internet for paid subscribers, Perfect 10 is no longer entitled to the enhanced protection available for an unpublished work."

3. *The Amount and Substantiality of the Portion Used:* The court held that the "use of the entire photographic image was reasonable in light of the purpose of a search engine. . . . [T]his factor favored neither party."

4. *Effect of Use on the Market:* The court noted that the District Court had held that Google's "use of thumbnails did not hurt Perfect 10's market for full-size images. . . . We agree."

The appellate court concluded:

> Google has put Perfect 10's thumbnail images (along with millions of other thumbnail images) to a use fundamentally different than the use intended by Perfect 10. In doing so, Google has provided a significant benefit to the public. Weighing this significant transformative use against the unproven use of Google thumbnails for cell phone downloads, and considering the other fair use factors, all in light of the purpose of copyright, we conclude that use of Perfect 10's thumbnails is a fair use. (*Perfect 10, Inc. v. Google, Inc.*, 508 F.3d1146 1168)

Throughout this tortuous litigation, Perfect 10 was seeking a preliminary injunction ordering Google to remove the thumbnail images. Following the Court of Appeals decision, the District Court denied the requested injunction (*Perfect 10, Inc. v. Google, Inc.,* No. CV 04 9484 AHM (SHx), C.D. Cal. 2010). That ruling was affirmed by the Court of Appeals (*Perfect 10, Inc. v. Google, Inc.,* 653 F.3d 976, 9th Cir. 2011), and the Supreme Court later denied a petition for a *writ of certiorari* (*Perfect 10, Inc. v. Google, Inc.,* 132 S.Ct. 1713, 2012). It had been nearly eight years since Perfect 10 filed its complaint. Google consistently contends that its selection and prioritization of others' work is protected by the First Amendment.

In the analysis of fair use, perhaps the most difficult part of the four-factor test to evaluate is the first, "the purpose and character of the use." It must be "transformative," as stated by the Court of Appeals in *Perfect 10 v. Google*. Though not mentioned in the statute, one form of transformative expression accepted by the Supreme Court is parody; the case involved was *Campbell v. Acuff-Rose Music Inc.*, 510 U.S. 569 (1994).

Luther R. Campbell, also known as Luke Skywalker, wrote a song called "Pretty Woman" for his rap music group 2 Live Crew, which he later described as an effort to satirize a rock ballad, "Oh Pretty Woman," by Roy Orbison and William Dees, which was popular twenty-five years earlier. They had assigned their rights to Acuff-Rose Music Inc., which registered the song for copyright protection. The 2 Live Crew recordings credited Orbison and Dees and the publisher of "Oh Pretty Woman." Nevertheless, Acuff-Rose sued for copyright infringement, and 2 Live Crew claimed fair use. The District Court for the Southern District of New York granted summary judgment for 2 Live Crew, but the Second Circuit Court of Appeals reversed.

The Supreme Court, in an artistic tour de force by Justice David Souter, unanimously reversed the appellate court, holding that "Pretty Woman" was a parody, transformative, and thus a fair use. Although Campbell saw his song as satire, Souter said no, it's a parody:

> For the purposes of copyright law, the nub of the definitions, and the heart of any parodist's claim to quote from existing material, is the use of some elements of a prior author's composition to create a new one that, at least in part, comments on that author's works. . . . Parody needs to mimic an original to make its point, and so has some claim to use the creation of its victim's (or collective victims') imagination, whereas satire can stand on its own two feet and so requires justification for the very act of borrowing. [footnote] Satire has been defined as a work "in which prevalent follies or vices are assailed with ridicule," Oxford English Dictionary . . . or are

"attacked through irony, derision, or wit," American Heritage Dictionary. (*Campbell v. Acuff-Rose Music Inc.*, 580)

Turning to some of the specific elements of the work at hand, Justice Souter continued:

2 Live Crew juxtaposes the romantic musings of a man whose fantasy comes true, with degrading taunts, a bawdy demand for sex, and a sigh of relief from paternal responsibility. The later words can be taken as a comment on the naiveté of the original of an earlier day, as a rejection of its sentiment that ignores the ugliness of street life and the debasement that it signifies. It is this joinder of reference and ridicule that marks off the author's choice of parody from the other types of comment and criticism that traditionally have had a claim to fair use protection as transformative works. (*Campbell v. Acuff-Rose Music Inc.*, 580–81)

Similarly, a takeoff on Margaret Mitchell's immortal *Gone With The Wind* was adjudged a parody. *The Wind Done Gone* was written by Alice Randall as the diary of a slave, presenting a forceful counter-thrust to Mitchell's portrayal of Southern society at the time of the Civil War. As the Eleventh Circuit Court of Appeals explained in great detail in *Suntrust Bank as Trustee of the Mitchell Trusts v. Houghton Mifflin Company*, 268 F.3d 1257 (11th Cir. 2001):

While told from a different perspective, more critically, the story is transformed into a very different tale, albeit much more abbreviated. Cynara's very language is a departure from Mitchell's original prose; she acts as the voice of Randall's inversion of GWTW. She is the vehicle of parody; she is its means—not its end. It is clear within the first fifty pages of Cynara's fictional diary that Randall's work flips GWTW's traditional race roles, portrays powerful whites as stupid or feckless, and generally sets out to demystify GWTW and strip the romanticism from Mitchell's specific account of this period of our history. . . . In GWTW, Scarlett O'Hara often expresses disgust with and condescension towards blacks; in TWDG, Other, Scarlett's counterpart, is herself of mixed descent. In GWTW, Ashley Wilkes is the initial object of Scarlett's affection; in TWDG, he is homosexual. In GWTW, Rhett Butler does not consort with black female characters and is portrayed as the captain of his own destiny. In TWDG, Cynara ends her affair with Rhett's counterpart, R., to begin a relationship with a black Congressman; R. ends up a washed out former cad. In TWDG, nearly every black character is given some redeeming quality—whether depth, wit, cunning, beauty, strength, or courage—that their GWTW analogues lacked. . . . It is hard to imagine how Randall could have specifically criticized GWTW without depending heavily upon copyrighted elements of that book. A parody is a work that seeks to comment upon or criticize another work by appropriating elements of the original. (*Suntrust Bank as Trustee of the Mitchell Trusts v. Houghton Mifflin Company,* 1270–71)

Having adjudged the new book "highly transformative" in the "purpose and character" analysis, the Court of Appeals gave short shrift to the three other fair-use factors, concluding that "a viable fair use defense is available."

To see the difference between a legally valid fair use parody and claimed parodies that failed to make the cut, we look to two of America's foremost twentieth-century authors, Dr. Seuss and J.D. Salinger.

In 1995, Alan Katz and Chris Wrinn wrote *The Cat NOT in the Hat!*, described as a satire of O.J. Simpson's trial in Los Angeles for the murder of his ex-wife and a friend. It was a tongue-in-cheek riff, all in Seuss-like verse, with illustrations, poking fun at all the principal players. "While Simpson is depicted 13 times in the Cat's distinctively scrunched and somewhat shabby red and white stove-pipe hat," the Ninth Circuit Court of Appeals stated in *Dr. Seuss Enterprises, L.P. v. Penguin Books USA, Inc. and Dove Audio, Inc.*, 109 F.3d 1394 (9th Cir. 1997), "the substance and content of *The Cat in the Hat* is not conjured up by the focus on the Brown-Goldman murders or the O.J. Simpson trial." The court held that despite the publisher's claim of parody, there was "no effort to create a transformative work with 'new expression, meaning, or message.'" It concluded: "We completely agree with the district court that Penguin and Dove's fair use defense is 'pure shtick' and that their post-hoc characterization of the work is 'completely unconvincing.'"

A 2009 book sought to capitalize on the enduring fame of J.D. Salinger's iconic 1951 coming-of-age novel, *Catcher in the Rye*. Fredrik Colting, using the pseudonym John David California, wrote and published under his own label what was billed as "a marvelous sequel" to *Catcher* called *60 Years Later: Coming Through the Rye*. Colting's protagonist was a 76-year-old called Mr. C, clearly an aging Holden Caulfield, Salinger's protagonist. Mr. C recalls events in Holden's early life, and *60 Years* has a familiar ring to it, starting within an institution, meandering through New York City, and ending in another institution. Colting did not seek Salinger's permission to adopt his character and story line. Though determinedly reclusive in rural New Hampshire since shortly after *Catcher* was published, Salinger emerged through his lawyers to seek an injunction blocking distribution of the book, alleging copyright violation. He died during the course of the litigation, but the J.D. Salinger Literary Trust pursued his cause.

In the U.S. District Court for the Southern District of New York, Judge

Deborah A. Batts meticulously applied the four-factor test of fair use, in *Salinger v. Colting*, 641 F. Supp.2d 250 (S.D.N.Y. 2009).

Purpose and Character of the Use

While Colting sought to define his novel as fitting within Justice Souter's description of parody as distinct from satire, Judge Batts thoughtfully disagreed:

> Unlike satire, which critiques and comments on aspects of society more broadly, parody sharpens its knives for the very work from which it borrows. . . . *Campbell* and its progeny define the limits of parody to include only those elements which criticize or comment upon the source author's works, rather than the author himself. . . . *60 Years,* however, contains no reasonably discernible rejoinder or specific criticism of any character or theme of *Catcher.* . . . [I]t can be argued that the contrast between Holden's authentic but critical and rebellious nature and his tendency toward depressive alienation is one of the key themes of *Catcher.* That many readers and critics have apparently idolized Caulfield for the former, despite—or perhaps because of—the latter, does not change the fact that those elements were already apparent in *Catcher.* It is hardly parodic to repeat that same exercise in contrast, just because society and the characters have aged. . . . Accordingly, the Court finds that *60 Years* contains no reasonably perceived parodic character as to *Catcher* and Holden Caulfield. (*Salinger v. Colting*, 256, 257)

The Nature of the Copyrighted Work

"Here there is no question" that *Catcher in the Rye* is a creative work that copyright is intended to protect, and "this factor weighs against a finding of fair use."

The Amount and Substantiality of the Portion Used in Relation to the Copyrighted Work as a Whole

"Defendants have taken well more from *Catcher,* in both substance and style, than is necessary for the alleged transformative purpose. . . . [L]ike Holden, Mr. C is a frequent liar, constantly complains, is out of shape, has trouble maneuvering in the dark, combs his hair with his hand to one side, wears the same red hunting cap, is obsessed with whether birds migrate for the winter, and likes the feeling of time standing still in museums." As a result of these and many other close similarities quoted by the court, "the third factor weighs heavily against a finding of fair use." (Notice how this analysis of "amount and substantiality" differs from the Supreme Court's word-count test applied to former President Ford's memoir.)

The Effect of the Use Upon the Potential Market for or Value of the Copyrighted Work

The court declared that the market for *Catcher in the Rye* would hardly be impaired by *60 Years,* but "it is quite likely that the publishing of *60 Years* and similar widespread works could substantially harm the market for a *Catcher* sequel or other derivative works. . . ." With Salinger still alive at that moment, the court acknowledged that he "has not demonstrated any interest in publishing a sequel or other derivative work of *Catcher,*" but he could change his mind. Therefore, the court concluded, "because it is likely that the publishing of *60 Years* would harm the potential market for sequels or other derivative works based upon *Catcher,* the fourth factor weighs, albeit only slightly, against fair use."

In sum, Judge Batts wrote, "while the Court does find some limited transformative character in *60 Years,* . . . it finds that the alleged parodic content is not reasonably perceivable, and that the limited non-parodic transformative content is unlikely to overcome the obvious commercial nature of the work, the likely injury to the potential market for derivative works of *Catcher,* and especially the substantial and pervasive extent to which *60 Years* borrows from *Catcher* and the character of Holden Caulfield."

Digital Millennium Copyright Act

Another significant aspect of the protracted *Perfect 10* litigation must be noted. In addition to its defense of fair use, Google relied on the Digital Millennium Copyright Act of 1998, an important statute that shields Internet service providers (ISPs) from liability for providing access to copyrighted material, provided the ISP removes the access as soon as it is properly notified of a violation. The Court of Appeals remanded this aspect of the case to the U.S. District Court for the Central District of California. In *Perfect 10, Inc. v. Google, Inc.*, No. CV 04 9484 AHM (SHx), C.D. Cal (2010), the District Court largely granted Google's motion for summary judgment on the grounds that Perfect 10's several notices of infringement sent to Google lacked sufficient specificity for Google to act on them. Denying Perfect 10's request for a preliminary injunction, the judge remarked, "To refer Google to more than 15,000 images appearing on the entirety of P10's website falls far short of identifying what may have been infringed." The trial judge also held that Perfect 10 had failed to prove the "irreparable harm" required for an injunction. The appellate court affirmed, in *Perfect 10, Inc. v. Google, Inc.*, 653 F.3d 976 (9th Cir. 2011).

While we're looking at copyright violation takedown requests, we will note that in August 2012, Google announced that it would start tallying the numbers of takedown requests received by other websites and would push repeat offenders down on its search results page. Also, in October 2012, Google stated that the number of URLs requested to be removed from its own website was rising rapidly, approaching an astonishing two million per week (Google 2012). Google also keeps track of the numbers of takedown requests received by YouTube, which it owns. If your video is posted to You-Tube without your authorization, you may file a complaint at the YouTube Copyright Center (YouTube 2012).

In 2010 the U.S. District Court for the Southern District of New York granted summary judgment to YouTube in a massive pair of copyright law-suits brought by Viacom International, Paramount Pictures Corporation, Black Entertainment Television, Football Association Premier League Ltd., Fédération Française de Tennis, and a gaggle of TV producers and music publishers. They alleged copyright infringement based on YouTube's show-ing of approximately 79,000 audiovisual clips between 2005 and 2008. The court, applying the Digital Millennium Copyright Act, held that YouTube was not culpable because "when they received specific notice that a particular item infringed a copyright, they swiftly removed it" and the company was not aware of other alleged copyright violations. But in April 2012 the Second Circuit Court of Appeals, in *Viacom International Inc. v. YouTube, Inc.*, 676 F.3d 19 (2d. Cir. 2012), vacated the summary judgment and remanded the case for further consideration by the trial court "because a reasonable jury could find that YouTube had actual knowledge or awareness of specific infringing activity on its website."

Writing for the court, Judge José A. Cabranes cited internal e-mails that recognized potential copyright problems. In one e-mail he said

> Google-YouTube video coordinator Patrick Walker requested that any "clearly infringing, official broadcast footage" from a list of top Premier League clubs—including Liverpool Football Club, Chelsea Football Club, Manchester United Football Club, and Arsenal Football Club—be taken down in advance of a meeting with the heads of "several major sports teams and leagues." YouTube founder Jawed Karim prepared a report in March 2006 which stated that, "[a]s of today[,] episodes and clips of the following well-known shows can still be found [on YouTube]: Family Guy, South Park,

MTV Cribs, Daily Show, Reno 911, [and] Dave Chapelle [sic]." . . . A reasonable juror could conclude from the March 2006 report that Karim knew of the presence of Viacom-owned material on YouTube . . . Furthermore, in a July 4, 2005 e-mail exchange, YouTube founder Chad Hurley sent an e-mail to his co-founders with the subject line "budlight commercials," and stated, "we need to reject these too." . . . Similarly, the Bud Light and space shuttle e-mails refer to particular clips in the context of correspondence about whether to remove infringing material from the website (*Viacom International Inc. v. YouTube, Inc.*, 33).

Significantly, in its remand order the appellate court also directed the trial court to consider a common-law concept called "willful blindness," described as an awareness that a person is "consciously avoiding" confirmation that a disputed fact is true. Judge Cabranes wrote, "we hold that the willful blindness doctrine may be applied, in appropriate circumstances, to demonstrate knowledge or awareness of specific instances of infringement under the DMCA." Does "willful blindness" sound a lot like "reckless disregard" of the truth, one of the "actual malice" prongs defined by Justice William Brennan in *New York Times v. Sullivan*?

On Using Fair Use

The numerous and sometimes lengthy opinion quotations earlier in this chapter are useful to help understand just how subjective the defense of fair use may be. Yet this defense is the journalist's best refuge when confronted by a claim of copyright infringement. Use it when you need it, but first minimize your exposure. Do not "patch write" (changing just an occasional word in an attempt to avoid verbatim quotation); paraphrase when possible, and use limited direct quotes. Attribute direct quotes to the author and to the original work. Link to that original. Unless a photo or video is explicitly made available for public use or copying, assume that any picture you find on the Internet is copyrighted, which it is. Do not permit your readers to post comments on your website or blog without your screening them; their violations of copyright or other laws could be attributed to you.

Questions for Discussion

1. For a professional journalist, is copyright law more foe than friend? What about for a blogger?
2. Does *Harper & Row v. Nation* provide clear guidance? Why or why not?
3. What's the most critical of the four tests for fair use?

4. Can you formulate your own definition of when a work is "transformative"?
5. What's the difference between parody and satire? List some examples from your own reading.
6. As a blogger, how can you protect yourself against legal liability for violations of copyright or other laws posted by your "commenters"?

References

Campbell v. Acuff-Rose Music Inc., 510 U.S. 569 (1994). http://www.law.cornell.edu/supct/html/92-1292.ZS.html.

Copyright Act, 17 USCS § 101 et seq. http://www.copyright.gov/title17/92chap1.html.

Copyright Term Extension Act (CTEA) (1998), 17 USCS § 304. http://www.copyright.gov/title17/92chap3.html.

Digital Millennium Copyright Act (DMCA) (1998), 17 USCS § 512. http://www.copyright.gov/title17/92chap5.html.

Dr. Seuss Enterprises, L.P. v. Penguin Books USA, Inc. and Dove Audio, Inc., 109 F.3d 1394 (9th Cir. 1997). http://www.leagle.com/xmlResult.aspx?xmldoc=1997 1503109F3d1394_11287.xml&docbase=CSLWAR2-1986-2006.

Eldred v. Ashcroft, 537 U.S. 186 (2003). http://supreme.justia.com/cases/federal/us/537/186/case.html.

Golan v. Holder, 132 S.Ct. 873 (2012). http://www.supremecourt.gov/opinions/11pdf/10-545.pdf.

Google, 2012. "Google Transparency Report: Removal Requests," http://www.google.com/transparencyreport/removals/copyright/ (accessed October 17, 2012).

Harper & Row, Publishers, Inc. v. Nation Enterprises, 471 U.S. 539 (1985). http://www.law.cornell.edu/copyright/cases/471_US_539.htm.

Perfect 10, Inc. v. Google, Inc., 508 F.3d 1146 (9th Cir. 2007). http://cyber.law.harvard.edu/people/tfisher/IP/2007%20Perfect%2010%20Abridged.pdf.

———. No. CV 04 9484 AHM (SHx) (C.D.Cal. 2010). http://www.iplitigationupdate.com/files/Uploads/Documents/Perfect%2010%20v%20Google.pdf.

———. 653 F.3d 976 (9th Cir. 2011). http://scholar.google.com/scholar_case?case=1 2081607724090797593&hl=en&as_sdt=2&as_vis=1&oi=scholarr.

———. 132 S.Ct. 1713 (2012). http://scholar.google.com/scholar_case?case=43821 14864426774450&hl=en&as_sdt=2&as_vis=1&oi=scholarr.

Salinger v. Colting, 641 F. Supp.2d 250 (S.D.N.Y. 2009). http://scholar.google.com/scholar_case?case=8887709316369349826&hl=en&as_sdt=2&as_vis=1&oi=scholarr.

Suntrust Bank as Trustee of the Mitchell Trusts v. Houghton Mifflin Company, 268 F.3d 1257 (11th Cir. 2001). http://www.yale.edu/lawweb/jbalkin/telecom/suntrustbank(appeal).pdf.

Viacom International Inc. v. YouTube, Inc., 676 F.3d 19 (2d. Cir. 2012). http://caselaw.findlaw.com/us-2nd-circuit/1597925.html.

YouTube, 2012. "Copyright on YouTube," http://www.youtube.com/yt/copyright/ (accessed April 6, 2013).

10

Access to Government Documents and Meetings

"A popular Government, without popular information, or the means of acquiring it, is but a Prologue to a Farce or a Tragedy; or, perhaps both. Knowledge will forever govern ignorance: And a people who mean to be their own Governors, must arm themselves with the power which knowledge gives."

—James Madison

As we have observed before, the United States, in both law and tradition, is hospitable to journalism. One strong indication is that the federal government and all states have freedom of information acts and open meetings acts. Freedom of information acts grant all citizens—not just journalists—access to many government files and documents, on request. Open meetings acts ensure that all meetings of public bodies, down to the town council and its committees, are both publicized and public. Most state open-meetings laws (but not the federal) have real teeth: a meeting not properly publicized in advance, or not open to the media and public, is not valid, so any actions taken there, such as votes on proposed legislation, can be nullified.

Federal Freedom of Information Act (FOIA) of 1966

The federal Freedom of Information Act (5 USCS § 552), was enacted in 1966 and amended in 1996 to require the use of electronic records on a national scale. The FOIA is intended to facilitate public and media access to government documents, though in recent years, at least partly because of some restrictive Supreme Court decisions, the government's rate of denial of document requests has risen.

The FOIA applies to all agencies in the executive branch of the federal government, including the Executive Office of the President, and all independent regulatory agencies, such as the Federal Communications Commission (FCC) and the Food and Drug Administration (FDA). However, Congress and the courts are excluded. The law applies to paper and electronic records maintained by each agency and by any outside records-management contractor. A person who seeks a record or document must submit a request in writing, in accordance with rules published by each agency, describing the document with reasonable specificity. The agency then has twenty working days to respond, or to request an extension, which is common. But there are exemptions, which we will deal with in a moment, under which an agency may deny a request. If that happens to you, you have the right to appeal to a review officer within the agency, and ultimately to the federal courts.

The exemptions, nine in number, have given rise to many court challenges and a number of Supreme Court decisions. These are the exemptions, stipulating the kinds of documents that the government may rightfully withhold:

1. National defense or foreign policy documents "specifically authorized under criteria established by an Executive order to be kept secret"
2. Documents "related solely to the internal personnel rules and practices of an agency"
3. Documents "specifically exempted from disclosure by statute," such as Central Intelligence Agency files, school records, and driver's license information
4. "Trade secrets and commercial or financial information" obtained by the government from a person or company on a confidential basis
5. "Inter-agency or intra-agency memorandums or letters" not available by law except to a party in litigation against the agency
6. "Personnel and medical files and similar files" whose disclosure "would constitute a clearly unwarranted invasion of personal privacy"
7. "Records or information compiled for law enforcement purposes" if disclosure would
   a. interfere with enforcement
   b. deprive a person of a fair trial
   c. constitute an unwarranted invasion of personal privacy
   d. disclose the identity of a confidential source
   e. disclose "techniques and procedures for law enforcement investigations or prosecutions"
   f. endanger someone's life or safety
8. Financial institutions' data gathered by government regulators
9. Oil and gas well information and data

The FOIA also provides that an agency, "to prevent a clearly unwarranted invasion of personal privacy . . . may delete identifying details when it makes available or publishes an opinion, statement of policy, interpretation, staff manual, instruction" or other records. Such deletions are commonly referred to as "redactions."

Let's look at several Supreme Court decisions interpreting the FOIA, both to see how the courts analyze FOIA questions as well as to learn what rules have been laid down.

"Agency records"

Columnist William Safire of the *New York Times,* the Reporters Committee for Freedom of the Press, and several other individual journalists and academic organizations wanted to obtain copies of summaries and transcripts of phone conversations by Henry Kissinger, President Richard Nixon's national security adviser on the White House staff, and later secretary of state. Kissinger was a formidable figure in the Nixon administration. He famously spearheaded the president's audacious opening of long-moribund relations with China, or Communist China as it was then called, by unexpectedly notifying reporters accompanying him on a visit to East Asia that he was ill and incommunicado, using that excuse to hide a covert, quick, and very successful trip to Beijing that laid the groundwork for a subsequent, historic visit there by Nixon himself.

In 1976 Safire requested the State Department to provide, according to the Supreme Court's opinion in *Kissinger v. Reporters Committee for Freedom of the Press*, 445 U.S. 136 (1980), "any transcripts of Kissinger's telephone conversations between January 21, 1969, and February 12, 1971, in which (1) Safire's name appeared or (2) Kissinger discussed the subject of information 'leaks' with certain named White House officials" including President Nixon, or Federal Bureau of Investigation Director J. Edgar Hoover. During that two-year period Kissinger was still at the White House, so the State Department turned down the request, saying the transcripts, though then housed at the State Department, were not "agency records subject to FOIA disclosure." Ironically, although the Supreme Court didn't mention it, Safire, too, was on the White House staff during that time, as a presidential speech writer. So in effect he was looking in on his own colleague. Safire appealed the refusal, but the U.S. Court of Appeals for the District of Columbia affirmed it, ruling that the FOIA did not apply to close presidential advisers. At the same time, though, the appellate court granted a request from the Reporters Committee for Freedom of the Press for Kissinger's State Department phone records.

The Supreme Court, reviewing both rulings, noted that the FOIA authorizes court intervention only in the event of "agency records improperly withheld." In a 5–2 decision, the Court stated it didn't need to decide, in regards to the Reporters Committee request, whether the White House phone records were "agency records" or whether they were "wrongfully removed," but it assumed, for the sake of argument, that they were, focusing then on the word "withheld."

The majority opinion by Justice William Rehnquist noted that under federal law records may not be removed from an agency without the permission of the Archivist of the United States, the overseer of the National Archives, and the remedy for recovery is a suit by the U.S. attorney general. In this case, the archivist had asked Kissinger to return the phone records, but Kissinger did not comply and the attorney general did not file suit against him. Rehnquist wrote, "Congress did not mean that an agency improperly withholds a document which has been removed from the possession of the agency prior to the filing of the FOIA request. In such a case, the agency has neither the custody nor control necessary to enable it to withhold." Furthermore, "An agency's failure to sue a third party to obtain possession is not a withholding under the Act." So the Court rejected the Reporters Committee request.

Regarding Safire's request, the Supreme Court, as courts often do in determining the meaning of a statute, turned to the "legislative history," meaning the congressional process of enacting the law. Among the principal sources of legislative history in the federal government are reports published by each congressional committee explaining in considerable detail each bill approved by the committee and thus recommended for passage. In this case the Supreme Court looked at the report of the joint House-Senate committee that resolved differences between versions of the bill passed by the House of Representatives and the Senate when they amended the FOIA in 1974. Noting that the FOIA explicitly *includes* the Executive Office of the President, Rehnquist wrote,

> The legislative history is unambiguous, however, in explaining that the "Executive Office" does not include the Office of the President. The Conference Report for the 1974 FOIA Amendments indicates that "the President's immediate personal staff or units in the Executive Office whose sole function is to advise and assist the President" are not included within the term "agency" under the FOIA. . . .
> Safire's request was limited to a period of time in which Kissinger was serving as Assistant to the President. Thus these telephone notes were not "agency records" when they were made. (*Kissinger v. Reporters Committee for Freedom of the Press*, 156)

In other words, the FOIA simply did not apply. The documents sought must be "agency records."

Exemptions from the FOIA

Now let's look at some cases dealing with the scope of specific exemptions from the FOIA.

One famous case hit the headlines some years ago. Air Force Academy officers uncovered an extensive, well-organized cheating ring and expelled 109 cadets for violating the Academy's ethics code. Subsequently, student editors and former editors of the *New York University Law Review*, researching an article on disciplinary systems and procedures at the three U.S. military academies, requested summaries of honor and ethics hearings at the Air Force Academy, with names and other identifying information deleted. Ironically, the student editor leading the research was First Lieutenant Michael Rose, a graduate of the Air Force Academy. The Academy rejected the law students' request. Pursuing the matter in a FOIA suit in the U.S. District Court for the Southern District of New York, in Manhattan, they were again rebuffed, the judge citing Exemption 2, which exempts internal personnel rules and practices, although the court ruled that Exemption 6, which excludes personnel and medical files "and similar files," did not apply. The Second Circuit Court of Appeals reversed as to Exemption 2, finding it inapplicable, and rejected Exemption 6 as well. It ordered the Academy to submit the requested documents to the trial judge for a confidential *in camera* inspection and redaction (blacking out) of personal information before the files would be released.

The case moved on to the Supreme Court. In *Department of the Air Force v. Rose*, 425 U.S. 352 (1976), a Court divided, 5–3, affirmed the Circuit Court's ruling. Justice William Brennan wrote for the majority:

> [W]e think that, at least where the situation is not one where disclosure may risk circumvention of agency regulation, Exemption 2 is not applicable to matters subject to such a genuine and significant public interest. . . . The case summaries . . . are not matter with merely internal significance. They do not concern only routine matters. . . . [As to Exemption 6] the case summaries name no names except in guilty cases, are widely disseminated for examination by fellow cadets, contain no facts except such as pertain to the alleged violation of the Honor or Ethics Codes, and are justified by the Academy solely for their value as an educational and instructional tool the better to train military officers for discharge of their important and exacting functions. Documents treated by the Agency in such a manner cannot reasonably be claimed to be within the common and congressional meaning of what constitutes a "personnel file" under Exemption 6. (*Department of the Air Force v. Rose,* 369–70, 377)

In fact, Exemption 6, raising questions of personal privacy, has received repeated attention from the Supreme Court.

In *Department of State v. Washington Post Co.*, 456 U.S. 595 (1982), the Court upheld the application of Exemption 6 against a request by the *Washington Post* to obtain "documents indicating whether Dr. Ali Behzadnia and Dr. Ibrahim Yazdi . . . hold valid U.S. passports." The two men were Iranian nationals then living in Iran. In a unanimous opinion, the Court held that the kind of personal information in a passport file satisfied the "similar files" of Exemption 6. However, the opinion went on, the lower courts had failed to consider "the effect of disclosure upon the privacy interests of Behzadnia and Yazdi, and we think that such balancing should be left to the Court of Appeals or to the District Court on remand."

The Supreme Court again agreed with the State Department's assertion of Exemption 6 in *Department of State v. Ray*, 502 U.S. 164 (1991). A Florida lawyer, Michael D. Ray, who represented Haitian nationals seeking asylum in the United States, requested the names of Haitians who had entered the U.S. illegally and were returned to Haiti, but the State Department redacted them from the records of confidential hearings it had delivered to him. The department believed that disclosing their names would identify them as having cooperated with the department's investigation of the autocratic Haitian government and might subject them to persecution. Citing *Rose,* Justice John Paul Stevens wrote for the Court that disclosure of the names would "constitute a clearly unwarranted invasion of the interviewees' privacy."

Exemption 7

However, when a corporation attempted to claim "personal privacy," the Supreme Court balked. The issue was Exemption 7, which exempts law enforcement records on no fewer than six different grounds, one of which, Exemption 7(C), guards against "unwarranted invasion of personal privacy." As related by Chief Justice John Roberts in *Federal Communications Commission v. AT&T, Inc.,* 131 S.Ct. 1177 (2011), "CompTel, a trade association, submitted a FOIA request for documents AT&T had provided to the Federal Communications Commission Enforcement Bureau during an investigation of that company. The Bureau found that Exemption 7(C) applied to individuals identified in AT&T's submissions but not to the company itself, concluding that corporations do not have 'personal privacy' interests as required by the exemption." The Court agreed, unanimously. Roberts continued: "We reject the argument that because 'person' is defined for purposes of FOIA to include a corporation, the phrase 'personal privacy' in Exemption 7(C) reaches corporations as well. The protection in FOIA against disclosure of law enforcement information on the ground that it would constitute an unwarranted invasion of personal privacy does not extend to corporations. We trust that AT&T will not take it personally."

The Supreme Court was more receptive to two other claims under Exemption 7(C). In *Department of Justice v. Reporters Committee for Freedom of the Press*, 489 U.S. 749 (1989), the Court recognized a personal privacy exemption for the criminal record, or rap sheet, of a member of a family company that allegedly had obtained defense contracts through a corrupt member of Congress. Justice John Paul Stevens wrote for a unanimous court that the FOIA was intended to permit public inspection of government functions: "Official information that sheds light on an agency's performance of its statutory duties falls squarely within that statutory purpose. That purpose, however, is not fostered by disclosure of information about private citizens that is accumulated in various governmental files but that reveals little or nothing about an agency's own conduct." The Court reversed the ruling of an appellate court.

In 1993 Vincent Foster, Jr., an old friend and top legal aide of President Bill Clinton's, was found dead in a park outside Washington of a gunshot wound to the head. A pistol was in his hand, and fragments of a torn-up, disconsolate letter of resignation in his briefcase. He left a wife and three children. His death stunned the president and the nation. Five separate government investigations concluded that Foster had taken his own life. But a lawyer named Allan Favish, deeming the investigations "grossly incomplete and untrustworthy," filed multiple FOIA requests for photographs of Foster's body taken at the scene by the U.S. Park Police. There was little disagreement that the photos constituted law enforcement records, but Foster's family opposed the requests under Exemption 7(C) on the grounds that disclosure "would set off another round of intense scrutiny by the media." Favish argued, however, that 7(C) protected only the privacy of the person whose pictures he sought, namely Foster himself, not his family.

In a unanimous opinion curiously short on precedents but long on compassion, the Supreme Court ruled against Favish. In *National Archives and Records Administration v. Favish*, 541 U.S. 157 (2004), Justice Anthony Kennedy evoked common practices when he stated:

> We have little difficulty, however, in finding in our case law and traditions the right of family members to direct and control disposition of the body of the deceased and to limit attempts to exploit pictures of the deceased family member's remains for public purposes. Burial rites or their counterparts have been respected in almost all civilizations from time immemorial. . . . In addition this well-established cultural tradition acknowledging a family's control over the body and death images of the deceased has long been recognized at common law. . . .

We are advised by the Government that child molesters, rapists, murderers, and other violent criminals often make FOIA requests for autopsies, photographs, and records of their deceased victims. Our holding ensures that the privacy interests of surviving family members would allow the Government to deny these gruesome requests in appropriate cases. We find it inconceivable that Congress could have intended a definition of "personal privacy" so narrow that it would allow convicted felons to obtain these materials without limitations at the expense of surviving family members' personal privacy. . . . [W]e hold that FOIA recognizes surviving family members' right to personal privacy with respect to their close relative's death-scene images. (*National Archives and Records Administration v. Favish*, 170)

The case of *Department of Justice v. Landano*, 508 U.S. 165 (1993) addressed another law enforcement exemption, 7(D), which covers documents that "could reasonably be expected to disclose the identity of a confidential source. . . ." Vincent Landano was convicted in a New Jersey court of murdering a Newark policeman in the course of a robbery. Landano contended that he did not participate in the robbery and that the killer was one Victor Forni, who had orchestrated the robbery. He asserted that the prosecutors had withheld evidence that might have exonerated him, in violation of a Supreme Court mandate. The Department of Justice claimed Exemption 7(D) on the grounds that all sources providing information to the Federal Bureau of Investigation in a criminal investigation should be presumed confidential. But the U.S. Circuit Court of Appeals for the Third Circuit, based in Philadelphia, rejected that blanket approach. It ruled that the government, to qualify for the exemption, had to provide "detailed explanations relating to each alleged confidential source," a ruling at variance with that of other circuit courts, so the Supreme Court, following its usual practice, granted a *writ of certiorari* to resolve the conflict among circuits. The Supreme Court took a middle ground, rejecting a need for "detailed explanations" but requiring some specific information about the case. Justice Sandra Day O'Connor wrote for a unanimous Court:

[W]e hold that the Government is not entitled to a presumption that a source is confidential within the meaning of Exemption 7(D) whenever the source provides information to the FBI in the course of a criminal investigation. More narrowly defined circumstances, however, can provide a basis for inferring confidentiality. For example, when circumstances such as the nature of the crime investigated and the witness' relation to it support an inference of confidentiality, the Government is entitled to a presumption. (*Department of Justice v. Landano*, 181)

Exemption 5

Exemption 5 was the issue at hand in *Department of the Interior v. Klamath Water Users Protective Association*, 532 U.S. 1 (2001), dealing with inter-agency or intra-agency memorandums or letters. The case put the Department of the Interior on the horns of a dilemma. On the one hand, the Department's Bureau of Indian Affairs, which administers lands and waters held in trust by the government for Indian tribes, filed claims on behalf of the Klamath Tribe in an Oregon court proceeding intended to allocate water rights to various users in the Klamath River Basin. At the same time the department's Bureau of Reclamation, as administrator of the Klamath Irrigation Project in Oregon and northern California, was responsible for allocation of water to various users in that basin. In that connection the Department consulted with the Klamath and other tribes seeking allocations.

The Klamath Water Users Protective Association, a nonprofit representing Klamath basin water users in competition with the tribes for water, filed a FOIA request to obtain copies of communications between the Bureau of Reclamation and the Indian tribes. The Bureau provided some documents but withheld others, invoking the attorney-client privilege and describing them as part of a deliberative process, thus allegedly protected by Exemption 5 as inter-agency or intra-agency communications. It likened the relationship between the Department and the Klamath Tribe to that of a consultant and its client, a relationship previously recognized by courts as falling under the intra-agency exception. But a unanimous Supreme Court, in an opinion by Justice David Souter, rejected the Department's representation of a client-consultant relationship:

> Since there is not enough water to satisfy everyone, the Government's position on behalf of the Tribe [in the Oregon litigation] is potentially adverse to other users, and it might ask for more or less on behalf of the Tribe depending on how it evaluated the tribal claim compared with the claims of its rivals. The ultimately adversarial character of tribal submissions to the Bureau therefore seems the only fair inference, as confirmed by the Department's acknowledgement that its "obligation to represent the Klamath Tribe necessarily coexists with the duty to protect other federal interests, including in particular its interests with respect to the Klamath Project." . . . The position of the Tribe as beneficiary is thus a far cry from the position of the paid consultant. (*Department of the Interior v. Klamath Water Users Protective Association*, 14–15)

In a final footnote Justice Souter added coyly: "nobody in the Federal Government should be surprised by this reading."

Exemption 2, Again

FOIA Exemption 2, as noted above, protects from disclosure material that is "related solely to the internal personnel rules and practices of an agency." The U.S. Navy stored weapons, ammunition and explosives at Naval Magazine Indian Island, a base on Puget Sound, near Seattle. According to the Supreme Court's opinion in *Milner v. Department of the Navy*, 131 S.Ct. 1259 (2011), Navy data "known as Explosive Safety Quantity Distance (ESQD) information . . . prescribes 'minimum separation distances' for explosives and helps the Navy design and construct storage facilities to prevent chain reactions in case of detonation. The ESQD calculations are often incorporated into specialized maps depicting the effects of hypothetical explosions."

So it was no surprise that at least one nearby resident, a man named Glen Milner, became curious about the explosives in his neighborhood and filed a FOIA request for ESQD information relating to Indian Island. The Navy turned him down, invoking Exemption 2. Justice Elena Kagan, writing for the Court in an 8–1 decision, remonstrated with the Navy:

> [A]ll the rules and practices referenced in Exemption 2 share a critical feature: They concern the conditions of employment in federal agencies— such matters as hiring and firing, work rules and discipline, compensation and benefits. . . . These data and maps calculate and visually portray the magnitude of hypothetical detonations. By no stretch of imagination do they relate to "personnel rules and practices," as that term is most naturally understood. They concern the physical rules governing explosives, not the workplace rules governing sailors. . . . (*Milner v. Department of the Navy*, 1265, 1266)

Helpfully, however, Justice Kagan went on to suggest that the Navy might utilize Exemption 1 (national security), or Exemption 3 (information kept secret under other statutes; she noted that this would require an act of Congress), or Exemption 7(F) (law enforcement records that might endanger someone's life or safety). Rarely does the Court advise so explicitly how to get around its own ruling.

How to File a Request

When the opportunity arises for you to file your own request for government documents, either under the federal FOIA or a similar state statute, you probably will find ample advice about how to do it on the website of the agency that has the documents. If not, ask the public information office about the proper procedure. For a federal filing, a good place to start is the website of the First Amendment Center: http://www.firstamendmentcenter.org/how-to-file-an-foia-request (Holliday 2004). The Reporters Committee for Freedom of the Press publishes a very helpful *Federal Open Government Guide,* available online for five dollars at http://www.rcfp.org/publications-order-form (Reporters Committee for Freedom of the Press 2012).

Open Meetings

As stated above, the federal government and all states have statutes requiring that meetings of government bodies be publicized in advance and open to the press and public. The federal Open Meetings Act (5 USCS § 552b) applies only to meetings of agencies whose members are appointed by the president, i.e., regulatory agencies such as the Federal Communications Commission and the Securities and Exchange Commission, and to meetings of federal advisory committees. State statutes, by contrast, are tougher and much more comprehensive in their reach.

Example: Illinois Statute

For instance, the Illinois Open Meetings Act (5 ILCS 120), declares that "It is the intent of this Act to protect the citizen's right to know," and covers "all legislative, executive, administrative or advisory bodies of the State, counties, townships, cities, villages, incorporated towns, school districts and all other municipal corporations, boards, bureaus, committees or commissions of this State, and any subsidiary bodies of any of the foregoing including but not limited to committees and subcommittees which are supported in whole or in part by tax revenue, or which expend tax revenue . . . ," although not the legislature. The statute applies to any discussion of public business by a majority of a quorum (i.e., more than half of a quorum, which ordinarily is equivalent to a majority of such a public body; so, in effect, more than a quarter of its members), whether it be in person, by video or telephone conference, by e-mail or Internet chat, or in any other way.

However, there are a number of specific exceptions in the Illinois statute where private meetings are allowed: meetings dealing with the hiring or dismissal of personnel; collective bargaining with union representatives; the purchase, lease, or sale of real estate; investments; financial audits; litigation; professional ethics; highly personal matters such as school disciplinary actions and prisoner reviews; and several other very narrow exceptions. But no final action may be taken at a closed meeting, meaning the actual vote must be taken subsequently in public.

Furthermore, the Illinois statute requires that each public body must give notice, including a posting on the body's website, at the beginning of each year, of the regular schedule of meetings for the year ahead, stipulating the date, time, and place. The agenda of each meeting must be announced publicly at least forty-eight hours before the meeting. Special meetings also require a forty-eight-hour public notice. Anyone may record the proceedings of any meeting. Minutes of each meeting must be approved by the members within thirty days and then be made available to the public within the next ten days. If a public body holds an illegal private meeting and purports to take official action, a citizen may bring a lawsuit to nullify that action, and the courts may issue such an order. This potent antidote is prescribed in other states, too. No such teeth exist in the federal open-meetings law.

Reporters under Siege

Although open-meetings laws are straightforward, requiring little judicial interpretation, one hard-fought dispute between a determined reporter and an obdurate village government rose as high as a federal appellate court. Noreen McBride covered the Village of Michiana, Michigan, for the *New Buffalo Times* and radio station WEFM. Some of her stories, as the opinion of the Sixth Circuit of Appeals later stated in *McBride v. Village of Michiana*, 100 F.3d 457 (6th Cir. 1996), "discussed the mishandling of public funds, violations of the Michigan Open Meetings Act, and efforts by village officials to encourage non-residents to vote in village elections."

Village officials tried to have McBride fired, or at least taken off the beat. When that failed, they tried to frustrate her coverage in ways that became almost ludicrous. They openly castigated her at a village council meeting. They ordered her out of a public meeting; she refused. They threatened to delay the start of the meeting until she left, and threatened to bodily remove her; she held her ground. Before the next meeting they removed the press table. They blocked her access to village employees and public records; they may have destroyed some records she wanted. And, McBride reported, the city building inspector threw a chair at her during a meeting. Whew! It is important to emphasize here that McBride confidently stood her ground; she refused to accede to actions she considered illegal. She set a good example for the profession. Like McBride, any reporter excluded from a public meeting should protest on the spot, at least orally, and promptly mount a legal challenge.

When the Michiana officials did not relent, McBride filed suit in federal court, claiming intimidation, a conspiracy to retaliate against her, and violation of her rights under the First Amendment and the Michigan Freedom of Information Act and Open Meetings Act. She testified that one village official said "she was from the south side of Chicago" and "'Don't mess with me, I will get you.'" Not to be outdone, the village officials retorted that their statements and actions were protected by that very same First Amendment, and they claimed immunity from prosecution for their actions as public officials. The U.S. District Court for the Western District of Michigan denied their immunity claim, and they appealed. The Sixth Circuit Court of Appeals, unable to find any precedents involving such bizarre hostility to the press, nevertheless had no trouble upholding McBride's rights. Responding to the village officials' assertion that "there was no clearly established law that their alleged actions were violative of the Plaintiff's constitutional rights," the court declared:

> Simply because no government official has heretofore deemed it acceptable to retaliate against and threaten a reporter for relating the activities of a local governmental body does not mean that the right of a member of the press to be free from such retaliation has not been "clearly established." Both the Supreme Court and this court have, in fact, consistently recognized that "retaliation by public officials against the exercise of First Amendment rights is itself a violation of the First Amendment." . . . Although no Supreme Court or Sixth Circuit decisions had, at that time, applied time-honored First Amendment principles to a situation *specifically* involving governmental retaliation against a news reporter, relevant pre-existing case law made the illegality of such retaliation apparent. . . . [A] reasonable governmental official committing those acts during the time period relevant to this litigation, would have understood that what was being done violated McBride's First Amendment rights. (*McBride v. Village of Michiana*, 460–61)

However, the appellate court added, its ruling did not impair the village officials' own right of free speech under the First Amendment. The court remanded the case to the trial court for further consideration of McBride's claims.

The finish was anticlimactic and disappointing, for McBride and for journalism generally. Acknowledging the First Amendment rights on both sides, the District Court in *McBride v. Village of Michiana*, 1998 WL 276139 (W.D. Mich. 1998) granted the village officials' motion for summary judgment against most of McBride's claims of intimidation and conspiracy to retaliate. Proven retaliation, of course, would have been unconstitutional, but the court faulted McBride for failing to offer sufficient evidence to support that claim. However, the court kept alive her claims under the state open-meetings and freedom of information statutes. There is no further legal record of this long and bitter wrangle, suggesting that the parties settled the remaining issues out of court. But the opportunity for a clear judicial declaration of journalists' rights was lost.

A similar dispute arose later in Kentucky, which also is within the Sixth Circuit, so the *McBride* case was cited as a precedent. Although the Kentucky case did not involve an open-meetings statute, it is worth noting here because retaliation again was alleged. Jim Strader, host of a long-running weekly radio program on hunting and fishing, persistently criticized the state's Department of Fish and Wildlife Resources for accepting hunters' phone reports of their kills, alleging that they were unreliable and facilitated poaching and over-harvesting. After warning Strader to back off, the department created its own hunting and fishing radio show in the same time slot as Strader's. He sued in federal court, alleging, among other things, a violation of his First Amendment rights by virtue of the department's retaliatory broadcast. But he lost because, like Noreen McBride, he failed to present sufficient evidence to back up his claim. In *Strader v. Kentucky Department of Fish and Wildlife Resources*, Civil Action No. 3:09–62-DCR (E.D. Ky. 2012), the district court granted summary judgment to the department, pointing out that "Strader admitted at his deposition that his show remains ranked number one in its time slot for the Louisville market and that *Kentucky Afield Radio* [the department's broadcast] has not hurt his listenership, ratings, or advertising sales. . . . Without evidence of injury, Strader's remaining retaliation claim cannot survive summary judgment."

What are we to make of these two peculiar cases, both involving angry government responses to critical but apparently honest, factual stories? The stories were not controverted. The press is supposed to criticize when it is warranted. Still, uncommon as they are, these cases should be heeded as requiring more than inconvenience or embarrassment in order to prevail on a press-obstruction claim against a government. The First Amendment and press-supportive statutes require facts, evidence, and proof of violation. A reporter sensing abridgment should retain notes and tapes, immediately make a record of what has happened, and proceed to quantify any real damage or loss that results.

Access to Prisons

Do the news media have a constitutional right of access to prisons? On three separate occasions the Supreme Court has said no. The third case, *Houchins v. KQED*, 438 U.S. 1 (1978), arose because the Ninth Circuit Court of Appeals "conceived" such a right, as the Supreme Court opinion put it, in the face of the Supreme Court's two previous denials of its existence.

KQED, in San Francisco, reported the suicide of an inmate in the Alameda

County Jail at Santa Rita. The story quoted a psychiatrist that conditions in the jail were responsible for illnesses of his patient-prisoners there, and also quoted a denial by the county sheriff. KQED then requested permission from the sheriff to visit the jail and take pictures. He refused. The station, joined by the Alameda and Oakland branches of the National Association for the Advancement of Colored People, filed suit against him under a federal civil rights statute, alleging a violation of the First Amendment. They contended the public was entitled to know the conditions at the jail. Both the District Court and the Circuit Court of Appeals agreed. But an exasperated Chief Justice Warren Burger, commanding only three other votes in a 4–3 decision, with two justices not participating, declared:

> The media are not a substitute for or an adjunct of government and, like the courts, they are "ill equipped" to deal with problems of prison administration. . . . We must not confuse the role of the media with that of government; each has special, crucial functions, each complementing—and sometimes conflicting with—the other. The public importance of conditions in penal facilities and the media's role of providing information afford no basis for reading into the Constitution a right of the public or the media to enter these institutions, with camera equipment, and take moving and still pictures of inmates for broadcast purposes. This Court has never intimated a First Amendment guarantee of a right of access to all sources of information within government control. (*Houchins v. KQED*, 8–9)

Why, you may wonder, if the two Supreme Court precedents were so clearly controlling in Chief Justice Burger's mind, would three justices dissent? Justice John Paul Stevens, writing for himself and Justices William Brennan and Lewis Powell, insisted that the issue in *Houchins v. KQED* was not press access but *public* access. Stevens said that because of the nature of the jail's population the public was entitled to know that the inmates' rights were properly protected:

> Some inmates—in Santa Rita, a substantial number—are pretrial detainees. Though confined pending trial, they have not been convicted of an offense against society and are entitled to the presumption of innocence. Certain penological objectives, *i.e.*, punishment, deterrence, and rehabilitation, which are legitimate in regard to convicted prisoners, are inapplicable to pretrial detainees. Society has a special interest in ensuring that unconvicted citizens are treated in accord with their status. . . . An official prison policy of concealing such knowledge from the public by arbitrarily cutting off the flow of information at its source abridges the freedom of speech and of the

press protected by the First and Fourteenth Amendments to the Constitution. (*Houchins v. KQED*, 37–38)

Despite this prison barrier, by and large both federal and state laws support media access to the workings of government.

Questions for Discussion

1. How has your state supreme court and your U.S. Circuit Court of Appeals ruled on freedom of information requests?
2. When writing a FOIA request, is it advisable to state your needs generally or specifically?
3. In framing a FOIA request, how could you strive to avoid being rejected under one of the stated exemptions?
4. On your first job, would it be better to ask an experienced reporter about how to interpret (and if necessary, pursue) the local open-meetings law or to just read the statute yourself?
5. If you're barred from entering a city council committee meeting, what will you do?

References

Department of the Air Force v. Rose, 425 U.S. 352 (1976). http://supreme.justia.com/cases/federal/us/425/352/case.html.
Department of the Interior v. Klamath Water Users Protective Association, 532 U.S. 1 (2001). http://supreme.justia.com/cases/federal/us/532/1/case.html.
Department of Justice v. Landano, 508 U.S. 165 (1993). http://supreme.justia.com/cases/federal/us/508/165/case.html.
Department of Justice v. Reporters Committee for Freedom of the Press, 489 U.S.749 (1989). http://caselaw.lp.findlaw.com/scripts/getcase.pl?court=us&vol=489&invol=749.
Department of State v. Ray, 502 U.S. 164 (1991). http://supreme.justia.com/cases/federal/us/502/164/case.html.
Department of State v. Washington Post Co., 456 U.S. 595 (1982). http://supreme.justia.com/cases/federal/us/456/595/case.html.
Federal Communications Commission v. AT&T, Inc., 131 S.Ct. 1177 (2011). http://www.supremecourt.gov/opinions/10pdf/09-1279.pdf.
Freedom of Information Act, 5 USCS § 552 et seq. http://www.law.cornell.edu/uscode/text/5/552.
Holliday, Taylor, "How to File an FOIA request," *Freedom of Information Issues* (First Amendment Center), November 16, 2004. http://www.firstamendmentcenter.org/how-to-file-an-foia-request (accessed April 10, 2013).
Houchins v. KQED, 438 U.S. 1 (1978). http://caselaw.lp.findlaw.com/scripts/getcase.pl?navby=case&court=us&vol=438&invol=1.

Illinois Open Meetings Act, 5 ILCS 120. http://www.ilga.gov/legislation/ilcs/ilcs3. asp?ActID=84&ChapterID=2.

Kissinger v. Reporters Committee for Freedom of the Press, 445 U.S. 136 (1980). http:// caselaw.lp.findlaw.com/cgi-bin/getcase.pl?court=us&vol=445&invol=136.

McBride v. Village of Michiana, 100 F.3d 457 (6th Cir. 1996). http://caselaw.lp.findlaw. com/scripts/getcase.pl?navby=search&case=/data2/circs/6th/960361p.html.

———, 1998 WL 276139 (W.D. Mich. 1998). 1998 U.S. Dist. LEXIS 6082; 26 Media L. Rep. 1833.

Milner v. Department of the Navy, 131 S.Ct. 1259 (2011). http://www.supremecourt. gov/opinions/10pdf/09-1163.pdf.

National Archives and Records Administration v. Favish, 541 U.S. 157 (2004). http:// www.law.cornell.edu/supct/html/02-954.ZO.html.

Open Meetings Act, 5 USCS § 552b. http://www.law.cornell.edu/uscode/text/5/552b.

Reporters Committee for Freedom of the Press, "Order Form," (2012). http://www. rcfp.org/publications-order-form (accessed April 10, 2013).

Strader v. Kentucky Department of Fish and Wildlife Resources, Civil Action No. 3:09–62-DCR (E.D. Ky. 2012). http://www.mmlk.com/James-Strader-v-KY-Dept-of-Fish-Wildlife.pdf.

11

Broadcast Regulation

" . . . as public convenience, interest, or necessity requires. . . ."
—Communications Act of 1934

Congress passed the Communications Act of 1934 to create the Federal Communications Commission, comprising five members appointed by the president, and to empower it to regulate broadcast station ownership, technical requirements, and in limited ways the content of programming. Inasmuch as our principal interest is the commission's programming rules, we have no need to dwell on the technical requirements pertaining to antennas and frequencies and such, but we will review ownership rules because ownership inevitably impacts programming.

The underlying rationale for government regulation of broadcasting is that the electromagnetic spectrum is limited and therefore should be subject to control in the public interest. So a broadcaster must obtain a license from the FCC. Licenses are granted for a period of eight years and in recent years have been routinely renewed. A license authorizes a station to broadcast on a certain frequency at a certain maximum power. For instance, AM (amplitude modulation) radio stations operate on the frequencies of 540 to 1700 kilohertz, or kHz (one thousand cycles per second). Power is specified, to a maximum of fifty thousand watts for twenty-four-hour ("clear channel") stations, which at night can be heard across much of the country; daytime-only stations have lower wattage limits and thus more limited reach.

Like all federal regulatory agencies, the FCC governs by majority vote and is empowered by Congress to issue regulations for the industry it regulates. A regulatory agency typically fashions new rules by first publishing them as proposals in the Federal Register, then accepting public comments and sometimes holding public hearings on them, after which it finalizes the rules and promulgates them. Agency regulations have the force of law in the regulated industry and may be enforced by fines or other penalties. Rulings of the FCC, like those of other federal regulatory agencies, may be appealed directly to circuit courts of appeals.

Ownership Rules

FCC rules limiting station ownership are enormously important to media companies if not (except in rare instances) to the general public. There are two kinds. One set of rules establishes requirements for ownership of radio and television stations. Owners must be U.S. citizens or corporations and possess (or obtain) the necessary technical skills and financing to own and operate a station. Other rules set limits on how many stations one party, typically a media company, may own. From time to time the FCC, sometimes mandated by Congress, changes these limit rules, almost always acceding to media companies' desires to bring more stations under one ownership. The Telecommunications Act of 1996 eliminated previous FCC limits on the nationwide numbers of television stations and radio stations that could be owned by a single company, and it established new, higher limits on the number of radio stations owned by a single company in radio markets of various sizes. As of 2012, the limits are these: In a radio market with forty-five or more commercial radio stations, eight commercial stations can be owned by a single company; in a market with thirty to forty-four commercial radio stations, it can be seven commercial stations; and so on to smaller and smaller markets.

Turning to television, an amendment to the Telecommunications Act of 1996 specified that TV stations *owned* (not the network affiliates) by one company may reach no more than thirty-nine percent of the national television audience. By FCC rule, a company may own up to two TV stations and six radio stations, or one TV station and seven radio stations, in a market that, after any proposed merger or combination, still has at least twenty independently owned media "voices." Other limitations are specified for smaller markets. Also, single ownership of two TV stations is allowed only if at least one of the stations is not among the top four in the market and at least eight independently owned stations would remain after any proposed combination.

More important, or at least more controversial, is the issue of "cross ownership." Since 1975 the FCC has barred any company from owning both a TV station and a newspaper in the same market, with "grandfather" exceptions granted to a few such combinations that existed at that time, such as the ownership of the *Chicago Tribune* and stations WGN and WGN-TV by the same parent company. The purpose of this cross-ownership rule was to maintain a diversity of news sources and views in each market.

With the proliferation of news sources in recent years, however, the FCC proposed to repeal the cross-ownership ban, a revocation ardently sought by media conglomerates. But the repeal has been blocked for several years by a protracted lawsuit, *Prometheus Radio Project v. Federal Communications*

Commission. In its most recent ruling on this case (652 F.3d 431, 3d Cir. 2011), the Third Circuit Court of Appeals, while acknowledging the desirability of repealing the rule, sent the matter back to the FCC to allow more time for public comment. In the meantime, exercising a specific authority granted by Congress, the FCC granted waivers of its cross-ownership ban to Gannett Company, Inc.'s newspaper-broadcast combination in Phoenix and to four Media General Inc. combinations in Myrtle Beach-Florence, South Carolina; Columbus, Georgia; Panama City, Florida; and in the Tri-Cities area of Tennessee and Virginia. The cross-ownership rule remains a moving target.

Content Regulation

Of more concern to the working journalist, Congress and the Federal Communications Commission impose some restrictions on broadcast content. They fall mainly into three categories: rules against indecency, political advertising requirements, and standards for children's programming.

Indecency

Because the airwaves are public, Congress has charged the FCC with regulating obscene, indecent, or profane programming. Obscenity is not an issue. It's not protected by the First Amendment and may not be broadcast at any time. The Supreme Court, in *Miller v. California*, 413 U.S. 15 (1973), defined obscenity as material that "appeals to the prurient interest; . . . depict[s] or describe[s], in a patently offensive way, sexual conduct specifically defined by applicable law; and . . . lack[s] serious literary, artistic, political or scientific value."

So the FCC's focus is on indecency, which is less offensive than obscenity. The FCC defines broadcast indecency—which does enjoy First Amendment protection and thus may not be totally banned—as "language or material that, in context, depicts or describes, in terms patently offensive as measured by contemporary community standards for the broadcast medium, sexual or excretory organs or activities." Thus indecent programming contains patently offensive sexual or excretory material that does not rise to the level of obscenity. To shield children from such programming, the FCC, mandated by Congress, requires that indecency be confined to the hours of 10 P.M. to 6 A.M., on both television and radio. A similar restriction applies to profanity, which the FCC defines as "language so grossly offensive to members of the public who actually hear it as to amount to a nuisance." The Communications Act empowers the FCC to fine violators as much as $325,000 per violation or per day of a continuing violation up to three million dollars.

However, enforcement is proving problematical today, though it was not initially. In an almost legendary case, *Federal Communications Commission v. Pacifica Foundation*, 438 U.S. 726 (1978), the Supreme Court upheld an FCC determination of indecency by a New York radio station that had aired, in mid-day, a monologue by comedian George Carlin defiantly uttering, repeatedly, "seven dirty words" intended to mock the FCC's indecency standard. Justice John Paul Stevens, writing the majority opinion, declared that "the language employed is, to most people, vulgar and offensive. It was chosen specifically for this quality, and it was repeated over and over as a sort of verbal shock treatment. The Commission did not err in characterizing the narrow category of language used here as 'patently offensive' to most people regardless of age."

As Americans' language became coarser in recent years, some occasional "dirty words," particularly in live entertainment and sports television broadcasts, were tolerated by the FCC under a new, more flexible policy allowing "fleeting expletives" and presumably "fleeting nudity." But that policy became bogged down in a decade-long series of disputes over its application by the commission, when it held that several TV broadcasts went too far. It issued indecency rulings against all four broadcast television networks; three of them proceeded to the Supreme Court together.

The first was Fox Television Stations, Inc., which carried live broadcasts of the Billboard Music Awards in 2002 and 2003. Both shows produced unscripted remarks that the FCC found indecent. The singer Cher exclaimed in her acceptance speech, "I've also had my critics for the last 40 years saying that I was on my way out every year. Right. So f*** 'em." A year later an award presenter, Nicole Richie, blurted out, "Have you ever tried to get cow s*** out of a Prada purse? It's not so f***ing simple."

Also in 2003, ABC television's *NYPD Blue* showed a woman's nude buttocks for seven seconds and momentarily the side of her breast, and, in an NBC broadcast of the Golden Globes Awards the singer Bono, winning for Best Original Song, exulted immodestly, "This is really, really, f***ing brilliant." Although it found all the broadcasts indecent, the FCC fined only the forty-five ABC affiliates that had broadcast the *NYPD* show, apparently because it was scripted rather than live, $27,000 each or a total of $1.2 million.

All three networks challenged the FCC findings, taking their cases to the Second Circuit Court of Appeals, then to the Supreme Court, which remanded them to the appellate court for further consideration. This time the Second Circuit found the FCC's policy so vague that it violated the First Amendment, so it was the FCC's turn to seek Supreme Court review.

In the meantime another FCC indecency ruling was being challenged elsewhere. In CBS's broadcast of the 2004 Super Bowl, halftime entertainment produced by MTV ended with Justin Timberlake singing to Janet Jackson, "gonna have you naked by the end of this song," and simultaneously tearing away part of her bustier. Jackson's bare right breast was exposed for nine-sixteenths of one second. The Commission fined CBS $500,000. CBS's appeal bounced to the Third Circuit Court of Appeals, then to the Supreme Court, and back to the Third Circuit. In *CBS Corp. v. Federal Communications Commission*, 663 F.3d 122 (3d Cir. 2011), the appellate court reaffirmed its earlier ruling that the Commission had not given adequate notice that its policy on "fleeting" indecency could be interpreted to apply to images as well as words. The court held that "the FCC arbitrarily and capriciously departed from its prior policy excepting fleeting broadcast material from the scope of actionable indecency." It vacated the Commission's order against CBS.

A few months later the Supreme Court, reviewing the FCC's indecency rulings against Fox, ABC, and NBC, similarly faulted the Commission for not making its policy clear. In *Federal Communications Commission v. Fox Television Stations, Inc.* and *FCC v. ABC, Inc.*, 132 S.Ct. 2307 (2012), a unanimous Court sidestepped the constitutional issue addressed by the Second Circuit, ruling simply that the Commission had failed to give the networks sufficient notice that its policy on fleeting expletives and fleeting nudity could be thus interpreted. Justice Anthony Kennedy, writing for the Court, stated that "the Commission's standards as applied to these broadcasts were vague, and the Commission's orders must be set aside. . . . In light of the Court's holding that the Commission's policy failed to provide fair notice it is unnecessary to reconsider *Pacifica* at this time." Kennedy added: "this opinion leaves the Commission free to modify its current indecency policy in light of its determination of the public interest and applicable legal requirements. And it leaves the courts free to review the current policy or any modified policy in light of its content and application." To be continued. Stay tuned.

Federal communications statutes do not authorize the FCC to regulate cable, satellite, and pay-per-view television, so its indecency rules do not apply in those realms. Thus in recent years the words on George Carlin's list, and other edgy language, have become common in made-for-cable shows. The Telecommunications Act of 1996 required cable TV operators to scramble "sexually-oriented" channels between 6 A.M. and 10 P.M., primarily to shield them from children, but the Supreme Court held that the requirement violated the First Amendment. In *United States v. Playboy Entertainment Group, Inc.*, 529 U.S. 803 (2000) the Court ruled, though only by 5–4, that because cable companies are able to block entirely any channel designated by a subscriber, the scrambling requirement was unnecessary. Writing for the majority, Justice Anthony Kennedy stated:

The history of the law of free expression is one of vindication in cases involving speech that many citizens may find shabby, offensive, or even ugly. It follows that all content-based restrictions on speech must give us more than a moment's pause. If television broadcasts can expose children to the real risk of harmful exposure to indecent materials, even in their own home and without parental consent, there is a problem the Government can address. It must do so, however, in a way consistent with First Amendment principles. Here the Government has not met the burden the First Amendment imposes. (*United States v. Playboy Entertainment Group, Inc.* 826–27)

Political Advertising

Providing thoughtfully in the Communications Act for their own members' interests, Congress requires that broadcasters must provide equal advertising opportunities to candidates for the same public office, and that charges for commercial time, during the forty-five days prior to a primary election and the sixty days preceding a general election, must be the lowest charged by the station for other advertising in the same time slot. These requirements, the law stipulates, do not apply to "bona fide" news or interview broadcasts, including coverage of "political conventions and activities incidental thereto." Incidentally, it is this same section of the Communications Act that requires at the end of a TV campaign commercial "simultaneously, for a period no less than 4 seconds—(i) a clearly identifiable photographic or similar image of the candidate; and (ii) a clearly readable printed statement, identifying the candidate and stating that the candidate has approved the broadcast and that the candidate's authorized committee paid for the broadcast."

Children's Programming

Programming directed at children is limited in three respects:

1. The Children's Television Act of 1990 requires that "each commercial television broadcast licensee shall limit the duration of advertising in children's television programming to not more than 10.5 minutes per hour on weekends and not more than 12 minutes per hour on weekdays."
2. By rule the FCC requires that children's program advertising featuring a "program-related character" must be "sufficiently separated from the program itself to mitigate the impact of host selling."
3. Also by rule, the commission requires that each TV station must provide weekly at least three hours of programming "aired between 7:00 A.M. and 10:00 P.M., that has serving the educational and informational needs of children ages 16 and under as a significant purpose."

Cable and Internet Regulation

The communications statutes give the FCC only limited authority over cable television and the Internet, but journalists should be aware that their local community's cable franchise, which is the license to operate in a given area, is granted by the municipal government. The municipal council may—and customarily does—attach strings such as free provision of community access channels and coverage of local government meetings.

However, federal law does apply to certain aspects of cable operations. For instance, a Supreme Court decision authorizes a cable operator to reject indecent programming. Also, the Communications Act provides that cable operators desiring to carry local TV stations serving the same market must pay the broadcasters for their programming. On the other hand, if the cable operator is not interested in carrying a local broadcast signal but the broadcaster wants to be included, at the broadcaster's request the cable company must do so, though in that case no compensation is required. This is referred to as the "must-carry" rule. The advertising time limits of the Children's Television Act of 1990 also apply to cable TV. However, as noted above, the Supreme Court in *United States of America v. Playboy Entertainment Group, Inc.* declared unconstitutional a statutory requirement that cable operators scramble all "sexually-oriented" programming between 6 A.M. and 10 P.M.

While lacking clear legal authority to regulate broadband Internet service, the FCC boldly launched a bid to do so in 1998. Responding to complaints that Comcast Corp., the biggest provider of cable TV service, was favoring certain high-volume broadband customers to the disadvantage of others, the Commission ruled that Comcast had "significantly impeded consumers' ability to access the content and use the applications of their choice." It ordered the company to manage its network traffic without discriminating against peer-to-peer communications. Such a posture is often described as "network neutrality." To justify its action, the FCC claimed "ancillary authority" to act under broad policy statements found in the Communications Act of 1934 and the Telecommunications Act of 1996.

Not so fast, said the Circuit Court of Appeals for the District of Columbia in *Comcast Corp. v. Federal Communications Commission*, 600 F.3d 642 (D.C. Cir. 2010). It vacated the Commission's order on the grounds that it had no legal authority to take such an action. "Policy statements are just that—statements of policy. They are not delegations of regulatory authority," the court declared. It noted, with apparent satisfaction, that Comcast "defended its interference with peer-to-peer programs as necessary to manage scarce network capacity."

Undeterred, just a few months later a divided FCC restated its claim of legal authority over broadband service and announced rules to govern it that sounded much like net neutrality. The Commission's order, while encouraging informal settlement of any disputes under the new rules, reminded the industry that any enforcement actions could include assessment of forfeitures, or fines. Two of the five commissioners dissented. One of them, Robert M. McDowell, declared frankly that the FCC order "is designed to circumvent the D.C. Circuit's *Comcast* decision." He commented caustically: "I'm afraid that this leaky ship of an Order is attempting to sail through a regulatory fog without the necessary ballast of factual or legal substance. The courts will easily sink it."

This issue is worth watching, while bearing in mind that the FCC's recent rulings on major matters like cross-ownership and indecency, not to mention net neutrality itself, have taken a bad beating in the courts. On the other hand, it's important for broadcasters to recognize that the FCC's rules on political advertising and children's programming remain firmly in place.

Questions for Discussion

1. In what area is a TV journalist most likely to come up against FCC regulation?
2. Does the FCC have an impossible job trying to enforce indecency standards?
3. Should Congress reconsider its assignment of indecency policing to the FCC?
4. Why should a journalist care about the FCC's cross-ownership rule?
5. Is there any perceptible value or benefit in the FCC's relaxed limits on the numbers of stations owned by one company in a market?
6. What is the rationale behind the statutory limit of thirty-nine percent on the share of the national TV audience reached by stations *owned* by one company?

References

CBS Corp. v. Federal Communications Commission, 663 F.3d 122 (3d Cir. 2011). http://caselaw.findlaw.com/us-3rd-circuit/1584404.html.

Children's Television Act of 1990, 47 USCS § 303a. http://www.law.cornell.edu/uscode/text/47/303a.

Comcast Corp. v. FCC, 600 F.3d 642 (D.C. Cir. 2010). https://www.eff.org/files/Comcast%20v%20FCC%20(DC%20Cir%202010).pdf.

Communications Act, 47 USCS § 151 et seq. http://www.bing.com/search?q=47+USCS+%C2%A7+151&src=ie9tr.

Federal Communications Commission v. Fox Television Stations, Inc. and *FCC v. ABC, Inc.,* 132 S.Ct. 2307 (2012). http://supreme.justia.com/cases/federal/us/567/10-1293/opinion3.html.

Federal Communications Commission v. Pacifica Foundation, 438 U.S. 726 (1978). http://www.law.cornell.edu/supremecourt/text/438/726.

Miller v. California, 413 U.S. 15 (1973). http://caselaw.lp.findlaw.com/cgi-bin/getcase.pl?court=us&vol=413&invol=15.

Prometheus Radio Project v. Federal Communications Commission, 652 F.3d 431(3d Cir. 2011). http://www.ca3.uscourts.gov/opinarch/083078p.pdf.

Telecommunications Act of 1996, 47 USCS § 561. http://www.law.cornell.edu/uscode/text/47/561.

United States of America v. Playboy Entertainment Group, Inc., 529 U.S. 803 (2000). http://law2.umkc.edu/faculty/projects/ftrials/communications/playboy.html.

12

Citizens United
v. Federal Election Commission

*"Factions should be checked by permitting
them all to speak, and by entrusting the people
to judge what is true and what is false."*
—Justice Anthony Kennedy,
Citizens United v. Federal Election Commission, 2010

There's another aspect of the First Amendment, probably not envisioned by the Founding Fathers but now enormously important in American life. For journalists, especially those covering politics and government, this is black-letter law: corporations, too, have the right of free expression.

Opening Wedge

In 1976, the attorney general of Massachusetts, Francis X. Bellotti, informed two major banks and three corporations that he intended to enforce a state statute forbidding them to make expenditures to influence the vote on a referendum. At issue was a proposition to authorize a graduated state income tax on individuals to which the businesses were opposed. So they sued Attorney General Bellotti to have the statute declared unconstitutional as violative of the First and Fourteenth Amendments. However, the Supreme Judicial Court of Massachusetts upheld the statute, noting that banks and corporations were authorized to spend to influence a referendum under the statute only if the referendum had a material bearing on their business or property, and the court saw none. But the companies petitioned the U.S. Supreme Court to review the federal constitutional issue.

On First Amendment grounds, the Supreme Court reversed, though only by 5–4. For the majority in *First National Bank of Boston v. Bellotti,* 435 U.S. 765 (1978), Justice Lewis Powell wrote:

If the speakers here were not corporations, no one would suggest that the State could silence their proposed speech. It is the type of speech indispensable to decisionmaking in a democracy, and this is no less true because the speech comes from a corporation rather than an individual. The inherent worth of the speech in terms of its capacity for informing the public does not depend upon the identity of its source, whether corporation, association, union, or individual.

We thus find no support in the First or Fourteenth, or in the decisions of this Court, for the proposition that speech that otherwise would be within the protection of the First Amendment loses that protection simply because its source is a corporation that cannot prove, to the satisfaction of a court, a material effect on its business or property. . . . In the realm of protected speech, the legislature is constitutionally disqualified from dictating the subjects about which persons may speak and the speakers who may address a public issue. (*First National Bank of Boston v. Bellotti,* 784–85)

Dissenting, Justice Byron White, joined by Justices William Brennan and Thurgood Marshall, disagreed "that the First Amendment forbids state interference with managerial decisions of this kind. . . . There can be no doubt that corporate expenditures in connection with referenda immaterial to corporate business affairs fall clearly into the category of corporate activities which may be barred."

Years later this same sharp disagreement among the justices would resurface in a momentous decision based on *First National Bank v. Bellotti.*

Citizens United and *Hillary*

Fast forward to 2008. A not-for-profit corporation, Citizens United, produced a documentary video critical of U.S. Senator Hillary Clinton, who was then seeking the Democratic nomination for president, and advertised that it would make *Hillary* available through video-on-demand during the thirty days prior to the primary elections. It was a test case. The corporation was fully aware that the Bipartisan Campaign Reform Act of 2002 (BCRA, or the McCain-Feingold law) prohibited corporations and unions from using their funds to advocate on television or radio for the election or defeat of a candidate in that thirty-day period. So Citizens United sued the Federal Election Commission, seeking injunctive relief on the grounds that the statutory prohibition was unconstitutional. But the U.S. District Court in Washington granted summary judgment to the commission. The Supreme Court granted a *writ of certiorari.*

As in *Bellotti* thirty-five years earlier, the Supreme Court split 5–4, but the verdict was stunning. Quoting *Bellotti,* Justice Anthony Kennedy wrote for the majority in *Citizens United v. Federal Election Commission,* 558 U.S. 310 130S.Ct. 876 (2010), "political speech does not lose First Amendment protection 'simply because its source is a corporation.'" He went on: "It is important to note that the reasoning and holding of *Bellotti* did not rest on the existence of a viewpoint-discriminatory statute. It rested on the principle that the Government lacks the power to ban corporations from speaking." Rising to a near-feverish pitch, Kennedy exclaimed that "The censorship we now confront is vast in its reach. . . . By suppressing the speech of manifold corporations, both for-profit and nonprofit, the Government prevents their voices and viewpoints from reaching the public and advising voters on which persons or entities are hostile to their interests." He found it anomalous that corporations were forbidden to influence elections and public policy through advertisements while "Corporate executives and employees counsel Members of Congress and Presidential administrations on many issues, as a matter of routine and often in private." Going well beyond the question of the thirty-day ban, the Court ruled that the statute's limitations on corporate and union expenditures were unconstitutional.

In an angry dissent for himself and Justices Ruth Bader Ginsburg, Sonia Sotomayor, and Stephen Breyer, Justice John Paul Stevens railed at the majority's application of *Bellotti* and other precedents:

> The conceit that corporations must be treated identically to natural persons in the political sphere is not only inaccurate but also inadequate to justify the Court's disposition of this case.
>
> In the context of election to public office, the distinction between corporate and human speakers is significant. Although they make enormous contributions to our society, corporations are not actually members of it. They cannot vote or run for office. Because they may be managed and controlled by nonresidents, their interests may conflict in fundamental respects with the interests of eligible voters. . . . It might also be added that corporations have no consciences, no beliefs, no feelings, no thoughts, no desires. . . .
>
> Today's decision is backwards in many senses. It elevates the majority's agenda over the litigants' submissions, facial attacks over as-applied claims, broad constitutional theories over narrow statutory grounds, individual dissenting opinions over precedential holdings, assertion over tradition, absolutism over empiricism, rhetoric over reality. . . . While American democracy is imperfect, few outside the majority of this Court would have thought its flaws included a dearth of corporate money in politics. (*Citizens United v. Federal Election Commission,* 394, 466, 479)

PACs

Prior to this decision, the federal election law provided for the creation of Political Action Committees, or PACs. Often PACs were organized by a company, an industry, or some other existing entity, to promote its interests by making political contributions. Other PACs were formed anew solely to engage in political activity. PAC donors were limited by law to giving a maximum of $5,000 a year to a single committee, and a maximum of $46,200 in any two-year election cycle to *all* political committees and state and local party committees. Corporations and unions could organize PACs but could not contribute to them; only individuals could contribute. A PAC was limited to donating $5,000 each election (a primary election was counted separately) to a candidate or a campaign committee, $15,000 a year to a political party, and $5,000 per year to another PAC. But *Citizens United* tore the lids off, permitting corporations and unions to make unlimited political expenditures provided they are made independently, without coordinating with a candidate or a campaign committee.

Just two months later, applying *Citizens United* in a case called *Speech-Now.org v. Federal Election Commission*, 599 F.3d 686 (D.C. Cir. 2010), the Circuit Court of Appeals for the District of Columbia ruled that PACs that made no direct contributions to candidates or parties could *accept* unlimited contributions from individuals, unions, and corporations (for-profit or nonprofit) and *make* unlimited "independent" political expenditures. (The organization at issue, SpeechNow, was formed to support freedom of speech.) In a unanimous ruling by nine judges of the court, *SpeechNow* held that the election law's contribution limits "violate the First Amendment by preventing plaintiffs [the organizers and prospective contributors to SpeechNow] from donating to SpeechNow in excess of the limits and by prohibiting SpeechNow from accepting donations in excess of the limits." At the same time, though, the court upheld the law's reporting and disclosure requirements:

> [T]he public has an interest in knowing who is speaking about a candidate and who is funding that speech, no matter whether the contributions were made towards administrative expenses or independent expenditures. Further, requiring disclosure of such information deters and helps expose violations of other campaign finance restrictions, such as those barring contributions from foreign corporations or individuals. These are sufficiently important governmental interests to justify requiring SpeechNow to organize and report to the FEC as a political committee. (*SpeechNow.org v. Federal Election Commission*, 698)

Super PACs

The rulings in Citizens United and SpeechNow opened the door to the formation of many such unfettered PACs, officially identified as "independent expenditure-only committees" but soon dubbed "Super PACs." In the 2012 elections they raised and spent hundreds of millions of dollars, most of it contributed not by corporations but by very wealthy individuals. According to the Center for Responsive Politics, which tracks campaign finances as reported to the Federal Election Commission and the Internal Revenue Service, in 2011–2012 Sheldon and Miriam Adelson of Las Vegas gave $93.1 million; Harold and Annette Simmons of Dallas, $27 million; Bob and Doylene Perry of Houston, $24.5 million; Fred Eychaner of Chicago, $12.7 million; Michael R. Bloomberg of New York, $13.7 million; and John and Marlene Ricketts of Omaha, $13.1 million. Most of the donations were unregulated "soft money," and, except for Mr. Eychaner's and Mayor Bloomberg's contributions, most went to Republican or conservative causes (Center for Responsive Politics 2013).

Although these donors are clearly identified, the actual source of some corporate contributions to Super PACs isn't always clear. In a collaboration between the Center for Public Integrity and the Center for Responsive Politics, Michael Beckel and Reity O'Brien wrote on November 5, 2012:

> The biggest corporate contributor in the 2012 election so far doesn't appear to make anything—other than very large contributions to a conservative super PAC.
>
> Specialty Group Inc., of Knoxville, Tenn., donated nearly $5.3 million between Oct. 1 and Oct. 11 to Freedom Works for America, which is affiliated with former GOP House Majority Leader Dick Armey. . . .
>
> Specialty was formed only a month ago. Its "principal office" is a private home in Knoxville. It has no website. And the only name associated with it is that of its registered agent, William Rose, a lawyer whose phone number, listed in a legal directory, is disconnected.
>
> Rose released a press release Monday saying the company was created to "buy, sell, develop and invest in a variety of real estate ventures and investments."
>
> In the six-page statement, Rose said he was a "disappointed, yet staunchly patriotic, baby boomer" with concerns about the administration's handling of the terrorist attack on the U.S. diplomatic mission in Benghazi, Libya, as well as the Department of Justice's botched "Operation Fast and Furious" gunwalking program.
>
> Specialty is the biggest and most mysterious corporate donor to super PACs, but it is not unique.

A new analysis by the Center for Public Integrity and the Center for Responsive Politics shows that companies have contributed roughly $75 million to super PACs in the 2012 election cycle. . . . They spend the funds mostly on negative advertising.

The Centers' analysis found that 85 percent of money from companies flowed to GOP-aligned groups, 11 percent went to Democratic groups and the remainder went to organizations not aligned with either party. (Beckel and O'Brien 2012)

The Super PACs led the way in swelling total "outside" spending, meaning spending aside from that by party committees—from $300 million in the 2007–2008 election cycle to $1.3 billion in 2011–2012—far surpassing party spending of $245 million. The Center for Responsive Politics reported that the largest expenditures were made by the conservative American Crossroads/Crossroads GPS groups, organized by Republican activist Karl Rove ($195 million), and Restore Our Future, created and run by former top assistants to Republican presidential candidate Mitt Romney ($142 million). In third place was Priorities USA, which supported President Barack Obama, organized by two of his former White House aides ($77 million). By far the bulk of TV advertisements by these "outside" organizations was negative (Center for Responsive Politics 2012a).

Hard Money and Soft Money

Throughout the many complex court and FEC rulings on political campaigns and expenditures there are frequent references to "hard money" and "soft money." The top individual contributors listed above gave mostly soft money. It's an important distinction. Hard money refers to the regulated, limited, and reportable donations to federal candidates, parties, and PACs. Soft money, on the other hand, includes unregulated contributions to outside groups, but only to those that disclose their donors, such as Super PACs and tax-exempt organizations registered with the Internal Revenue Service under section 527 of the Internal Revenue Code.

527s

These "527s" are a political curiosity, and are not well known. They are limited to such political activities as voter mobilization and issue advocacy. So, although they may not support or oppose candidates by name, 527s may advocate or criticize *public issues* with which candidates are known to identify. However, they must disclose their donors. According to the Center for

Responsive Politics, the leading donors to 527s in the 2011–2012 election cycle were mostly labor unions: the Service Employees International Union was on top ($6.2 million); National Association of Realtors ($5.3 million); Plumbers/Pipefitters Union ($4.4 million); Carpenters and Joiners Union, International Brotherhood of Electrical Workers, and United Food and Commercial Workers ($2 million each) (Center for Responsive Politics 2012b).

"Social Welfare" Organizations

Then there's another category of tax-exempt organizations that need *not* disclose their donors: section 501(c)(4) organizations. Not to be confused with 501(c)(3) organizations, the more common tax-exempt charitable and educational groups (which may not participate in politics), those registered under 501(c)(4) are "social welfare" organizations that are permitted to engage in political activity, provided that it is not their principal purpose, though enforcement of that requirement seems murky. Kim Barker of *ProPublica* wrote on August 12, 2012 about this "darkest corner of American political fundraising":

> Forget super PACs, their much-hyped cousins, which can take unlimited contributions but must name their donors. More money is being spent on TV advertising in the presidential race by social welfare nonprofits, known as 501(c)(4)s for their section of the tax code, than by any other type of independent group.... Our examination shows that dozens of these groups do little or nothing to justify the subsidies they receive from taxpayers. Instead, they are pouring much of their resources, directly or indirectly, into political races at the local, state and federal level. (Barker 2012)

Similarly, Robert Maguire and Viveca Novak of the Center for Responsive Politics reported on October 25, 2012:

> Outside spending so far this election cycle, by super PACs and other groups, has eclipsed that in all previous cycles combined at this point, going back to 1990. And in that universe, money spent by groups that don't disclose their donors is playing a far bigger role than it ever has. . . . This week, spending by Crossroads GPS, Americans for Prosperity, Patriot Majority and other nondisclosing groups broke $200 million. Almost all of it—88 percent—went for attack ads, and 83 percent of that negative spending was directed against Democrats. On the flip side, nearly three-quarters of the shadow money spent to *support* candidates went to help Republicans. And that's counting only the spending that has to be reported to the Federal Election Commission: ads explicitly calling for a candidate's election or

defeat, plus "issue ads" that feature a candidate and run in the weeks before an election. Millions more have been spent on issue ads running far enough before an election that they don't need to be reported anywhere. (Maguire and Novak 2012)

Follow the Money

What's the working journalist to make of all this? Perhaps most importantly, as the above excerpts indicate, in these days of big-money elections, the huge political donations and expenditures can make good stories in and of themselves. Although this chapter deals only with federal law and disclosures, most states have similar requirements and records open to the press and public. Mining the data may be arduous, but worthwhile.

Second, when covering a political campaign, addressing the candidates' financing, donors, and expenditures is necessary these days. It was said long ago that "money is the mother's milk of politics," and that's true now more than ever. It may help explain, better than the speeches and position papers, why a candidate is ahead—or behind—in the polls.

Also, campaign finance records tell us a lot about the connections between government and business, unions, other special-interest groups, and well-to-do individuals—most of whom give money, especially when the amounts are large, to gain access and favorable treatment, presumably at the expense of others with less clout and lucre to plead their case. Follow the money into the next session of the legislature: For instance, connecting the dots between the National Rifle Association's political contributions and legislators' votes on gun control could be illuminating. Gunshot victims and prospective targets, meaning the general public, have no countervailing influence. No state or local campaign finance law could be as complex as the federal, but understanding *Citizens United* and its First Amendment implications is an excellent introduction to the whole subject.

Questions for Discussion

1. What are the public sources of information on campaign contributions?
2. What's the difference between a 501(c)(4) and a 527?
3. What would be an authoritative source that advises on local campaign finance law by state?
4. Where can contribution records be found?
5. How would an apparent failure to report an in-kind (goods or services) contribution to a campaign be documented?

References

Barker, Kim, "How Nonprofits Spend Millions on Elections and Call It Public Welfare," *ProPublica* (August 18, 2012). http://www.propublica.org/article/how-nonprofits-spend-millions-on-elections-and-call-it-public-welfare/ (accessed January 11, 2013).

Beckel, Michael, and Reity O'Brien, "Mystery Firm Is Election's Top Corporate Donor at $5.3 Million," Center for Public Integrity and Center for Responsive Politics (November 5, 2012). http://www.opensecrets.org/news/2012/11/mystery-firm-is-elections-top-corpo.html#.UJlXxNrpsX4.email (accessed January 11, 2013).

Bipartisan Campaign Reform Act of 2002, Pub.L. 107-155, 2 USCS § 441a. http://www.law.cornell.edu/uscode/text/2/441a.

Center for Responsive Politics, "Outside Spending," OpenSecrets.org (2012a). http://www.opensecrets.org/outsidespending/index.php (accessed January 11, 2013).

———, "Top Contributors to Federally Focused 527 Organizations, 2012 Election Cycle," OpenSecrets.org (November 13, 2012b). http://www.opensecrets.org/527s/527contribs.php (accessed January 11, 2013).

———, "Top Overall Individual Contributors," OpenSecrets.org (2013). http://www.opensecrets.org/overview/topindivs_overall.php (accessed January 11, 2013).

Citizens United v. Federal Election Commission, 558 U.S. 310, 130 S.Ct. 876 (2010). http://www.law.cornell.edu/supct/html/08-205.ZX1.html.

First National Bank of Boston v. Bellotti, 435 U.S. 765 (1978). http://caselaw.lp.findlaw.com/cgi-bin/getcase.pl?court=us&vol=435&invol=765.

Maguire, Robert and Viveca Novak, "The Shadow Money Trail," Center for Responsive Politics, OpenSecrets.org (October 25, 2012). http://www.opensecrets.org/news/2012/10/shadow-moneys-top-10-candidates.html (accessed January 11, 2013).

SpeechNow.org v. Federal Election Commission, 599 F.3d 797 (D.C. Cir. 2010). http://www.fec.gov/law/litigation/speechnow_ac_opinion.pdf.

13

The Ethical Journalist

"Whenever the people are well-informed,
they can be trusted with their own government."
—Thomas Jefferson

We inherit a rich tradition—historic, legal, and ethical—of high journalistic purpose in our democracy. Gaps in journalist's privilege protection notwithstanding, the courts are usually on the side of press freedom, often fervently. However, we have noted instances in which a court's ruling about what's legal may not comport with a more personal judgment about what's ethical or fair.

Promises, Promises

Much of what we have seen is played out in an important and most unusual Supreme Court confrontation called *Cohen v. Cowles Media Co.*, 501 U.S. 663 (1991). Resonating here are familiar strains of precedents on invasion of privacy and freedom of the press, but the case turns on an old common law principle that we haven't seen before, a principle sounding in both law and ethics. It involves a reporter's broken promise of confidentiality. But this situation differs from the journalist's privilege cases that we read about in Chapter 8 because there was no third party trying to extract the source's name, thus no question of a testimonial privilege. In fact, the newspaper itself revealed the source's name—quite voluntarily.

Reporters Lori Sturdevant of the *Minneapolis Star and Tribune* and Bill Salisbury of the *Saint Paul Dispatch* were approached shortly before election day 1982 by Dan Cohen, public relations director for the advertising agency handling the campaign of the Republican candidate for governor, Wheelock Whitney, Jr. Cohen offered to give the reporters some damaging documents about a Democratic candidate, but he wanted, not surprisingly, a promise of confidentiality. Both reporters assented. Cohen then turned over copies of public court records concerning Marlene Johnson, the Democratic-Farmer-Labor candidate for lieutenant governor. One record showed that she had been charged in 1969 with unlawful assembly; another showed that she had been convicted in 1970 of petty theft.

Both newspapers promptly interviewed Marlene Johnson. She said both matters were minor. The unlawful assembly charges stemmed from her participation in a protest of an alleged failure to hire minority workers on municipal construction projects. The charges were dismissed. The petty theft conviction was for leaving a store without paying for six dollars' worth of sewing materials. She said she was emotionally distraught at the time, and her conviction was later vacated.

With the election fast approaching, the newspapers were faced with a dilemma. Don't print the story? Print it and protect the source, as promised? Or print it and break the promise, revealing Cohen's name? A *Tribune* editor discussed the question with a small group in the newsroom, not including Sturdevant. They felt that if the *Tribune* didn't run the story, the paper could be accused of suppressing information damaging to the DFL party. They also rejected the idea of ascribing the story to an unnamed Whitney supporter or Whitney campaign member. Sturdevant lodged an adamant objection to dishonoring her promise to Cohen, insisting that if the paper ran the story, her name shouldn't be on it. At the direction of her editor, Sturdevant called Cohen and tried to persuade him to release her from her promise, but he wouldn't budge.

Just five days before the election, the *Tribune* ran the story on the front page, naming Cohen and his ad agency, under the headline, "Marlene Johnson Arrests Disclosed by Whitney Ally." The byline was merely "Staff Writer." Over at the *Dispatch,* there was no hand-wringing, but it went ahead, too, also naming the source, over Salisbury's objection. The Associated Press, which also had been approached by Cohen, ran the story without naming him. WCCO-TV got the documents, too, but decided to honor its reporter's promise to Cohen by not airing the story. The day the stories appeared, Cohen was fired from the ad agency.

Cohen sued the publishers of the two newspapers, alleging fraudulent misrepresentation and breach of contract. The jury came down hard on the newspapers, awarding him two hundred thousand dollars in compensatory damages and a half million dollars in punitive damages. But a court of appeals reversed the fraud finding and the punitive damages award, and then the Minnesota Supreme Court set aside the breach of contract and the compensatory damages, apparently leaving Cohen with nothing.

However, during oral argument one of the State Supreme Court justices had asked about a common-law doctrine called "estoppel." Estoppel, universally recognized in American law, prevents a person from changing his legal position after benefitting from his original position, and the Minnesota court decided the case by interpreting a form of estoppel called "promissory estoppel". The court explained it: "a promise expected or reasonably expected to induce definite action by the promisee that does induce action is binding if injustice can be avoided only by enforcing the promise." (Cohen v. Cowles Media Co., 457 N.W. 2d 199, 203-04 (1990). Applied here, this appears to mean that a reporter's promise of confidentiality is enforceable if breaking it would be unjust. But in its decision the Minnesota Supreme Court said promissory estoppel, though it would ordinarily apply to such facts, was not applicable because enforcing the reporters' promise would violate the newspapers' First Amendment rights.

Nevertheless, this proved the key to the decision of the U.S. Supreme Court. There the newspapers argued that their reporters had obtained truthful information about a matter of public significance, citing *Smith v. Daily Mail, Florida Star v. B.J.F.,* and *Landmark Communications v. Virginia,* three invasion-of-privacy cases won by the press. However, in a 5–4 decision, Justice Byron White questioned whether the documents at issue in *Cohen v. Cowles Media Co.* were obtained legally. He stated that the case was not controlled by the Court's privacy decisions but "by the equally well-established line of decisions holding that generally applicable laws do not offend the First Amendment simply because their enforcement against the press has incidental effects on its ability to gather and report the news."

Also citing *Branzburg v. Hayes,* White continued, "Neither does the First Amendment relieve a newspaper reporter of the obligation shared by all citizens to respond to a grand jury subpoena and answer questions relevant to a criminal investigation, even though the reporter might be required to reveal a confidential source. . . . The press, like others interested in publishing, may not publish copyrighted material without obeying the copyright laws." White went on to recite other Supreme Court holdings that media companies were not excused from obeying federal labor laws, antitrust laws, and tax laws. "Accordingly," White declared, "enforcement of such general laws against the press is not subject to stricter scrutiny than would be applied to enforcement against other persons or organizations. . . . There can be little doubt that the Minnesota doctrine of promissory estoppel is a law of general applicability. It does not target or single out the press." So the U.S. Supreme Court reversed the Minnesota Supreme Court and sent the case back for further consideration in light of promissory estoppel.

As with so many other Supreme Court cases involving the press, there were strong dissents. Justice Harry Blackmun, a Minnesota native, contended the state supreme court got it right. In an opinion joined by Justice David Souter and Justice Thurgood Marshall, Blackmun cited another privacy case, *Hustler Magazine v. Falwell,* and insisted that "the law may not be enforced to punish the expression of truthful information or opinion. In the instant case, it is undisputed that the publication at issue was true."

Despite the split, the Court's holding is important. The First Amendment does not excuse journalists—or their employers—from breaking promises or complying with all rules applying to all people, or to all companies. (Incidentally, Dan Cohen's candidate, Wheelock Whitney, Jr., lost the election.)

No Government Discrimination

The Supreme Court did not mention it, but it might also have mentioned *Grosjean v. American Press Co.,* 297 U.S. 233 (1936) for the opposite reason: neither may government discriminate against the press. This case, though only the Court's second pro-press ruling (after *Near v. Minnesota* in 1931), was a resounding affirmation of freedom of the press. The Louisiana legislature, under the thumb of a colorful populist politician named Huey "Kingfish" Long, struck back at the state's major newspapers for criticizing Long (then a U.S. senator, formerly governor), by imposing a tax on the gross receipts of all papers with a circulation exceeding 20,000 per week. Carefully drawn, the tax hit only the state's largest thirteen papers, the ones that had been critical, and no others.

The Supreme Court—the conservative 1930s Supreme Court that President Franklin Roosevelt would later confront with his "court-packing" plan to add more justices—wouldn't hear of it. In a unanimous opinion by Justice George Sutherland, the Court foresaw the practical harm of such a tax: "First, its effect is to curtail the amount of revenue realized from advertising, and, second, its direct tendency is to restrict circulation. This is plain enough when we consider that, if it were increased to a high degree, as it could be if valid, it well might result in destroying both advertising and circulation." Then the Court looked back in English history to evoke John Milton's "Appeal for the Liberty of Unlicensed Printing" (his famous *Areopagitica,* published in 1644), in which he, according to Justice Sutherland's paraphrase, "declared the impossibility of finding any man base enough to accept the office of censor and at the same time good enough to be allowed to perform its duties." The Court also referred to a 1712 statute by which "Parliament imposed a tax upon all newspapers and upon advertisements. That the main purpose of these taxes was to suppress the publication of comments and criticisms objectionable to the Crown does not admit of doubt."

Ruling the tax a violation of the due process clause of the Fourteenth Amendment, Justice Sutherland closed with this emphatic peroration:

The tax here involved is bad not because it takes money from the pockets of the appellees. If that were all, a wholly different question would be presented. It is bad because, in the light of its history and of its present setting, it is seen to be a deliberate and calculated device in the guise of a tax to limit the circulation of information to which the public is entitled in virtue of the constitutional guaranties. A free press stands as one of the great interpreters between the government and the people. To allow it to be fettered is to fetter ourselves. (*Grosjean v. American Press Co.,* 248)

Today's Environment

The balance that the Constitution and the Supreme Court have struck for journalists: no dispensation from generally-applicable laws, even though they might impose a burden on journalistic operations (for example, reporters—like everyone else—must respect police and fire lines at emergency scenes), but no special burdens or restrictions either. As a corollary, of course, reporters' promises of confidentiality must be honored. This is apart from any legal pressure that might be applied by prosecutors or other litigants demanding to know the names of confidential sources.

All things considered, the legal and ethical standards of today's American journalism frame an agreeable environment in which to work. Employers are generally robustly supportive of the rights of their reporters, photographers, and editors. Now that you have some understanding of the limits and risks in practicing journalism, its legal and ethical standards require continuing attention on your part. One aspect of this obligation is the need to learn and observe the expectations of your company. Know the code of conduct or code of ethics. When rules are not clear, be sure to ask your editor for clarification. For example, if you're covering business, it may not be entirely clear what constitutes a conflict of interest: how much stock ownership by you or your family would constitute a conflict?

Another professional expectation is to be informed of applicable local laws, including pertinent court rulings. Although we've looked at many federal cases, the reality is that the law governing the everyday workings of the profession is primarily state law—libel, invasion of privacy, journalist's privilege, freedom of information, open meetings, maybe product disparagement.

In particular, learn the reach of the shield law, whether statutory or common law; criminal as well as civil proceedings. The federal courts aren't always uniform in interpreting statutes—in particular, journalist's privilege cases—even Supreme Court rulings. Know the relevant rulings of the federal courts governing your area; they may differ. For instance, in the Chicago area, the Seventh Circuit Court of Appeals recognizes no journalist's privilege, but in New York and San Francisco the U.S. Courts of Appeals see things differently.

Your employer is concerned about these legal rules, too, and should have literature—maybe it's part of the code of conduct booklet—informing the staff what the legislature and the courts have said on all these matters. But booklet or no, realize that you cannot know with certainty the details of all your legal rights and limitations, and carry them around in your head.

What this text should equip you to do, however, is to recognize ethical or legal questions that may arise in your everyday routine. Sometimes you'll be able to anticipate the questions or choices you will need to make, but if you don't have a ready answer, discuss these issues in advance with your editor or manager, maybe even the company lawyer, until you're comfortable with your decisions.

Of course, there will also be instances where you need to come up with quick answers to unexpected dilemmas. Should I video tape the body? Can I trust my source well enough to quote him anonymously if that's the bargain to which I've agreed? (Maybe some more phone calls will obviate the need to rely on a nameless source.) Should I momentarily ignore the obligation to identify myself as a reporter if it will help get a spontaneous quote? Can I safely enter private property with a concealed camera or recorder? Can I expect that the highway patrol will give me a dispensation if I violate the speed limit to get to a disaster scene? How much is the lunch bill my source has just offered to pay, and is it more than the company's limit on an allowable gift? The best policy is to recognize that these moments will arise and that your conscience will be your guide.

Even on your first job, you are not just an order-taker. You will have lots of decisions and professional judgments to make: Which stories to write, and which to spike; which sources (even obnoxious ones) to trust, and which to justifiably ignore. Some of these considerations merely call for good journalism: seek the truth, verify, be fair. That's ethical journalism, too. At some point, good journalism and sound ethical standards overlap, or at the very least they go hand in hand.

References

Cohen v. Cowles Media Co., 457 N.W. 2d 199 (Minn. 1990). http://scholar.google. comscholar_case?case=11094080409851792106&hl=en&as_sdt=2&as_ vis=1&oi=scholar.

Cohen v. Cowles Media Co., 501 U.S. 663 (1991). http://supreme.justia.com/cases/ federal/us/501/663/case.html.

Grosjean v. American Press Co., 297 U.S. 233 (1936). http://www.law.cornell.edu/ supct/html/historics/USSC_CR_0297_0233_ZO.html.

Milton, John, *Areopagitica: A Speech of Mr. John Milton for the Liberty of Unlicensed Printing to the Parliament of England* (1644).

Bibliography

Ali v. Playgirl, Inc., 447 F. Supp. 723 (S.D. N.Y. 1978).

American Jurisprudence, second edition (AmJur 2d), Lawyers Cooperative Publishing/Bancroft Whitney.

Anonymous Online Speakers, In re, 661 F.3d 1168 (9th Cir. 2011).

Aristotle. 2009. *Aristotle: The Nicomachean Ethics,* Trans. by William David Ross, Oxford: Oxford University Press.

Associated Press v. Walker, 388 U.S. 130 (1967).

Atomic Energy Act, 42 U.S.C. § 2280.

Baker v. F & F Investment, 470 F.2d 778 (2d Cir. 1972).

Balk, Alfred. 1962. "Confessions of a Block-Buster," *Saturday Evening Post,* July 14.

Barker, Kim. 2012. "How Nonprofits Spend Millions on Elections and Call It Public Welfare." ProPublica, August 18. http://www.propublica.org/article/how-nonprofits-spend-millions-on-elections-and-call-it-public-welfare/ (accessed January 11, 2013).

Barry, Dan, David Barstow, Jonathan D. Glater, Adam Liptak, and Jacques Steinberg. 2003. "CORRECTING THE RECORD; Times Reporter Who Resigned Leaves Long Trail of Deception." *The New York Times,* May 11. http://www.nytimes.com/2003/05/11/us/correcting-the-record-times-reporter-who-resigned-leaves-long-trail-of-deception.html?pagewanted=all&src=pm (accessed December 1, 2012).

Bartnicki v. Vopper, 532 U.S. 514 (2001).

Beck, Susan. 1997. "Trial and Errors." *The American Lawyer,* June, p. 42.

Beckel, Michael, and Reity O'Brien. 2012. "Mystery Firm Is Election's Top Corporate Donor at $5.3 Million." Center for Public Integrity and Center for Responsive Politics, November 5. http://www.opensecrets.org/news/2012/11/mystery-firm-is-elections-top-corpo.html#.UJlXxNrpsX4.email (accessed January 11, 2013).

Bentham, Jeremy. 2010. *The Principles of Morals and Legislation.* Charleston: Nabu Press.

Bipartisan Campaign Reform Act of 2002, Pub.L. 107–155, 2 USCS § 441a. http://www.law.cornell.edu/uscode/text/2/441a.

Black's Law Dictionary, Free Online Legal Dictionary 2d edition, ed. Bryan A. Garner. St. Paul: West. http://thelawdictionary.org/tort/.

Blumenthal v. Drudge, 186 F.R.D. 236 (D.D.C. 1999).

Bose Corp. v. Consumers Union of United States, Inc., 466 U.S. 485 (1984).

Branzburg v. Hayes, 408 U.S. 665 (1972).

Brown & Williamson Tobacco Corporation v. Walter Jacobson and CBS, Inc., 14 Media L. Rep. 1497 (7th Cir. 1987).

Bush v. Gore, 531 U.S. 98 (2000).

California Civil Code § 47. http://law.onecle.com/california/civil/47.html.

Campbell v. Acuff-Rose Music Inc., 510 U.S. 569 (1994).

Cantrell v. Forest City Publishing Co., 419 U.S. 245 (1974).

Carey v. Hume, 492 F.2d 631 (D.C. Cir. 1974).

CBS Corp. v. Federal Communications Commission, 663 F.3d 122 (3d Cir. 2011).

Center for Responsive Politics. 2013. "Top Overall Individual Contributors." http://www.opensecrets.org/overview/topindivs_overall.php (accessed January 11, 2013).

———. 2012a. "Outside Spending." http://www.opensecrets.org/outsidespending/index.php (accessed January 11, 2013).

———. 2012b. "Top Contributors to Federally Focused 527 Organizations, 2012 Election Cycle." November 13. http://www.opensecrets.org/527s/527contribs.php (accessed January 11, 2013).

Chandler v. Florida, 449 U.S. 560 (1981).

Cher v. Forum International, Ltd., 692 F.2d 634 (9th Cir. 1982).

Children's Television Act of 1990, 47 USCS § 303.

Christians, Clifford G., Mark Fackler, Kathy Brittain Richardson, and Peggy J. Kreshel. 2011. *Media Ethics: Cases and Moral Reasoning,* 8th ed. Boston: Allyn & Bacon.

Citizens United v. Federal Election Commission, 558 U.S. 310, 130 S.Ct. 876 (2010).

Cohen v. Cowles Media Co., 501 U.S. 663 (1991).

Comcast Corp. v. FCC, 600 F.3d 642 (D.C. Cir. 2010).

Communications Act, 47 USCS § 151 et seq.

———. 1915. *The Ethics of Confucius.* Trans. by Miles Menander Dawson, New York: G. P. Putnam's Sons, 1915.

Confucius. 1999. *The Analects of Confucius: A Philosophical Translation.* Trans. by Roger T. Ames and Henry Rosemont, Jr., New York: Ballantine Books.

Conradt, Patricia v. NBC Universal, Inc., 536 F.Supp.2d 380 (S.D. N.Y. 2008).

Copyright Act, 17 USCS § 101 et seq.

Copyright Term Extension Act (CTEA) (1998), 17 USCS § 304.

Cox Broadcasting Corp. v. Cohn, 420 U.S. 469 (1975).

Crump v. Beckley Newspapers, Inc., 173 W.Va. 699 (1983).

Curtis Publishing Co. v. Butts and *Associated Press v. Walker,* 388 U.S. 130 (1967).

Department of the Air Force v. Rose, 425 U.S. 352 (1976).

Department of the Interior v. Klamath Water Users Protective Association, 532 U.S. 1 (2001).

Department of Justice v. Landano, 508 U.S. 165 (1993).

Department of Justice v. Reporters Committee for Freedom of the Press, 489 U.S.749 (1989).

Department of State v. Ray, 502 U.S. 164 (1991).

Department of State v. Washington Post, 456 U.S. 595 (1982).

Desnick v. American Broadcasting Companies, Inc., 233 F.3d 514 (7th Cir. 2000).

Deteresa v. American Broadcasting Companies, Inc., 121 F.3d 460 (9th Cir. 1997).

Dietemann v. Time, Inc., 449 F.2d 245 (9th Cir. 1971).

Digital Millennium Copyright Act (DMCA) (1998), 17 USCS § 512.

Doe v. Cahill, 884 A.2d 451 (Del. 2005).

Dow Jones & Company. 2012. "Code of Conduct." http://www.dowjones.com/code-conduct.asp (accessed December 1, 2012).

Dr. Seuss Enterprises, L.P. v. Penguin Books USA, Inc. and Dove Audio, Inc., 109 F.3d 1394 (9th Cir. 1997).

Eastwood v. Superior Court of Los Angeles County, 198 Cal.Rptr. 342 (1983).

Eldred v. Ashcroft, 537 U.S. 186 (2003).

Estes v. Texas, 381 U.S. 532 (1965).

Federal Communications Commission v. AT&T, Inc., 131 S.Ct. 1177 (2011).

Federal Communications Commission v. Fox Television Stations, Inc. and *FCC v. ABC, Inc.,* 132 S.Ct. 2307 (2012).

Federal Communications Commission v. Pacifica Foundation, 438 U.S. 726 (1978).

First National Bank of Boston v. Bellotti, 435 U.S. 765 (1978).

Florida Star v. B.J.F., 491 U.S. 524 (1989).

Food Lion v. Capital Cities/ABC, Inc., 194 F.3d 505 (4th Cir. 1999).

Freedom of Information Act, 5 USCS § 552 et seq.

Galella v. Onassis, 487 F.2d 986 (2d Cir. 1973).

Gertz v. Robert Welch, Inc., 418 U.S. 323 (1974); 680 F.2d 527 (7th Cir. 1982).

Gannett Co., Inc. v. DePasquale, 443 U.S. 368 (1979).

Golan v. Holder, 132 S.Ct. 873 (2012).

Gonzales v. National Broadcasting Company, Inc., 194 F.3d 29 (2d Cir. 1998).

Google. 2012. "Google Transparency Report: Removal Requests." http://www.google.com/transparencyreport/removals/copyright/ (accessed October 17, 2012).

Gore v. Harris, 772 So.2d 1243 (Fla. 2000).

Griswold v. Connecticut, 381 U.S. 479 (1965).

Grosjean v. American Press Co., 297 U.S. 233 (1936).

Harper & Row, Publishers, Inc. v. Nation Enterprises, 471 U.S. 539 (1985).

Harte-Hanks Communications, Inc. v. Connaughton, 491 U.S. 657 (1989).

Hoffman v. Capital Cities/ABC, Incorporated and L.A. Magazine, Inc., 255 F.3d 1180 (9th Cir. 2001).

Holliday, Taylor. 2004. "How to File an FOIA request." Freedom of Information Issues (First Amendment Center), November 16. http://www.firstamendmentcenter.org/how-to-file-an-foia-request. Accessed April 10, 2013.

Houchins v. KQED, 438 U.S. 1 (1978).

Hustler Magazine and Larry C. Flynt v. Jerry Falwell, 485 U.S. 46 (1988).

Illinois Open Meetings Act, 5 ILCS 120.

Irvin v. Dowd, 359 U.S. 394 (1959); 366 U.S. 717 (1961).

Jennings v. Telegram-Tribune Company, 164 Cal.App.3d 119 (1985).

Johns-Byrne Company v. TechnoBuffalo LLC, No. 2011 L 009161 (Ill. Circ. Ct. July 13, 2012).

Kant, Immanuel. 2010. *The Works of Immanuel Kant,* Kindle ed. Trans. by T.K. Abbott. Hustonville, KY: Golgotha.

KOVR-TV, Inc. v. Superior Court of Sacramento County, 31 Cal.App.4th 1023 (1995).

Kissinger v. Reporters Committee for Freedom of the Press, 445 U.S. 136 (1980).

Landmark Communications, Inc. v. Virginia, 435 U.S. 829 (1978).

LaRouche v. National Broadcasting Co., 780 F.2d 1134 (4th Cir. 1986).

Leggett, Vanessa v. United States, 535 U.S. 1011 (2002).

Locke, John. 2010. "A Letter Concerning Toleration." In *The Work of John Locke,* Kindle ed. Seattle: Amazon Digital Services.

Lyon, Andrea D. 2011. "Criminal Coverage: News Media, Legal Commentary, and the Crucible of the Presumption of Innocence." *Reynolds Courts & Media Law Journal* 1(4): 427–42.

Maguire, Robert and Viveca Novak. 2012. "The Shadow Money Trail." Center for Responsive Politics, October 25. http://www.opensecrets.org/news/2012/10/shadow-moneys-top-10-candidates.html (accessed January 11, 2013).

Masson v. New Yorker Magazine, 501 U.S. 406 (1991); 85 F.3d 1394 (9th Cir. 1996).

McBride v. Village of Michiana, 100 F.3d 457 (6th Cir. 1996); 1998 WL 276139 (W.D. Mich. 1998).

Medical Laboratory Management Consultants v. American Broadcasting Companies, Inc., Diane Sawyer, et al., 306 F.3d 806 (9th Cir. 2002).

Milkovich v. Lorain Journal, 497 U.S. 1 (1990).

Mill, John Stuart. 2012. *Utilitarianism,* Kindle ed. Seattle: Amazon Digital Services.

Miller v. California, 413 U.S. 15 (1973).

Miller, Brownie v. National Broadcasting Company, 187 Cal. App.3d 1463 (1986).

Miller, Judith, In re Grand Jury Subpoena, 397 F.3d 964 (D.C. Cir. 2005).

Milner v. Department of the Navy, 131 S.Ct. 1259 (2011).

Milton, John. 1644. *Areopagitica: A Speech of Mr. John Milton for the Liberty of Unlicensed Printing to the Parliament of England.*

MMAR Group, Inc. v. Dow, Jones & Co., Inc. and Laura Jereski, 187 F.R.D. 282 (S.D. Tex. April 8, 1999).

Montana v. San Jose Mercury News, Inc., 34 Cal. App.4th 790 (1995).

Mortgage Specialists, Inc. v. Implode-Explode Heavy Industries, Inc., 160 N.H. 277 (2010).

Multimedia WMAZ, Inc. v. Kubach, 212 Ga. App. 707 (1994).

National Archives and Records Administration v. Favish, 541 U.S. 157 (2004).

Near v. Minnesota, 283 U.S. 697 (1931).

Nebraska Press Association v. Stuart, 427 U.S. 539 (1976).

New York Civil Rights Law, § 79-h (c).

New York Times Company. 2005. "The New York Times Company Policy on Ethics in Journalism." October. http://www.nytimes.com/nytco/press/ethics.html (accessed December 1, 2012).

New York Times Co. v. Sullivan, 376 U.S. 24 (1964).

New York Times Co. v. United States, 403 U.S. 713 (1971).

Nixon v. Warner Communications, Inc., 435 U.S. 589 (1978).

Obsidian Finance Group, LLC v. Cox, No. CV-11–57-HZ (D. Ore. 2011).

O'Grady v. Superior Court, 139 Cal. App.4th 1423 (2006).

Oklahoma Publishing Co. v. Oklahoma County District Court, 430 U.S. 308 (1977).

Open Meetings Act, 5 USCS § 552b.

Patterson v. Colorado, 205 U.S. 454 (1907).

Peavy v. WFAA-TV, 221 F.3d 158 (5th Cir. 2000).

Peoples Bank and Trust Company of Mountain Home, as Conservator of the Estate of Nellie Mitchell, an Aged Person v. Globe International Publishing, Inc., doing business as "Sun," 978 F.2d 1065 (8th Cir. 1992).

Perfect 10, Inc. v. Google, Inc., 508 F.3d 1146 (9th Cir. 2007); No. CV 04 9484 AHM (SHx) (C.D. Cal. 2010); 653 F.3d 976 (9th Cir. 2011); 132 S.Ct. 1713 (2012).

Press-Enterprise Co. v. Superior Court, 464 U.S. 501 (1984); 478 U.S. 1 (1986).

Price v. Time, Inc., 416 F.3d 1327 (11th Cir. 2005).

Procter & Gamble Company v. Bankers Trust Company, 78 F.3d 219 (6th Cir. 1996).

Prometheus Radio Project v. Federal Communications Commission, 652 F.3d 431 (3d Cir. 2011).

Radio Television Digital News Association. 2012. "Code of Ethics." http://rtdna.org/article/rtdna_code_of_ethics (accessed December 1, 2012).

Rawls, John. 1971. *A Theory of Justice.* Cambridge: Harvard.

Reporters Committee for Freedom of the Press. 2012. "Order Form." http://www.rcfp.org/publications-order-form. Accessed April 10, 2013.

Restatement of the Law, Second, Torts. 1977. Philadelphia: American Law Institute.

Richmond Newspapers, Inc. v. Virginia, 448 U.S. 555 (1980).

Rideau v. Louisiana, 373 U.S. 723 (1963).

Risen, James, In re: Grand Jury Subpoena, 39 Media L. Rep. 1945 (E.D. Va. 2011).

Risen, James. 2006. *State of War: The Secret History of the CIA and the Bush Administration.* New York: Free Press.

Roe v. Wade, 410 U.S. 113 (1973).

Salinger v. Colting, 641 F.Supp.2d 250 (S.D. N.Y. 2009).

Sanders v. American Broadcasting Companies, Inc., 20 Cal.4th 907 (1999).

Sheppard v. Maxwell, 384 U.S. 333 (1966).

Shoen v. Shoen, 5 F.3d 1289 (9th Cir. 1993).

Shulman v. Group W Productions, Inc., 18 Cal.4th 200 (1998).

Sikelianos, Nikolas, In re Subpeona Directed to the Associated Press, v. City of New York, 36 Media L. Rep. 2087 (S.D. N.Y. 2008).

Smith v. Daily Mail Publishing Co., 443 U.S. 97 (1979).

Society of Professional Journalists (SPJ). 1996. "SPJ Code of Ethics." http://www.spj.org/ethicscode.asp (accessed May 20, 2013).

Spahn v. Messner, 21 N.Y.2d 124 (1967).

SpeechNow.org v. Federal Election Commission, 599 F.3d 797 (D.C. Cir. 2010).

Stewart v. NYT Broadcast Holdings, L.L.C., and Griffin Communications, L.L.C., 2010 Okla. Civ.App. 89, 240 P.3d 722 (2010).

Strader v. Kentucky Department of Fish and Wildlife Resources, Civil Action No. 3:09–62-DCR (E.D. Ky. 2012).

Suntrust Bank as Trustee of the Mitchell Trusts v. Houghton Mifflin Company, 268 F.3d 1257 (11th Cir. 2001).

Taricani, Jim, In re: Special Proceedings, 373 F.3d 37 (lst Cir. 2004). http://caselaw.findlaw.com/us-1st-circuit/1378300.html.

Telecommunications Act of 1996, 47 USCS § 561.

Texas Beef Group v. Oprah Winfrey, 11 F.Supp.2d 858 (N.D. Tex. 1998); 212 F.3d 597 (2000).

Thomas, Marlo. 2002. *The Right Words at the Right Time.* New York: Altria Books.

Time, Inc. v. Firestone, 424 U.S. 448 (1976).

Time, Inc. v. Hill, 385 U.S. 374 (1967).

Tiwari v. NBC Universal, Inc., No. C-08–3988 EMC (N.D. Cal. 2011).

Toledo Newspaper Company v. United States, 247 U.S. 402 (1918).

TooMuchMedia v. Hale, 206 N.J. 209 (2011).

United States of America v. Kaczynski, 154 F.3d 930 (9th Cir. 1998).

United States of America v. New York Times Company, 444 F.2d 544 (2d Cir. June 23, 1971).

United States of America v. Noriega and Cable News Network, 917 F.2d 1543 (11th Cir. 1990).

United States of America v. Playboy Entertainment Group, Inc., 529 U.S. 803 (2000).

United States of America v. Progressive, Inc., 486 F. Supp. 5 (W.D. Wis.1979).

United States of America v. Washington Post Company, 446 F.2d 1327 (D.C. Cir. June 23, 1971).

Veilleux v. National Broadcasting Company, 206 F.3d 92 (1st Cir. 2000).

Viacom International Inc. v. YouTube, Inc., 676 F.3d 19 (2d Cir. 2012).

Waller v. Georgia, 467 U.S. 39 (1984).

Warren, Samuel D., and Louis D. Brandeis. 1890. "The Right to Privacy." IV *Harvard Law Review* 5, December 15.

Wen Ho Lee v. Department of Justice, 413 F.3d 53 (D.C. Cir. 2005).

Wolf v. United States, 201 Fed.Appx. 430 (9th Cir. 2006).

Yeakey v. Hearst Communications, Inc., 156 Wn. App. 787 (2010).

YouTube. 2012. "Copyright on YouTube." http://www.youtube.com/yt/copyright/.

Zacchini v. Scripps-Howard Broadcasting Co., 433 U.S. 562, 578 (1977).

Zerilli v. Smith, 656 F.2d 705 (D.C. Cir. 1981).

Index

About the Author

Joe Mathewson teaches courses in the ethics and law of journalism in the Medill School of Journalism, Media, Integrated Marketing Communications at Northwestern University. A former Supreme Court correspondent for the *Wall Street Journal*, he is the author of *The Supreme Court and the Press: The Indispensable Conflict* (2011). He's a contributor to chicagohistoryjournal. com, having written pieces on Chicago-based Supreme Court cases involving prominent lawyers and other Chicagoans. In New York, Washington, and Chicago, Mathewson covered business for the *Wall Street Journal*. He was a WBBM-TV reporter and press secretary to Illinois governor Richard B. Ogilvie. He authored a book on Chicago politics, *Up Against Daley* (1974), as well as op-eds and Sunday magazine articles for the *Chicago Tribune* and the *Chicago Sun-Times*. He has contributed to CNN.com, Editor and Publisher online, and Businessweek.com. He has been a Cook County commissioner, Illinois assistant attorney general for media relations, a director of several community banks, a principal of a minority-owned broker-dealer, and a securities arbitrator for the National Association of Securities Dealers. He formerly practiced commercial and banking law in Chicago. Mathewson has degrees from Dartmouth and the University of Chicago Law School, and did graduate work in European politics and economies at the Bologna Center of John Hopkins University's School of Advanced International Studies in Italy. He served ten years as a trustee of Dartmouth College and chaired the Illinois State Advisory Committee to the U.S. Civil Rights Commission.